MUSIC FOR FUN
MUSIC FOR LEARNING

SECOND EDITION
For Regular and Special Classrooms

Lois Birkenshaw

Holt, Rinehart and Winston of Canada, Limited   Toronto

Canadian Cataloguing in Publication Data

Birkenshaw, Lois, date
   Music for fun, music for learning

"For regular and special classrooms."
Includes songs with unacc. melodies and chord symbols.

Bibliography: p.
Discography: p.

Includes index.
ISBN 0-03-920001-9 pa.

1. School music – Instruction and study – Canada.
2. School song-books, Canadian. I. Title.

MT925.B57 1977   372.8'7'044   C77-001027-X

Copyright © 1974, 1977 by
Holt, Rinehart and Winston of Canada, Limited
55 Horner Avenue
Toronto, Ontario M8Z 4X6

Holt, Rinehart and Winston, Incorporated
383 Madison Avenue
New York, N.Y. 10017

Holt-Saunders Limited
1 St. Annes Road
Eastbourne, East Sussex
England BN213UN

Holt-Saunders Pty. Limited
9 Waltham Street
Artarmon, New South Wales
Australia 2064

ISBN 0-03-920001-9

Printed in Canada

3 4 5   81 80

Acknowledgements

ALLYN AND BACON, INC. "There Was An Old Witch" from THIS IS MUSIC, Book II, by William R. Sur, Mary R. Tolbert, William R. Fischer, and Adeline McCall. © Copyright 1961 by Allyn and Bacon, Inc. Used by permission.

AMERICAN BOOK COMPANY. "Brownies and Witches", words by Mayme Christenson, music by J. Wolverton, "Making Valentines", words and music by J. Wolverton. Used by permission of American Book Company.

AUGENER LIMITED. "Jig-Jog-Jig-Jog" by Paul Edmonds, Augener Limited.

A & C BLACK LIMITED. "Shoo Fly" and "Shoe Game" from *Singing Rhymes for Recreation* compiled by Janet Tobitt and published by A & C Black Limited (London, England).

THE CLARENDON PRESS. "There Was A Man In Our Town" reprinted from *The Oxford Nursery Rhyme Book* edited by Iona and Peter Opie by permission of The Clarendon Press, Oxford. "Mary At the Door", "Bumpety Bumpety Bump", "Pease Porridge Hot", "To Market To Market" and "Daisy Charm" reprinted from *The Oxford Dictionary of Nursery Rhymes* edited by Iona and Peter Opie by permission of The Clarendon Press, Oxford.

THE JOHN DAY COMPANY, INC. "Snow". Copyright © 1932 by The John Day Company, Inc. Reprinted from THE GOLDEN FLUTE by Alice Wilkins by permission of The John Day Company, Inc., an Intext publisher.

DOUBLEDAY & COMPANY, INC. and THE SOCIETY OF AUTHORS. "Witch, Witch" from FIFTY-ONE NEW NURSERY RHYMES by Rose Fyleman. Copyright 1932 by Doubleday & Company, Inc. Reprinted by permission of Doubleday & Company, Inc. and The Society of Authors as the literary representative of the Estate of Rose Fyleman.

GINN AND COMPANY. "Jingle at the Windows" from *Tuning Up* of THE WORLD OF MUSIC series, © Copyright 1943, 1936, by Ginn and Company Xerox Corporation; © Copyright Renewed, 1964, by Mabelle Glenn and Earl L. Baker. Used with permission.

HART PUBLISHING COMPANY, INC. "Paw Paw Patch" from *A Treasury of Songs*, Hart Publishing Company, Inc., New York City.

HOLT, RINEHART AND WINSTON OF CANADA, LIMITED. "C-C-C-C-Cold" by John Wood from SONGTIME 4 by Vera Russell, Lansing MacDowell, John Wood, Charles Winter. Copyright © 1963 by Holt, Rinehart and Winston of Canada, Limited.

JEWISH EDUCATION PRESS. "My Dreydel", words by S.S. Grossman, music by S.E. Goldfarb. Permission granted by Jewish Education Press, Board of Jewish Education of New York.

LITTLE, BROWN AND COMPANY. "The Umbrella Brigade" by Laura E. Richards from TIRRA LIRRA, Little, Brown and Company, Publishers.

ROBERT B. LUCE, INC. "Hands on Shoulders", "My Hands", "Up the Steps We Go", "The Little Witches", "Eensy Weensy Spider" from *Let's Do Fingerplays* by Marion F. Grayson, Robert B. Luce, Inc., Publishers. Reprinted by permission of Robert B. Luce, Inc.

MACMILLAN PUBLISHING CO., INC. "Teddy Bear" reprinted with permission of Macmillan Publishing Co., Inc. from JUMP THE ROPE JINGLES by Emma Victor Worstell. © Emma Victor Worstell 1960.

Illustrations and Cover:
Bob Seguin

TABLE OF CONTENTS

INTRODUCTION

Music. Have you ever considered what your life would be like without music? No folk songs; no jazz; no symphonies; no opera; no carols, hymns or religious songs; no rock and roll; no sing songs. Impossible you say? Perhaps, but if you could walk around some of our elementary schools today or look into homes across the nation you might not consider this to be quite as far fetched as it sounds.

True, our children are bombarded, as are all of us, with recorded music in stores, subways, from television, radio and record player, but the vast majority of this, is just for background and not for listening to. It is the rare home today in which the child learns the folklore of his culture: the rhymes, songs, games and fingerplays which used to be part of every child's birthright. Many schools, also, seem to be putting the emphasis on subjects such as reading, math and spelling and music has been relegated to the status of a "frill".

The result of this, is that many of the children in the regular classes — let alone those in classes for "special children" — are not being exposed to an active music program either at home or at school.

By an active music program I mean one which uses melody, rhythm, movement and speech to involve the whole child. This total involvement and integration of these four elements should be integral in the childhood experience. Who ever has seen a normal child listen to music without moving, or bounce a ball without chanting a rhyme, or chant a rhyme without making a little song out of it? If, indeed, this total involvement is not present, this just might be a clue to the presence of some handicap in that child: deafness, learning disability, gross motor problems, cerebral palsy, etc.

Rhythm is the underlying, vital force in the world. Gaining inner rhythmic sureness is one of the most important tasks of the young child — a pre-condition to success in reading, writing or any other learning. He or she achieves this, by chanting words, word patterns, nonsense rhymes, poetry, by singing little songs, by clapping or walking to the beat of the music, etc.

Movement is another vital element of learning. The child first discovers himself, how he moves, how the various parts of his body function, the fact that he has two sides (laterality) which he can learn to control and wonders of wonders, he can then walk and move on his own.

The child next moves out into the environment and manipulates it (by movement). This is how he discovers and learns. Music, movement, rhythm and speech are all necessary to aid this discovery.

Music can help develop auditory awareness and listening skills.

Music can help speech, both the development of speech and the remediation.

Music can teach concepts: colours, animal sounds, counting, sequencing, geography, etc.

Music can give the joy of creation.

Finally, through an involvement in an active music program, the child learns to participate in a group on his or her own level of achievement and experiences the delight and satisfaction this brings.

MUSIC IN SPECIAL EDUCATION

If music is so important in the training of children who are normal, how much more necessary and useful it is in working with children with problems.

These children have missed out in the early training and experiences just by the very nature of their handicap.

Deaf and aphasic children cannot hear or cannot process in their brains the rhymes, games and songs. They also miss the many rhythmic clues of the world around them, so the emphasis on coordinative work and speech is of vital importance to them.

Children with learning disabilities and those who are orthopedically handicapped, need the special emphasis on coordinative and gross motor work found in this type of program.

Retarded children are left behind when normal children play games and sing songs. They need involvement in all phases of music and physical development and in addition, can be taught much valuable information such as colours, names of animals, the alphabet, etc., through music.

Emotionally disturbed children can be calmed down by selecting suitable music and through the non-threatening medium of music, can learn to relate in a significant way to another person and, eventually, to participate constructively in a group.

All handicapped children can experience the joy of creativity and the satisfaction of achievement gained through music. For some, this is a novel experience indeed.

The above points are true for severely handicapped children and also for those with minimal handicaps or those who are just slow to develop. These children are often found in the regular classroom, and the teacher can select activities which help them overcome some difficulty while the rest of the class just has fun.

An active music program is particularly useful in working in inner city classes.

Music, therefore, should be included as an integral part of each child's life both in and out of school. This book's emphasis is on some of the practical results which can come from an active, well-rounded music program. It is also meant to point out what has, to date, not been universally recognized — that much valuable learning in other phases of the child's development can be promoted with such a music program.

HOW TO USE THIS BOOK

The activities found here are fun to do and, at the same time, are carefully designed to help the child attain motor, auditory and rhythmic skills through the many games, songs, dances, rhythmic activities and speech activities. The explanations have been kept simple, so no great skill is necessary to use them — all you need is enthusiasm.

The ideas have been tried with handicapped as well as with other children and it has been found that every child enjoys this kind of musical activity because each can take part on his own level: a simple drum beat is as important to the final result as a complicated xylophone pattern. Everyone can gain a feeling of self-worth and accomplishment.

The activities have been arbitrarily placed into sections for the sake of clarity but it is very difficult to pigeonhole them, as they always tend to overlap in certain areas. Cross references have been provided wherever possible and each activity has been tied to a particular skill.

The ideas are numbered for easy reference. Some sections are progressive and your teaching will be more successful if one step is mastered before you go on to the next. There are often many different games which reinforce the same concept. This ensures that, while the slower members of the group are gaining practice in a skill, the others will not become bored.

Most songs, games, speech activities or poems have one or more side headings adjacent to the main text. These headings (e.g. Directionality, Action song, Visual discrimination) indicate the concepts, other than those mentioned in the specific section title, that the activities will promote. If the heading is right next to the text (see a.), then it applies to that specific paragraph. However, if the heading is placed closer to the edge of the page (see b.), it indicates that the whole following section would be pertinent. As these headings have been used in organizing the **Index**, they should make finding appropriate activities much easier.

a. Side headings

b. Side headings.

Choose the ideas and songs with which you feel comfortable and try these with your children. If it is possible, ideas should be chosen from different sections for presentation in the same lesson period. That is, don't work all the way through **Relaxation** one week and go on to **Coordination, Spatial Relationship and Body Rhythm** the next week. Do some relaxation exercises, some body awareness and some listening games one week as you teach a song. The next week, you might try some different relaxation exercises, an auditory sequencing song and a poem. Don't forget to review the previous activities. Children love repetition.

See the section **Sample Lesson Plans** on page 237 for some specific ideas on how to combine activities from various sections of the book to plan lessons presenting concepts which become progressively more difficult.

EXPLANATION OF SOME UNFAMILIAR TERMS

Body Awareness is the knowledge of the various external parts of the body (i.e. hands, feet, arms, head, elbow, etc.) and how they function.

Body Image is the concept of the body and its position in space. The child must learn from observation how the parts of his body move in relationship to each other and in relationship to the outside world. An accurate knowledge of this, is necessary in order to initiate any controlled movement whatever.

Body Spatial Relationship involves the ability to move oneself around one's environment efficiently. For a child, this means that he has developed in movement skills to the point where he does not bump into desks, chairs, lamps, etc. as he proceeds through life. He can walk through a maze, over and under jungle gym equipment, etc. Many skills enter into this: for instance, body awareness, body image, directionality and position of body in space. The underdevelopment of any one of these skills can make the child appear clumsy.

Laterality is the motor awareness of the two sides of the body. A child has to learn to distinguish between the left and right concepts in his own body and to control the two sides simultaneously and separately.

Directionality is the projection of laterality from the body into space. Understanding of the differences between left and right in the child's own body leads, by way of visual and tactual exploration, to the ability to distinguish directional differences in the space around him. It is also the ability to distinguish up from down, forward from backward.

Midline is simply the centre of the body. Often a child can perform actions very well on each side of his body but when the actions cross the midline they become confused and jerky.

Pentatonic Scale. It is generally agreed that as the child's voice develops the first interval he sings is Soh-Me. Lah is then added and the three note taunt of the schoolyard is arrived at: Soh Soh Me Lah Soh Me, (G, G, E, A, G, E). The next two notes to be added are Doh and Ray and the five note or pentatonic scale is the result. There are several forms of this scale but the most common is: Doh, Ray, Me, Soh, Lah. (In the key of C this would be: C, D, E, G, A.)

This scale is found in the folk songs of many countries. It is easy to sing and is, therefore, very useful in working with children.

Rhythmic notation has been used throughout when there was no pitch or melody involved.

$|$ is just a fast way of writing ♩ and similarly ⊓ means ♫ . The "feet" are not needed when there is no melody present. Children find it very easy to understand and write this notation. Both the symbols ⸯ and ✗ indicate a quarter note rest.

I hope that the use of the ideas presented will help make your music time more relaxed and happy, for without this kind of atmosphere, no learning will take place. Music is too precious an area of experience to be ruined by a dreary, crabby, unimaginative and negative approach. If you enjoy music yourself, this feeling of enthusiasm will be imparted to the children.

LET'S SING

"Let's Sing". These are magic words for children, for singing is as natural as breathing for the young child. Anyone who has stood in a schoolyard and listened to the children's calls, their skipping and ball bouncing rhymes and their songs is well aware of this fact. We should capitalize on this love of singing by bringing it into our activities with children every day. So many good things happen when children sing.

Singing time is a social time. In this era of individualized timetables it is often the only period in the day when everyone comes together to do one thing. Singing encourages group participation and is an excellent way of reaching a withdrawn child. Singing is also an important means of promoting good speech.

Singing releases tensions and relaxes everyone. Sing after a particularly hard period of work to provide an outlet for pent-up energy. The games and activities associated with songs also give children an acceptable outlet for excess energy and, at the same time, help develop awareness and motor coordination skills.

With children, singing and moving should always be combined. It is, in fact, almost impossible for a young child not to move when he sings or even when he listens to music. Let the children act out the meaning of the songs, make up dances, walk or clap the beat, rock or sway to the music, or anything at all, but let them move.

The sections **Singing** and **Songs** deal more specifically with song material and its presentation but this section was included at the beginning to stress the importance of singing. Since it is often easier to do rhythmic activities and even speech and poetry, we tend to forget that the voice was man's first instrument and that singing should come before all else.

Many people say: "But I have no time for a music period." The answer to this is to have short singing sessions several times a day incorporating a few of the rhythm, speech and movement ideas along with the singing. The benefits from such a program will be great and the time spent will be more than justified.

In the classroom, sing while the children are putting on their boots, while they are lining up for recess or going on a bus. Sing a song about a policeman or fireman during a lesson on community helpers. Sing a folk song from the country presently being studied in the geography class. Surely it is as important to know some songs of the country as it is to know the number of pounds of bacon exported or the number of towns with over 10,000 inhabitants.

Many teachers say: "But I can't sing!" or "I can't even carry a tune." This is a real problem but it can be overcome. Children don't mind if you are not very good at music. Often, in an older class, there is one child who can take the lead or there is a teacher down the hall who would come in and introduce a song to your class. Records and tapes are not as real to the children as the actual voice but songs *can* be learned from them. There are many excellent recordings and tapes available. (See **Records**, page 225, for some suggestions.)

Use a piano (one finger if necessary), an autoharp, ukelele, recorder, or anything that will help you present the song confidently. Although, admittedly, the piano does present problems, the other instruments are easy to play.

LET'S SING!

RELAXATION

CONTENTS

All lessons should begin with some form of relaxation because a tense body cannot learn. If you sense that the children have started to "tighten" during a lesson you should have them relax and begin again. This is true in working with all subjects — mathematics, reading and spelling as well as music — and is particularly important when working with exceptional children.

There are many relaxation exercises but the following few are especially useful. They should be done *slowly!*

A. GENERAL RELAXATION

Try to create some space for these exercises. There is nothing worse than trying to move in a cramped setting; the whole purpose of the exercises would be defeated. The best place in the school setting is the gym but, to make a gross understatement, it is not always available. So, push the chairs back and let's begin.

Move to a Song

Have some children sing a well-known song while others move any way they wish to the rhythm and mood of the song. Singing a well-known song like this encourages relaxed movement because the song is part of the child and he can concentrate on just the movement.

Spatial relationship

Feathers

Give each child a feather. (Coloured feathers can be purchased at craft stores.) Have the child blow his feather up in the air and try to keep it up by blowing. This encourages breath control and lots of movement.

Breath control

Rag Doll

Have the children move like a rag doll or some floppy animal. Alternate this with moving stiffly like a wooden soldier. This exercise will help the tense child feel the contrast in movement.

Have the children move like a rag doll while repeating the following very slowly:

"I'm an old rag doll and I have no bones at all."

Balloons

Spatial relationship

Give each child a balloon. Have him keep it up in the air either by blowing or hitting it with hands. This exercise should be done in a room with a lot of space and can be accompanied by music from records. Waltz music which gives a good steady beat but is also relaxing is a good choice: *i.e. The Skaters' Waltz, The Blue Danube* by Strauss or the "Waltz" from *Copelia* by Delibes.

Scarves

Similar relaxed movements can also be encouraged by having the children move to music, holding light, brightly coloured chiffon scarves.

Shake Out

Body awareness

Have the children stand and "shake out" parts of the body starting with the hands, feet and head and finally involving the whole body. Name the individual body parts as you work with them.

Have the children lift and lower their shoulders. First, one at a time, then both together. Do this slowly. Make big circles with alternate shoulders. Say: "Imagine you have a pencil stuck to your shoulders and you are drawing a circle on the wall."

Have the children sit or stand. Let the head fall loosely forward, slowly, a few times. Let the head fall backward, then from side to side, always slowly. Make very slow circles in different directions with the head (so that the children will not get dizzy). Tell the children to allow their mouths to open as their heads go back. The feeling of relaxation will be greater.

Balloon Pricking

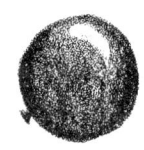

Have the children lie on the floor like collapsed balloons. As the teacher plays softly on a drum, the "balloons" are blown up and get bigger and bigger. The teacher plays a loud bang on the drum to "prick" the balloons and they all collapse again. Repeat.

Instead of "pricking" the balloons, let them go. They fly away. The children imitate this in movement.

B.   BREATHING EXERCISES

— Breathe like a big fat man. (Stomach and chest move out, shoulders remain still.)
— Breathe out as long as you can without making a noise.
— Breathe out as long as you can, making the "th" sound. This helps the child to control his breathing.

Breath control
— Combine breathing with an arm motion. Raise your arms slowly as you breathe in, lower them as you breathe out, or raise your arms like a swan.
— Breathe out slowly as if you are going to blow out a candle but do not quite blow it out.

COORDINATION, SPATIAL RELATIONSHIP AND BODY RHYTHM

CONTENTS

This section deals with games to help develop the child's coordination, and his awareness of his own body, its image and its relationship to other objects and position in space in general. The sense of left and right (laterality), up and down, sideways, behind *etc.* and the projection of these concepts outward from the body to the surroundings (directionality) is necessary to the child's growth.

The development of rhythmic sureness is also very important. A child should be able to adapt his rhythm to those of other people. He should be able to walk to the steady beat of a drum or song and to clap to the word rhythm of a song.

By the time children are seven or eight they should have enough experience with movement and rhythm to have enabled them to develop in these important areas and to have provided themselves with much information about their environment. They should have sung songs, said rhymes, played games, skipped, run, jumped, climbed trees and played hop scotch. Children with these experiences seem "at home" in their environment and have a relaxed and easy manner.

There are many children who have some problem such as emotional disturbance, brain damage, autistic tendencies or who are just slow in maturing: others may have had a restricted early life, perhaps because they grew up in an apartment, with no provision made for free play. These children do not move in a relaxed way so they should be given concentrated work in rhythmic movement. Psychologists such as Prof. William Condon of Pittsburg feel that if a person cannot synchronize his "body language" with other people's he will never be able to communicate properly.* This conclusion is based on the realization that we actually communicate far more with gestures and expression than with words.

Other psychologists such as Newell C. Kephart and Bryant J. Cratty feel that a foundation of movement skills and inner rhythmic sureness must be laid before other learning processes such as reading or mathematics can be added.**

The suggestions which follow are very useful in working with kindergarten, primary and junior grade children. Besides helping rhythmic sureness and coordination, these games will also help the development of laterality, directionality, position of body in

*Davis, Flora *Inside Intuition: What We Know about Non-verbal Communication* McGraw-Hill, New York, 1973.

**Cratty, Bryant J. *Active Learning* Prentice-Hall, Englewood Cliffs, New Jersey, 1971, page 7.

space, body awareness and listening skills. If the different properties of the sounds are discussed and listed (loud, soft, high, low), reading and language development can be reinforced at the same time.

Great care must be taken when working with children not to force them to adapt their rhythm to someone else's before they are ready. For instance, do not take their hands and "help" them play in time. It won't work and will only result in making them stiff and resistant. Do not single them out as being "off the beat"; it will only make them more self-conscious and add to the problem.

Eventually, if the learning situation is kept very relaxed and work in rhythmic movement is done regularly, most children will acquire these motor skills, a well-developed rhythmic sureness, and the ability to keep the beat. For some it will be a long time in coming.

A. IMITATING EACH CHILD'S RHYTHM OR BEAT

Have the children sit in a circle. Talk about the different ways they can move when coming to school or going to the store — walking, running, skipping *etc*.

Have each child demonstrate his way in turn. Imitate the rhythm of the child's feet on a drum or sticks. The other children then clap this rhythm.

For children who are having problems with rhythm, a great amount of time must be spent at this stage. Some children are upset when they find themselves keeping the same rhythm as someone else and will immediately change their own. Eventually the child will learn to accept another person joining him in his rhythm and then, finally, the child will learn to imitate another person's rhythm.

If it is possible to work individually with the child, his progress will be much faster. In time, most children will be able to imitate the leader's rhythm if lots of practice is provided.

B. FOLLOW ME
(using simple body movements)

The children imitate the movements of the leader, changing when the leader changes.

Keep the tempo fairly slow so that no one becomes confused and tense.

At first, keep the rhythm at a steady walking beat. Later, you may add more difficult rhythms.

Do the following in sequence, making sure that each step is conquered before going on to the next.

Body awareness
Auditory sequencing
Body levels

1. Pat Knees
   Pat knees in a fairly slow, relaxed tempo.
   The children imitate.

2. Clapping
   This must be done softly. You can use different parts of the hands such as the edges, two fingers in the palm, *etc*.

3. Combine 1 and 2
   Keep this slow, simple and relaxed.
   e.g. pat, clap, pat, clap;
   or pat, clap, clap, clap; pat, clap, clap, clap.

4. Snapping Fingers
   This is difficult for some children.
   Keep the tempo slow.

5. Combine 1, 2, and 4
   Keep the pattern simple.
   e.g. pat, clap, snap, snap,
   pat, clap, snap, snap.

6. Stamping Feet
   Do this first sitting down, as there is a problem of balance.

7. Combine 1, 2, 4 and 6

The above progression might take a long time to work through: from many months or, in some cases, many years. Combinations such as pat, clap, snap, clap, are very difficult, even for a child who has no problems, but they can be mastered if worked at slowly and consistently.

The child's rate of progress in these exercises is very difficult to predict. It depends on many factors — maturity, emotional stability, other problems the child might have, such as impaired hearing, cerebral palsy, inner ear problems affecting balance, the amount of time which is spent working with the child and so on. If, however, work is done in this type of activity every day, all children should show dramatic improvement in two to three months.

C. ECHOES

A big problem in a book of this kind lies in deciding how to organize different concepts. Echoes could follow here because they provide excellent training in coordination but they have been included in **Auditory Awareness** because they are perfect for listening, auditory sequencing, and memory.

Echoes are a logical step after Follow Me, so do try some at this point. You will find the explanation on page 37.

D. BALANCE

Laterality

Have the children just rock slowly back and forth to the words "rock, rock, rock, rock" or to a slow rocking-type song like a lullaby or a sea song. Playing a record of slow waltzlike music and having the children move to it is also excellent.

Have the children do this first sitting down, then kneeling and, finally, standing.

Walking slowly in a "rolling" gait also provides good practice in balancing. Do this to the beat of a song, poem, record or drum.

To reinforce the concept of left and right have the children say "left, right, left, right" while they are doing the exercises.

E. MOVE TO DRUM RHYTHMS
(This game could also be played with sticks and other instruments.)

Auditory awareness

Do the following in sequence.

1. Walking
    Play the drums in a good swinging, walking beat. The children listen first, then walk to this, trying to match their walk to the rhythm of the drum.

2. Stopping
    When the drum stops, the children stop. Children with learning disabilities often have trouble stopping an activity. It is very important to master this skill. To practise moving and then stopping to the sound of a drum is very helpful. All children can benefit from this kind of activity.

3. Running
   Play the drum quickly for the running beat. The children learn to listen for the difference between the sound for walking and that for running.

4. Jumping
   This is hard sometimes to distinguish from the walking tempo as small children jump almost as fast as they walk. Play the drum in a more forceful manner to indicate the "jump". You might have to tell them that this is a jumping beat.

5. Skipping and Galloping
   The beats for these are uneven and the children will recognize them very quickly.

6. Sliding
   This can be indicated by making a "swishing" sound on the drumhead with the flat of the hand.

Auditory awareness

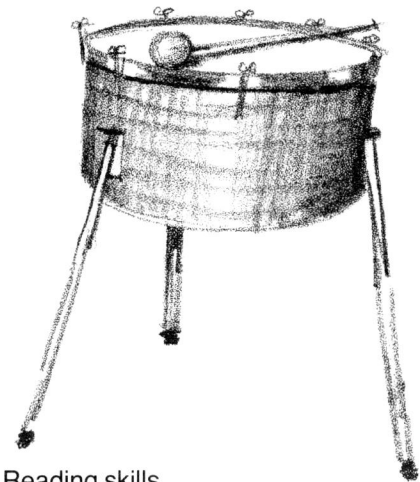

Reading skills

At first, stop after each type of movement before changing to another. When the children have acquired this skill, you can then change from one to another with no stops in between.

Reading skills can be reinforced by adding the following:
1. Make cards with words describing the activity (walk, run, skip).
2. Hold up one card; the child guesses which activity it describes; the child who is correct does the action to a drum accompaniment, then is allowed to choose the next card to play. Many other games of this type are possible.

F. WALK BEAT OF SONGS OR POEMS

Have the children sing a song or recite a poem they know so well that they don't have to think as they sing it — it is part of them. Have them walk around on the beat at the same time.

Suitable songs might be:
Baa Baa Black Sheep
Frère Jacques
Twinkle, Twinkle Little Star

Suitable poems might include:
Pease Porridge Hot
Humpty Dumpty
Jack and Jill

Give one child who is on the beat a drum to play to reinforce the sound of the beat. Most children will walk on the beat naturally, but for those who are having trouble, the above is a good exercise.

See **Singing**, page 51, for a description of catching the beat in different parts of the body while singing.

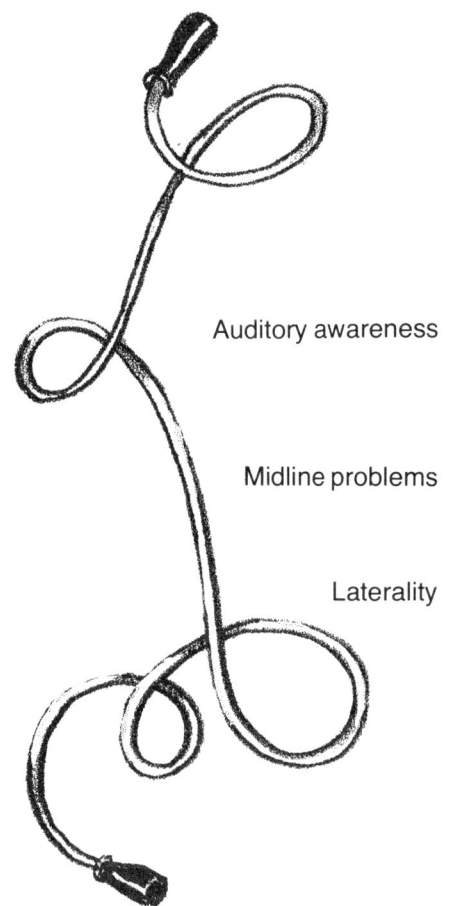

G. KEEP THE BEAT WITH ROPES OR HOOPS

Auditory awareness

Have a group of children stand holding a rope or hoop. The size of the group will vary according to the children's ages and emotional control but four or five children is usually a good number. The hoop or rope should be held loosely in their hands with the palms up so that there is less temptation to yank it.

Midline problems

The children stand still and move the hoop or rope gently from side to side to the beat of a song or poem which is well known to them. This game can also be done to the words "pull, pull" chanted by someone or to a drum beat.

Laterality

If left and right concepts need reinforcing, say "left, right, left, right" as the children sway from side to side.

This kind of group activity helps a child who has problems with moving to a steady beat, because he can be "pulled" in time with the other children.

H. SCARVES

Lightweight, brightly coloured chiffon or nylon scarves can be used not only to encourage relaxation (see page 8) but also in coordination and spatial relationship exercises. Try the following ideas.

The children roll their scarves into a ball, throw them up into the air and imitate the movement the scarves make as they float slowly down.

The children roll their scarves up into a ball, throw them up into the air and catch them on one hand, the other hand, one foot, the other foot, their heads, one shoulder, their backs, *etc*.

Reading

The children move their scarves high above their heads or low behind them or at the side, as they are instructed. This not only helps develop spatial concepts but can be made a reading exercise if cards printed with the directions high, low, left side, right side, behind, *etc*. are held up at the same time.

Make cards with the following shapes on them.

Shape perception

○ △ ▭ ∞ 8 ☐ Show them to the children and ask them to move their scarves to make these shapes in the air. Change hands with the scarves so practice is given with both sides of the body.

I. CIRCLES, SQUARES AND TRIANGLES

"When the drum starts, keep the beat with your feet and walk around in a circle (square, triangle, rectangle)." Many children find it difficult to imagine these shapes well enough to walk out the pattern on the floor.

Vary the game by requesting that they make a *small* triangle, a *large* rectangle, *etc.* This brings in yet another concept — that of relative size.

Shape perception

J. SEND THE MESSAGE

This is a variation of the old party game in which someone whispers a message to the person beside him, who in turn whispers to the person beside him and so on to the last person, who says the message out loud. The trick is to have the last person's message correspond with the first person's message.

Several children stand in a line. (The number of children in the line depends on their ages and abilities.)

The child at the end taps a "message" (a short rhythm) on the back of the child in front of him. This second child repeats the rhythm on the back of the next child and so on up to the front. The front child then claps (or plays on a drum) the "message" he received.

If there is a problem, you can watch to see where the breakdown occurs and help that child specifically when his turn comes.

Children enjoy this game.

K. MIRROR

The following exercises are excellent for developing body awareness and coordination skills. They must be done slowly and each step must be mastered before you move on to the next. They may appear simple but each involves three distinct steps: (1) differentiation of body parts (2) control and (3) coordination necessary to imitate.

Body awareness
Laterality

Follow With Your Eyes

Begin by sitting or standing facing the child. Have a ball or bean bag in one hand; hold it out to one side, move it up, down, in, out, around. Transfer it to the other hand and repeat the actions on the opposite side. The child just follows it with his eyes.

Mirror

Directionality
Attention span

The child becomes a "mirror" of you and copies exactly the actions he sees. This time no object is held in the hands.

Do the following in sequence:

1. Move one hand slowly up, down, to the side, around, wiggle the fingers, wave the hand *etc*. The child copies the action using the hand (and arm) on the same side.
2. Repeat with the other hand.
3. Repeat with one foot and then the other. Do this exercise sitting down, or balance becomes a problem.
4. After a lot of practice with one hand or one foot at a time, try two hands together. First, move them in the same direction and do the same actions with them. Later, try with hands going in different directions and doing different actions. This step is difficult for some children. Do not rush into it until the child is ready.
5. Again, when the child is ready, and after much practice doing the preceding steps, combine the actions of one hand and one foot. At first, combine those on the same side, then those on opposite sides.

Group participation

Let children try these games in partners, trying to mirror each other's actions.

L. ADDITIONAL EXERCISES FOR SPECIFIC PROBLEMS

Sometimes children have special problems in coordination and psychologists recommend that they perform certain exercises to overcome these. Here are some examples.

I   Special Exercises Done to Music

Music can help the child relax and control his movements so that he moves smoothly. Exercises will also become more enjoyable when set to music.

One example is "Angels in the Snow" described in the book *The Slow Learner in the Classroom*.* The child lies on his back on the floor and with one arm makes sweeping motions along the floor, up and out to the side, up over his head and back down again. The exercise is repeated with the other arm, then the two together. One leg, then both legs, make the same sweeping motions out to the side and back; repeat, starting with the other leg, then both legs. When the children are ready, one leg and one

*Kephart, Newell C. *The Slow Learner in the Classroom* Charles E. Merrill Co., Columbus, Ohio, 1960, page 98.

arm are combined and finally both legs and both arms. This is, of course, an old children's game and when done lying in the snow the resulting imprint is called "an angel".

Records of waltz music and semipopular music which have a lively beat but do not intrude on the concentration are a good choice here. MUZAK and other companies which sell background music to commercial firms and stores use this principle of background music to aid performance. This is to be deplored in most instances but here we can make good use of it.

II   Ball Bouncing, Throwing and Catching

Many children have trouble throwing and catching a ball. These few exercises will help.

a.   Ball Bouncing

Choose a short poem, a well-known song or a record with a strong, definite beat: a march, for instance. Have the children practise the ball bouncing skills to this accompaniment, bouncing on the strong beat.

Do these in sequence:

1. Bounce, catch, bounce, catch (repeat).
2. Bounce, catch, throw in air, catch (repeat).
3. Bounce, catch with right hand (repeat).
4. Bounce, catch with left hand (repeat).
5. Bounce and catch while walking, first in any direction, then along a line. Do the action with both hands, then with right only, then left only, then in fast time without catching in between.

Almost any of the well-known nursery rhymes and children's songs are suitable for ball bouncing because they have such a definite beat but, in addition, there are many songs and poems in children's folklore which are designed especially to be accompanied by ball bouncing. Some of these are: *One, Two, Three, Alora, Ordinary Movings* and *Help! Murder! Police!* Others may be found in children's song collections such as *Sally Go Round the Sun,* (see **Books**, page 233) which has one section devoted to them.

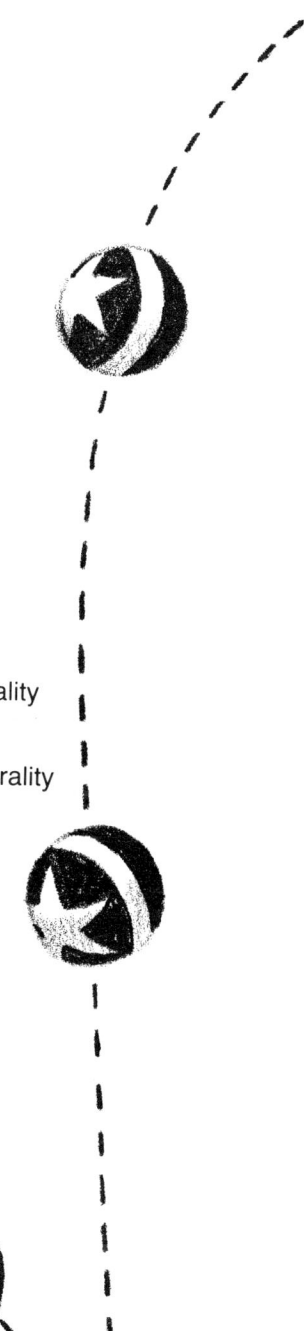

Laterality

Laterality

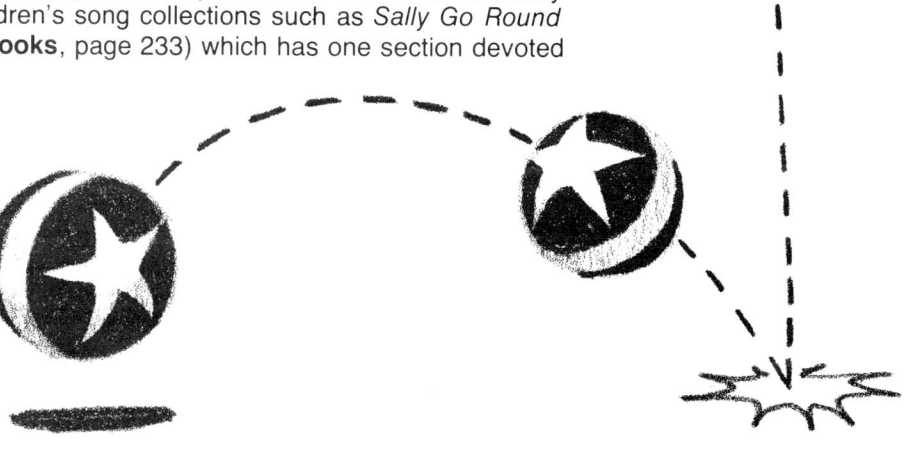

19

The next two exercises can be performed well to a short song such as *Li'l Liza Jane* (see **Songs**, page 71) or to a short poem like the following:

Happiness

John had
Great Big
Waterproof
Boots on;
John had a
Great Big
Waterproof
Hat;
John had a
Great Big
Waterproof
Mackintosh —
And that
(Said John)
is
That.

A. A. Milne

Directionality

6. Bounce and catch on the beat walking sideways to the right for the first phrase of four lines, to the left for the second, to the right for the third phrase and to the left for the fourth.

Midline

7. Have a child stand on a balance board. Have him bounce and catch the ball starting on one side and working around the front to the other side while saying the poem. It might take the whole poem to get around at first, but later the child will be able to start on the left and get around to the right on the first phrase, back to the left for the second, and so on.

b. **Ball Throwing and Catching**
Sing this song with the children.

Make a Circle

Group participation

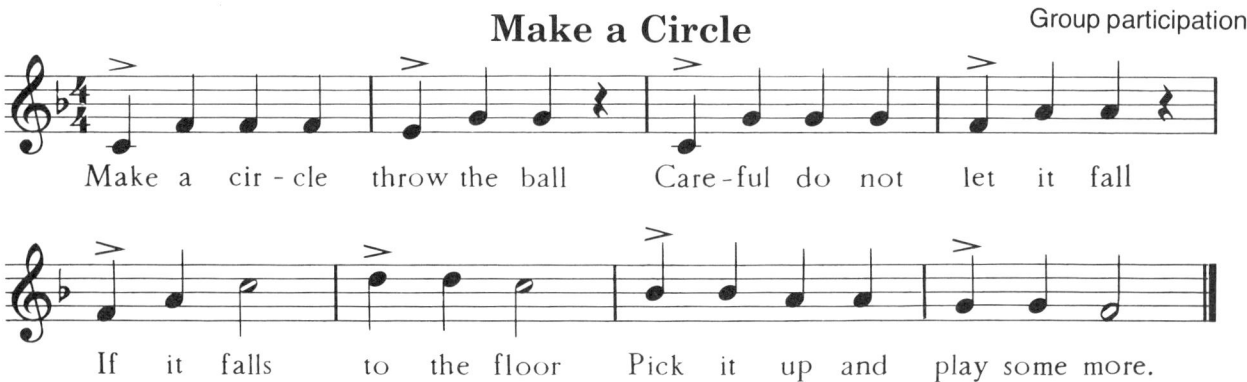

Make a cir-cle throw the ball   Care-ful do not   let it   fall

If   it   falls   to   the   floor   Pick   it   up   and   play some more.

I have changed the words from "take your seat and play no more" to "pick it up and play some more". If you are trying to teach skills to someone who lacks them it makes little sense to put the child "out" of the game because he has not mastered them.

Have the children make a circle.
1. One person stands in the middle and throws a ball to each child in turn on the strong beat. The child returns the throw on the next strong beat as well.
2. The game can be changed by changing the words and actions to "roll the ball" or "bounce the ball".
3. Instead of having a person in the middle, the ball can be bounced or thrown from child to child in turn around the circle.

III   Imitating Animals, Machines and Things

Much useful and creative movement can be done by having the children imitate the movement of certain animals, machines, growing flowers, *etc.* A poem or song about an animal or machine is often a good starting place:
The Train
Hickory Dickory Dock (Nursery Rhyme)
The Elephant (see below)
Bell Horses
Jig Jog Jig Jog
Horses Horses
Are You Sleeping? (clocks)

Those marked * will be found in **Poems**, pages 139-159, or **Songs**, pages 55-128.

This activity can be structured to encourage children to practise the movements recommended for motor development by psychologists such as Newell C. Kephart (*op. cit.* page 18): *i.e.* the duck walk and the elephant walk.

In the duck walk the child squats down with his hands either on his knees or his waist or sticking out behind him, in imitation of the duck's tail feathers. Keeping this position he "waddles forward".

The elephant walk can be done very simply with each child bending over and making a "trunk" from his outstretched arms. He walks slowly swaying the trunk back and forth. In a more complicated version two children can combine by one wrapping his legs around the waist of another child. The first child lets his head hang down and then puts his head, shoulders and arms between the legs of the second child, holding onto the second child's legs. The second child then lets himself fall forward on his hands and proceeds to "walk" on all fours with stiff knees.

Do the duck walk to the following poem:

Six Little Ducks

Six little ducks went swimming one day
Over the pond and far away.
Mother duck said "Quack, quack, quack"
And five little ducks came swimming right back.

Repeat until "no little ducks" come swimming right back.

Try a poem such as "The Elephant" and have the children imitate an elephant's walk:

The Elephant

The elephant walks like this, like that
He's terribly big and he's terribly fat.
He has no fingers, he has no toes,
But goodness gracious, WHAT A NOSE.

IV   Midline Problems

Many children, even in the regular classrooms, often have trouble crossing over the midline of the body to perform a task on the other side. Children with severe disabilities simply cannot operate on the side of the body opposite to the hand performing the task. The following ideas will help this problem through the use of music and rhythm.

Laterality
Directionality
Midline

Walk and Swing
Have the children walk a slow beat to a song or record and have them swing their arms alternately from side to side across their bodies.

Pat Your Knees
Practise patting knees in the following order:
1. With the right hand, pat alternate knees: right, left, right, left.
2. Do the same with left hand: left, right, left, right.
3. Do this with both hands together crossing over hands and alternating knees.
4. The right hand pats the right knee, left shoulder, right knee, left shoulder alternately.
5. The left hand pats the left knee, right shoulder, left knee, right shoulder alternately.

These exercises can be more fun if they are done to the beat of a poem or song.

Alternate Clap

Clap hands together on one side of the body and then the other, alternately.

Cymbals

Play large cymbals. This helps to bring the hands together in the middle.

Accompaniments can be devised which cross the midline. These should be repetitive and are best played on a fairly large instrument, such as an alto xylophone, alto metallophone, bass xylophone or bass metallophone.

Laterality

Right hand only

C Major

Left hand only

C Major

V   Circles

The child must learn that the circle is drawn with constant rhythm.*

When children with problems are practising the drawing of circles, whether in the air, on the board, or on paper, it sometimes helps things go more smoothly if this exercise is accompanied by music. Sing a song or play a well-known record which is in $\frac{3}{4}$ or $\frac{6}{8}$ time. This gives a cyclic rhythm and is perfect for circle drawing. *Humpty Dumpty* or *Here We Go Round the Mulberry Bush* are good examples of songs; records such as a Strauss waltz or *The Skater's Waltz* would be excellent as well.

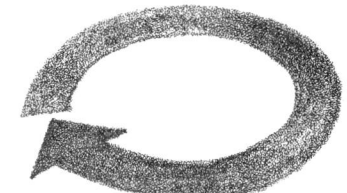

This exercise is sometimes easier if the circles are drawn in finger paint or liquid soap. This is especially true when it is used with children with cerebral palsy or other coordinative disabilities.

M. AUDITORY AWARENESS AND LISTENING SKILLS

Many of the activities in the section **Let's Listen** could just as well have been included in this section. Try the following:

Presence and Absence of Sound
— Freeze like a ball or the letter Z. (See page 28 for a description of these games.)
— Musical *Simon Says*. (See page 29.)

---

*Kephart, Newell C. *op. cit.* page 18.

Developing Awareness of Fast and Slow
    (See page 31.)

High and Low
— Moving to high and low sounds. (See page 33.)
— Relating high and low sounds to different parts of body and moving accordingly. (See page 34.)
— Songs and poems. (See page 34.)

LET'S LISTEN

CONTENTS

All experience with music could be classed as developing auditory awareness and listening skills, but simply exposing children to music today is not enough. Because every child is surrounded by music from radio, records, TV and MUZAK from his earliest years, he quickly learns to shut most of this sound out. This is particularly true of children with problems or those from the congested areas of our cities where the ability to blank out sound becomes a matter of survival. Before any formal learning can take place the ability to listen to and to differentiate between sounds must be consciously taught. What better way than through music? The following ideas are fun to do and they work well with the average child as well as with groups of exceptional boys and girls.

Listening skills can be roughly divided into three main categories: auditory awareness, auditory discrimination and auditory sequencing and memory. The first, auditory awareness, is concerned with the simple recognition of the presence of sound. The second, auditory discrimination, requires the ability to distinguish between sounds and to group them into categories such as fast-slow, loud-soft, high-low *etc*. The third section, auditory sequencing, deals with the ability to reproduce a sequence of sounds in the correct order and therefore requires the exercise of auditory memory as well.

A. AUDITORY AWARENESS

Presence and Absence of Sound

Exploring Sound

Laterality
Directionality

Have "portable" sound makers available i.e., sticks, small drums, tambourines, shakers, finger cymbals, etc. The children choose one, explore its sound and move to the quality of its sound. This game can be done with a partner. One person "moves" the other with his sound, high, low, fast, slow, to the left, to the right, etc.

Freeze

Have the children walk to a drum beat and stop or "freeze" when the drum stops. Use the sound of a piano, xylophone, record, sticks, *etc.* instead of the drum.

Freeze Like an Object

Body awareness
Coordination

This is a variation of "Freeze" above, but this time, tell children to freeze like a "tree", a "ball", a "dog", the number "2", the letter "S", the letter "L" and so on. This maintains interest and reinforces number and letter shapes when these concepts are used with slightly older children.

Freeze High and Low

Body levels
Spatial relationship

Have the children "freeze" with the body at a high level, using the space above their bodies. They can also work down low or in the middle.

Freeze Like a Figure

Have the children "freeze" in the shape of stick figures which are drawn on cards. One of the cards is held up by someone when the music stops so that the children can see it.

These figures can be kneeling, bending over, have arms outstretched or hands over heads, *etc*.

Examples of figures to put on cards in the above exercise.

Musical Chairs

This excellent party game can be varied by having the children jump into hoops placed on the floor when the music stops, instead of searching for a chair. Remember always to have one fewer chair or hoop than the number of children playing.

This is a game of elimination, but the eliminating is accomplished by an impersonal force in the music, and not by an authority figure (teacher, camp leader, etc.), or a lack of skill on the child's part. Have those eliminated, stay involved by taking turns running the record player or by clapping the beat of the music etc.

Different Directions

Play some music, as in musical chairs. Each child moves in any direction he wants. When the music stops have the children change direction and move in that new direction when the music starts again. You can help them think of different ways to move by suggesting that they go backwards, forwards, to one side, to the other side, diagonally, *etc*.

Directionality
Spatial relationship

When Did the Sound Stop?

Play an instrument such as a large cymbal, triangle, large gong or metallophone which has a ringing tone. The children listen and put their hands up when they can no longer hear the sound. The challenge here is that they must realize that the sound continues after the playing has stopped.

Simon Says

"Simon Says" is a favourite game with children. The leader says "Simon says do this" and makes a movement (puts hands out; lifts one foot up; bends over; or claps hands, *etc*.). The children imitate. The leader says "Simon says do this." and performs another movement. The children imitate.

Body awareness

Concentration

The trick, of course, comes when the leader says simply: "Do this" without first saying "Simon says". If the child imitates at this command, he is wrong.

When a child makes a mistake, don't put him out of the game. He is the one who needs the practice, not the child who is always the winner.

Musical Simon Says

This is very similar, with music added, and is very helpful for developing listening skills.

Body awareness

Concentration

Instead of moving to a spoken command ("Simon says do this"), children move only when they hear a certain note played on a piano, xylophone, glockenspiel, pitch pipe, or other tuned instrument. Give instructions, along with this note, to "Touch your knees. Touch your head." *etc*. The children do the action only when they hear the note — no note, no action. In these games let different children take turns being leader.

Never put the child out of the game when playing this, especially children with problems, because they will never get the practice they need. Just say: "Try again and really listen this time."

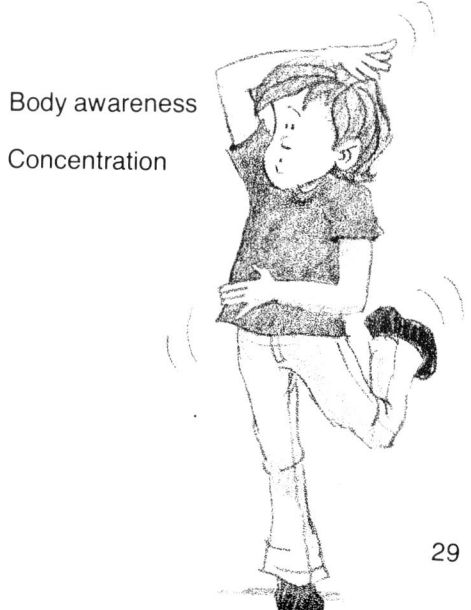

29

I Distinguishing Between Sounds

Auditory discrimination is very difficult for some children but it will improve with practice.

Listen to different sounds: outside (cars, sirens, birds, rain, thunder, dogs barking), and inside (feet walking, chalk scratching on the chalkboard, radiator thunking, people talking). The list is endless. The children must be very quiet in order to hear. Have the children describe one of the sounds in movement. The very act of moving tends to help the child concentrate better on listening. Simple listening is often a passive act, but when movement is added, it becomes an activity of conscious involvement. Have them imitate the sound, talk about it and even make a list of all the sounds if they are at that stage in reading readiness.

These games help language development, as much useful language is gained if the sounds are discovered and their properties listed (whirring, scrunching, loud, scratchy, thumping, sizzling, *etc*.).

Room Tap

Tap objects around the room — chalkboard, glass, desk, windows. Have the children identify what is being done with their eyes shut. They must listen very carefully to distinguish the differences.

Found Sounds

Have the children bring things that make interesting sounds from their home or street. Help them to discover some really unusual ones — such as clanging garbage can lids, balloons making a whistling sound as the air is let out — as well as the more ordinary ones — of rattling pots and pans or tapping flower pots. Listen to the sounds, discuss the differences and experiment with combining the sounds in different ways.

Language development

Which One is Playing?

Play instruments with sharply contrasting sounds, such as maracas and a drum, or xylophone and sticks. Put the instruments and players out of sight of the other children and have them tell you which instrument is playing. Have the children describe in movement the kind of sound each instrument makes.

Which One Stopped?

Play several instruments together. The number of instruments depends on the proficiency of the children. Let the children hear these instruments singly, then together, so that they know what sounds each instrument makes and what the total sound is like. Next, put the instruments and players out of sight of the other children and have them all play together. At a signal, one child stops while the others continue. The trick is to guess which instrument stopped playing.

What's in the Can?

Fill the cans with different items such as beans, small stones, cereal, rice, *etc*. Cover them and then have the children identify each one by sound alone.

Musical Simon Says
(for distinguishing between sounds)

This game (already described on page 29) can be easily adapted for distinguishing between similar sounds.

Play one note (*i.e.* G). Have the children hum this note so that they know what note to listen for. This note (the "key" note) alone is the one they must hear each time before they move to the command of the leader: "Touch your teeth. Touch your elbow" and so on. If another ("wrong") note is sounded with the command, they must not move.

Body awareness

At first choose just one "wrong" note, many tones away from the note they are to listen for. Gradually, as the game is learned, move this "other" note closer to the key one. The closer the notes, the harder the game.

When everybody is fairly proficient, play *two* "wrong" notes, one higher and one lower than the key note. At first, play notes that are many tones away from the key note, and then gradually move them closer and closer.

Any melodic instrument may be used in this game; glockenspiel, xylophone, metallophone, piano, guitar, *etc*.

II   Developing Awareness of Fast and Slow and of Different Rhythms

For ideas to help children become aware of walking, running and skipping rhythms, *etc*. and to express the difference between these rhythms in movement, see **Coordination, Spatial Relationship and Body Rhythm**, section E, Move to Drum Rhythms, page 14.

Fast and Slow
(singing, taped or recorded)

Have the children sing a song which is well known to them. Sing it at different tempos: at normal pace, very slowly or very quickly. Have them listen to the difference and discuss the change.

If a tape recorder or record player is available, play music or sounds at normal speed, then at faster and slower speeds. Discuss the difference and perhaps have the children move to the sounds.

Imitate Movement of Animals
(domestic, farm, circus, jungle or zoo)

Language development

Discuss how each animal moves — quickly, slowly, heavily, lightly. Imitate this movement. Try to find a sound effect on an instrument to accompany the movement.

Body awareness
Coordination

Look in **Songs** for examples which call for imitative movement of animals in their lyrics.

Spatial relationship

The children can also listen to records, such as Saint Saëns *Carnival of the Animals*, and imitate in movement the animals described in the music.

Have the children make a picture of the sound and movement with paints or crayons or on the chalkboard *i.e.:*

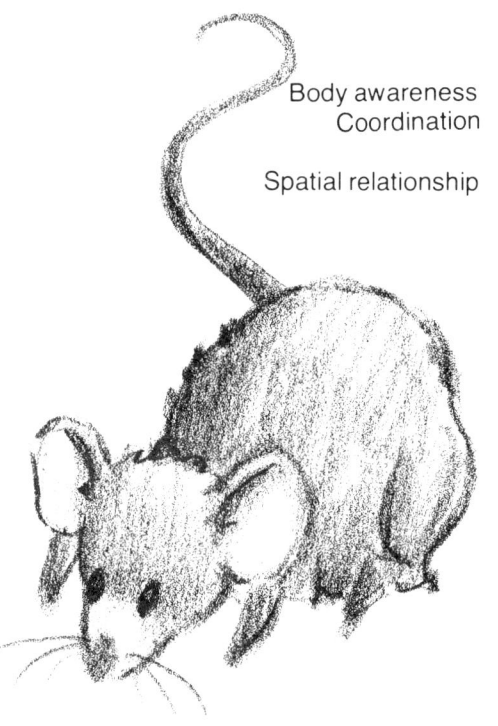

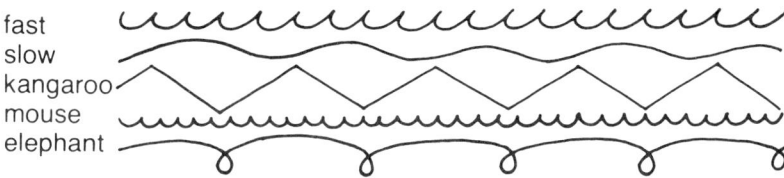

fast
slow
kangaroo
mouse
elephant

The attempt to draw or paint the sound reinforces awareness of its qualities.

III   Developing Awareness of Loud, and Soft, and Becoming Louder and Softer

Language development

Awareness of the concepts of loud and soft comes from listening to many sounds and describing them in language. Children should be encouraged to talk about sounds around them and to decide whether they are loud or soft.

Have the children describe in movement the feeling of loud and soft sounds when played on a drum, piano, or sticks, *etc*. They will usually make large, open movements for loud, and small, closed ones for soft.

In and Out for Loud and Soft
Here is a game to help awareness of sounds becoming louder and softer. Have the children stand in a circle with space in front and behind them. Someone stands in the middle and plays a drum. When the drummer plays loudly, the children move into the centre; when he plays softly, they back out of the circle.

When this game is mastered, it can be made more challenging by playing loudly or softly but in different rhythms: *i.e.*, skip-

Spatial relationship

ping, running, *etc*. Children have to listen to two things — "how" to move and "in which direction" (in or out). You could say "move up high" or "down low" as the children are listening for

Coordination

the loud or soft sounds. This also makes the game much harder.

Reading

Use flash cards with the words "loud", "soft", *etc*. written on them.

Encourage the children to draw or paint these concepts.

Visual awareness

Some interesting patterns will develop.

IV Developing Awareness of High and Low Sounds

High and Low in Movement

Do these in sequence.

Use the words "up" and "down" if the children are not ready for "high" and "low".

1. Have the children talk about objects which are high and low. First outside (clouds or sky *vs* ground or rocks) then inside (ceilings *vs* floors). Have them talk about and imitate high and low sounds around them (birds singing *vs* large dog barking; police car siren *vs* chuffing of bulldozer).

   Language development

2. Play a pattern of notes from low to high then back to low again. Relate this to something the children know — an elevator going up and down in their apartment, a sleigh being dragged up the hill slowly then going back down the hill quickly or someone walking up and down stairs. Have them move their hands or whole body high and low as they hear the sounds.

   Spatial relationship

3. Play notes ascending and descending the scale but play each note several times. The children should try to sing these with you at the same time.

   Singing

   If the notes are repeated in a rhythmic pattern such as:

   | | ⊓ | or   ⊓ | ⊓ |

   the game becomes more interesting, especially for older children.

4. Play two notes, one high, one low. Ask "Which note is on the roof? Which is in the basement? Show me with your hands." Position yourself so that the children cannot see the notes being played. The exercise will thus be completely auditory.

5. Play a "dance" rhythm first on low notes then on high notes. Have the children move to this — doing a "low" dance or a "high" dance. Do not change from one to the other too quickly.

   Spatial relationship

Scarves

Light nylon or chiffon scarves can be used to add interest to these exercises. The children move with them high or low as the music dictates.

Spatial relationship

Hoops

Two children hold a large hoop upright about two feet from the ground for "high". Another two children hold a hoop upright resting on the ground for "low". Depending on which note is played the rest of the children have to choose the high hoop to climb through or the low hoop to crawl through.

Spatial relationship

Have the children show the concept of high and low visually by drawing and pointing, *etc*.

Visual awareness

High and Low Sounds and Body Levels

After the children are at ease putting together movements with various parts of the body — patting knees, stamping, clapping, snapping fingers (see **Coordination, Spatial Relationship and Body Rhythm**, page 13) — these body levels can be related to high and low notes. Children move only when the key note is sounded.

Stamp — lowest note.
Pat knees — next lowest.
Clap — medium high.
Snap fingers — highest.

These notes can be played on any melodic instrument; a piano (one finger), a xylophone, a slide whistle, or they can be sung (if you are sure you can sing the same note every time).

Play one note very slowly as many as eight or sixteen times: e.g., the lowest note, for stamping. Change to the note for clapping and play many times before going back to the first note. The children listen and change their body movements also. Combine only two different movements and their corresponding notes at first and don't change too quickly from one to the other. Later, after several weeks of listening practice, three or four notes can be combined in a pattern, with the children listening and changing their activity when the note changes.

Make sure that you have everyone listen to the individual notes separately at first, so that they are familiar with each sound.

Direct this game from behind a screen so that the children cannot see you playing. Their responses should be based solely on auditory recognition.

High and Low in Poems and Songs

There are many songs and poems which can help the children to develop the concepts of high and low or up and down. Some of these follow. The movement showing the concept should always be performed as well.

Poems

Sliding

Down the slide
We ride, we ride
Round we run and then
Up we pop
To reach the top
Down we come again.

Activities

The children pretend to slide down, run around to the back, climb up to the top and slide down again.

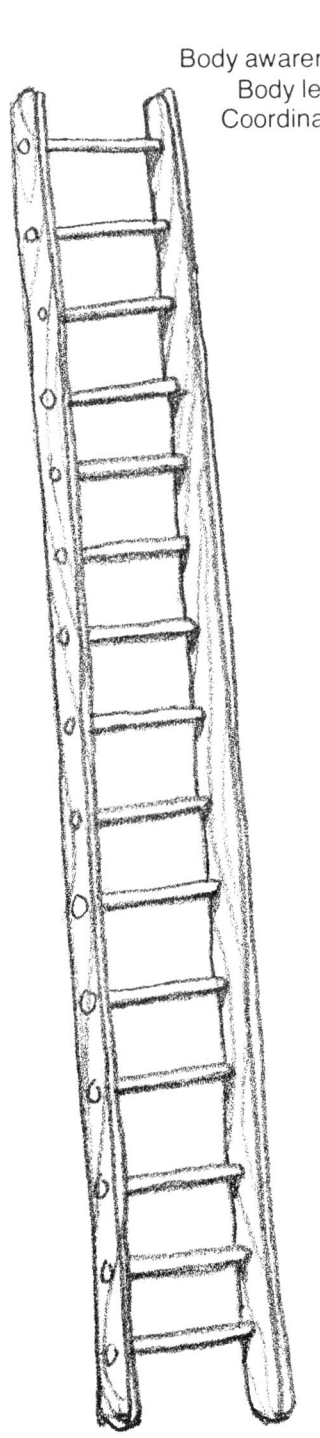

Body awareness
Body levels
Coordination

34

The Ladder

The ladder's high
And so
I go up step by step
And very slow
But when I'm at the top at last
I can come down . . . . . .
Very fast!

Activities

The children pretend to "climb" up the ladder with their hands as they say the poem letting their hands drop at the last line.

You could at the same time play the notes of a xylophone from low to high very slowly until the last line of the poem. At this point, slide the mallet very quickly over the notes top to bottom.

Songs

Bounce the Ball

Have the children sing the song and tell which words have the high notes and which the low notes. Show high, low and middle with the position of the hands.

Draw Sound Pictures

After a song has been learned well, the picture of the melody can be drawn in the air with the hand. This shows very vividly whether or or not the concept of high or low notes is clear in the child's mind.

Visual awareness

The picture of the melody can also of course be drawn on paper or the chalkboard. Children enjoy this activity.

Draw the picture of a melody heard on a record. This is harder, as the record player is much more impersonal than an instrument which the children can see being played and, of course, far more remote than the singing voice. See also **Singing**, page 53.

Singing

For a description of singing high and low tones see **Singing** under "Call and Response", page 49.

Hot and Cold

Variations on the old game "Hot and Cold" to teach "high" and "low". Have one child go out of the room or hide his eyes. Another child hides some article, such as a chalkboard brush, somewhere in the room. The first child has to find it but no verbal hints can be given. Instead, a third child plays a xylophone — low tones when the seeker is "cold" or far away from the hiding place, getting higher and higher as the seeker gets closer or "warm". Repeat the game with different children.

This is a very popular game, especially with boys, and it teaches listening skills and high and low concepts so painlessly.

(This game can also be played with the concepts "loud" and "soft".)

Reading

Whenever practical, flash cards with the words "high", "low" or "up" and "down" should be shown to the children as they perform the activity, to reinforce language development in all these games.

C. AUDITORY SEQUENCING

All children need to develop the ability to reproduce a sequence of sounds in the correct order, pattern and number. This skill is a fundamental one to be mastered before a child can learn to read, solve step-by-step problems in arithmetic or even speak correctly. It is a very difficult skill for many, involving, as it does, perception, memory and a motor activity of some sort (speech, singing or movement). For children with problems, there may be a breakdown in one or all of the foregoing steps, but most children can learn to play the following games if they are presented slowly enough.

I   Follow Me

"Follow Me" is an excellent sequencing exercise and should be performed as a preliminary to "Echoes". Children should be able to do sequences in movement as well as in sound.

For a fuller explanation of this, see **Coordination, Spatial Relationship and Body Rhythm**, page 12. Briefly, the leader performs some action: patting knees, clapping, stamping, hopping on one foot, *etc.* The children imitate, changing when the leader does.

Keep the action very simple at first, performing just a steady beat. Later, when everyone is more proficient, vary the patterns by making these fast or slow, or loud or soft, and so on.

If you find some children becoming tense, slow down the tempo and make the patterns simple again or stop altogether and do some relaxation exercises.

II   Echoes or Copycat

After the children are fairly proficient in "Follow Me", echoes can be tried. These are tremendously useful from Kindergarten to Grade 8 for developing coordination, auditory discrimination and auditory sequencing and a sense of phrasing. Besides all this, they are fun to do and involve everyone in the class.

They can be done in many ways: in movement by clapping hands, stamping feet, touching head, snapping fingers; in singing; or on instruments — percussion, such as drums and wood blocks, or melodic, such as xylophone, glockenspiels, *etc.*

Echoes can be tried on a one-to-one basis, or with the whole class. They can be worked in different metres: $\frac{2}{4}$ $\frac{4}{4}$ $\frac{6}{8}$ $\frac{3}{4}$ $\frac{5}{4}$ or $\frac{7}{8}$

Guard against doing the exercises too quickly. The children may become tense. Keep the tempo relaxed.

The important thing to remember is to allow each child some success. Do not make the exercises too difficult and always end with one or two that are so simple that every child can do them with ease.

Movement Echoes

Movement echoes are almost self-explanatory and are limited only by the space available. You perform a certain movement: high, low, fast, slow, running across the room, shaking hands over head, turning around, jumping up and down, and so on. The children copy. Later, one child can give the echoes to the rest.

Sequencing

Keep the movement simple at first, combining only one or two different motions. More complicated patterns can be tried later.

Coordination

Use different levels, different speeds, different forces (strong or weak motions).

Spatial relationship

Echoes Using Different Parts of the Body

Do the following exercises in sequence.
1. Clap a number of times in a steady pattern — two, three, four or five. Start with two counts and have the children echo. Increase the number as the children become proficient.

Coordination

2. Clap a simple 4 beat pattern:

| | | 𝄾
1   2   3   rest   Children echo: 1   2   3   rest

Attention span

3. Add notes of different lengths:

(a) | ⊓ | 𝄾 Children repeat: | ⊓ | 𝄾

(b) ⊓⊓ | 𝄾 Children repeat: ⊓⊓ | 𝄾

If trouble is encountered at this stage, put words to the pattern: | ⊓ | | | | 𝄾   ⊓ | | 𝄾

(a) Come, Maryanne or (b) Peter Marg Barbara Fred

(c) ⊓   ⊓ |
    We like playing ball.

Any word pattern will do as long as the rhythm and accents are suitable, and the content appeals to the children.

4. When the children can perform these echoes easily by clapping, combine different body motions such as patting knees, snapping, touching shoulders *etc*.

e.g. $\frac{4}{4}$ | | | 𝄾 $\frac{4}{4}$ ⊓   ⊓ | 𝄾
        pat, clap, pat, or   clap clap clap clap snap

or $\frac{4}{4}$ | | | 𝄾 $\frac{4}{4}$ | ⊓ | 𝄾
    stamp, stamp, clap or   pat, clap clap snap.

5. Make patterns longer (only if children are very proficient in shorter versions).

(a) $\frac{4}{4}$ | ⊓ | | ⊓⊓ | echo $\frac{4}{4}$ | ⊓ | | ⊓⊓ | |

or even (b) $\frac{4}{4}$ ⊓⊓ | | ⊓ | ⊓ | ⊓⊓ | | | | 𝄾

echo $\frac{4}{4}$ ⊓⊓ | | ⊓ | ⊓ | ⊓⊓ | | | | 𝄾

6. Clap or play these in different metres if you feel confident. Have the children echo.

$\frac{3}{4}$ | ⊓ | | ⊓ | | | | | 𝄾 𝄾

or $\frac{6}{8}$ ⊓⊓ | ♪ | ♪ | 𝄿

or even $\frac{7}{8}$ ⊓ ⊓ | ♪ | ⊓ | 𝄿

38

Dominance on One Side of Body

There are some children who can perform echoes on one side of the body and not on the other. Do not be concerned with those who have only slight difficulty because this problem will solve itself in time if the regular program of echoes is followed. However, sometimes, certain children are so dominant on one side that the other is almost useless. These must be given extra help.

Try the following in sequence:

1. Echo with one hand, patting knee, or tapping table.

2. Echo the same with just the other hand.

3. When ready, try doing both hands alternately. Change smoothly from one side to the other.

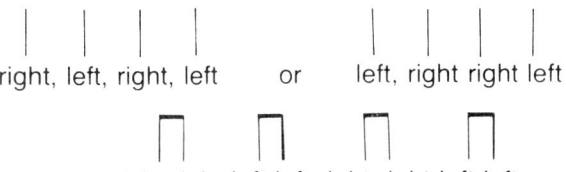

right, left, right, left   or   left, right right left

or   right right left left right right left left.

Have the children echo.

4. Combine left and right feet the same way.

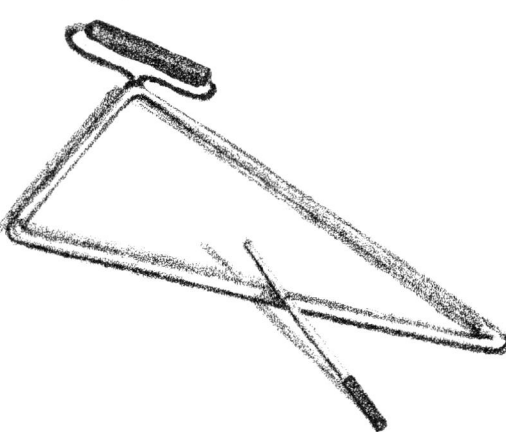

Laterality

Playing Echoes on Percussion Instruments

Rhythms similar to those above can be played on drums, sticks, triangles or some other percussion instrument. The children echo, also on a percussion instrument.

Boys in particular enjoy this activity. Often they will echo on drums long before they will clap a rhythm. This is especially the case with older boys who have learning or emotional problems.

Singing Echoes

Use syllables with a neutral vowel such as "loo", "lah" or "dum di dum" and begin simply. Gradually introduce more difficult notes and more complicated patterns.
Here are some examples to try.

Tone matching

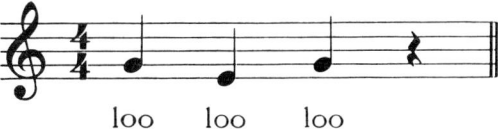

loo   loo   loo

loo   loo   loo loo loo

39

lah lah lah lah lah lah

dum di dum di dum

loo loo loo loo loo

lah lah lah lah

See **Singing**, page 49, Call and Response, for more examples of patterns that might be used as echoes.

Playing Echoes on Melodic Instruments

Begin very simply. Since there is no difference between echoing a pattern on a drum, and echoing it on one note on a xylophone, glockenspiel or chime bar, you should begin with one note.

Use glockenspiels, xylophones or chime bars.

Play: Children echo on instruments

Play:

Children echo

Echoes on two notes follow:

Play: Children echo.

Play: Children echo.

When playing patterns with three or more notes, step-by-step progressions are easier than leaps, so do something like the following:

40

Play: Children echo.

Play: Children echo.

Play   Children echo.

Then try: Children echo.

Finally, work up to patterns as difficult as your children can handle. Try the following if your children are ready:

Play

Children echo.

All the examples for singing and melodic instrumental echoes are given here in $\frac{4}{4}$ time. Try them also in different metres, such as $\frac{6}{8}$ $\frac{4}{4}$ $\frac{3}{4}$ etc.

Success in Echoes

To help each child succeed in echoes make at least the last beat of every pattern a rest. The children can catch their breath, keep relaxed and have time to organize their thoughts before repeating. As the children become more proficient, they will be able to echo patterns with the last beat filled in.

Keep the tempo fairly slow and relaxed and the patterns easy.

Sometimes, with young children, it helps to say: "My turn . . . " "Your turn . . . " This keeps them from starting too soon.

If you have trouble thinking of patterns to do for echoes, try them at first at home alone in a room with the door shut. It helps to say words to a song or a poem silently to yourself and clap the rhythm of the words.

41

Children as Leaders

After the children have had some experience, they can give the pattern for echoing to each other (in pairs or in small groups) or to the whole class. They are much less inhibited than adults.

Puppets

Children love puppets. Give some echoes using a puppet to spark interest. Emotionally disturbed, autistic and withdrawn children will sometimes respond to a puppet where they will not relate to a person. Puppets are particularly successful in reaching retarded children.

III   Songs

There are many excellent sequencing songs that count or catalogue in order either forwards or backwards. Try some of these well-known selections.

   Apples Pears and Oranges
   Barnyard Song (I had a cat and the cat pleased me)
   One Finger One Thumb Keep Moving
   She'll Be Coming Round the Mountain
   The Green Grass Grows All Around All Around
   There's a Hole in the Bottom of the Sea
   There's a Hole in the Bucket
   The Twelve Days of Christmas (A Partridge in a Pear Tree)

It is helpful to make pictures of the different components of the song in the beginning so the children can follow visually as the song is sung.

Singing play songs with definite movements or dance patterns which have to be learned in sequence and recalled in sequence can be very helpful.

See **Songs**, page 87, for ideas for these game songs. Some good examples are:

   Li'l Liza Jane
   Rig a Jig Jig
   Go In and Out the Windows
   Punchinello

The old favourites are also excellent.

   A-Hunting We Will Go
   Here We Go Round the Mulberry Bush
   The Farmer in the Dell
   London Bridge

*Songs marked * can be found in **Songs**, page 55. Many songs and poems which appear in this and following lists throughout the book are so well-known that they can be found in many popular song books. They have therefore not been given specific references.

IV   Stories and Poems

Many poems are sequencing poems and many stories are cumulative and have to be remembered in sequence. Some examples are:

Stories

Drummer Hoff
The Gingerbread Boy
　(American version of *Johnny Cake*)
Henny Penny
Johnny Cake
The Old Woman and Her Pig

Poems

My Father is a Garbage Man

My father is a garbage man — pheew.
My mother is a baker — pheew, yum yum.
My sister is a hairdresser
　　— pheew, yum, yum, curl, curl.
My brother is a cowboy
　　— pheew, yum yum, curl curl, bang bang.
My baby is a cry baby
　　— pheew, yum yum, curl curl, bang bang,
whaaaaaaaaaa!

I Went Downtown to See Miss Brown

I went downtown to see Miss Brown.
She gave me a nickel to buy a pickle.
The pickle was sour: she gave me a flower.
The flower was dead: she gave me a thread.
The thread was black: she gave me a smack.
The smack was hard: she gave me a card,
And this is what the card said to do:
　Lady, turn around, turn around, turn around.
　Lady, touch the ground, touch the ground, touch the ground.
　Lady, show your shoe, show your shoe, show your shoe.
　Lady, that will do, that will do, that will do.

These well-known sequencing poems are also popular with children:

Sequencing

Girl Guide Girl Guide (dressed in blue)
　— a skipping rhyme.
The Three Little Kittens (lost their mittens)
This Is the House that Jack Built

V   Other Ideas for Sequencing Practice

Coordination

Movement Sequence

Have the child reproduce a series of movements: *e.g.*, run eight steps, walk eight steps, jump four times. The number of movements in the series can be increased as the child becomes more proficient.

Simple motions can be used instead. "Touch your head, touch your shoulders, clap your hands, pat your knees." The children have to repeat these in the same order.

Instrument Sequence

Play several instruments in order. The child has to play these in the same order. Do this where the child can see them at first, then hide the instruments; the child has to recognize the order by listening, and repeat it. The number of instruments used depends on the age and ability of the children. Often two will be enough.

Reading

Word Puzzle

Make a set of cards for the words of a short song. The child has to put these in the correct order. This, of course, requires *reading* as well but it is not a difficult task after the child has learned the song.

Glasses

Put different amounts of water in several glasses. Put a piece of paper around the glasses so the children cannot see the level of the water. The children tap the sides and discover which are high and which are low in pitch. They can then arrange these in sequence, high to low.

Bottles

Put various amounts of water in bottles. Have paper around bottles as above. The children discover the pitch of each by blowing across the top and then they arrange the bottles in sequence.

Mystery Tunes

Clap the rhythm of the first phrase or so of a song or poem well-known to the children. They guess which it is. Some ideas might include *Frère Jacques, Row, Row, Row Your Boat, Humpty Dumpty, Baa Baa Black Sheep*, or a song they have learned recently. The only clue will be the rhythm sequence.

Sing a well-known song to "loo", not using the words. The children guess the name of the song from the melody or sequence of notes.

Sing or play two well-known songs. Ask the children: "Are they the same or different?"

These are good games to use in short periods of time, perhaps while waiting for the recess or lunch bell or while driving in a car or bus.

SINGING

CONTENTS

All young children love to sing. This is especially true of handicapped children who, you will find, are some of the most enthusiastic singers around.

We must be careful to encourage this love by giving all children enjoyable experiences while singing. Never tell a child not to sing! Too many adults are "tone deaf" because some tactless perfectionist told them to stand in the back row and "just mouth the words".

Some of the benefits to be derived from singing are discussed in **Let's Sing**, page 1.

There are many games and activities that can be done with songs to make them more enjoyable, and many ideas for selecting and presenting them will improve the children's singing.

A. CHOOSING SUITABLE SONGS

Choose your songs, keeping the following points in mind:

1. Songs for young children must be easy to sing: no great interval leaps or tricky rhythms at first.
2. Songs must have a limited range. Begin with songs having two or three notes only, such as *Rain Rain Go Away, A Tisket, A Tasket,* or *Ring Around a Rosie.* Next try some in the pentatonic or 5 note range, such as *Li'l Liza Jane* and *Jingle at the Windows.* Songs with six or eight notes can be tried next, but watch that they are easy enough for the children to sing without too much effort.
3. Choose songs in a fairly low pitch at first or transpose songs written in a higher range down to a suitable key. Most children can sing in tune in the lower range "A" below middle "C" to "A" above, and almost all handicapped children have very low voices. If the song is pitched too high there will be many "out-of-tuners".
4. Pick songs which lend themselves to movement.
5. Pick songs with lots of repetition of words and music. Children love repetition.

*Songs marked * can be found in **Songs**, page 55.

47

6. Choose songs which interest the children:
   — songs using the children's names
   — songs about animals or things easily imitated in action or sound
   — songs with actions, dance patterns or games
   — songs with lots of rhythmic content
   — quiet songs for reflective qualities as a contrast to lively rhythmic music
   — Songs about things that happen in the world around us.

Remember, if after giving a song a fair trial, the children still do not want to sing it, then forget that song and find another. The possible repertoire is too vast to waste time on songs no one likes.

B. THREE NOTE SONGS

Everyone's natural voice progression begins with three note calls.

The words change and are usually derogatory in meaning, but children sing these notes in tune — perhaps in a very low voice, but in tune.

Many children's songs are based on these notes:

e.g.   *Star Light Star Bright*
   Rain Rain Go Away
   Ring Around a Rosie
   A Tisket a Tasket *

Tinker, Tailor

Nursery Rhyme

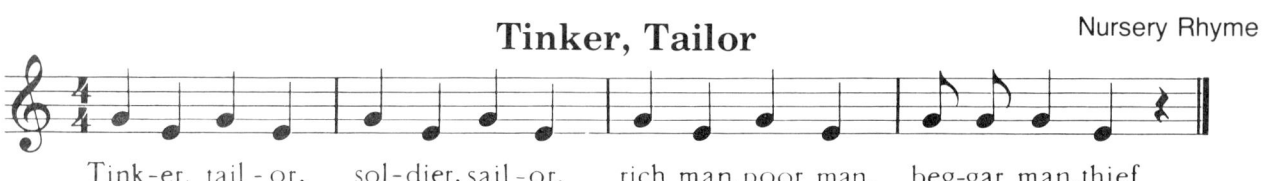

*See **Songs**, for more examples of 3-note songs.

Because most children can sing these notes easily, leading music educators such as Carl Orff and Zoltán Kodály have collected folk songs and composed many of their own for children, using just *soh, me* and *lah*.

Mother Goose rhymes can be set to these notes as can many other rhymes and jingles. Have the children compose their own. They will like them better anyway.

C. CALL AND RESPONSE OR TONE MATCHING

Many enjoyable games can be played using the three notes in a call and response activity.

1. Roll call.

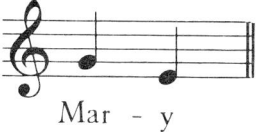

Mar - y

Here I am

Auditory discrimination

2. Questions.

Question

Who had toast for break - fast?

Language development

Speech

Answer

We had toast for break - fast.

or

We did.

Question

How man-y peo-ple have red on?

Answer

I do.

Sing these calls in many different keys — high and low. You will find many children will be able to sing them in tune in the low range but not in the high. Match the low tones of these children by singing the calls in their range, then gradually raise the notes and bring the pitch up. It may take anywhere from several weeks to several years to achieve this with some children but eventually the ability to sing in tune will come to all.

If you feel that you cannot sing even these notes in tune, then help yourself by playing them on a piano (one finger), a recorder, a xylophone, or even by blowing on a pitch pipe. Try to sound these in many keys.

G G E A G E
Who is wear-ing blue pants?

E E C# F# E C#
Who is wear-ing green socks?

C C A D C A A
Who has brought their lunch mon-ey?

F D G F D
Where are you go - ing?

Gradually extend the number of notes used until the full octave is employed.

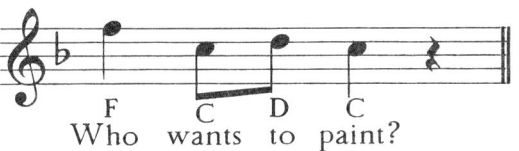

F C D C
Who wants to paint?

C D E F G G G
Who is go - ing home for lunch?

Once the idea is grasped, this game of three note calls is endless and can be used to teach many things such as colours, number concepts *etc*.

D. SOME GENERAL IDEAS FOR TEACHING AND SINGING SONGS

I   Introducing Songs

This can be done formally in a singing period by singing the song directly to the children or playing it from a record. Sometimes a new song can be introduced casually while children are doing something else: *i.e.* lining up for recess, putting books away or cleaning up the campsite.

The use of hand puppets is an enjoyable activity for all children and can sometimes encourage a withdrawn, emotionally disturbed or autistic child to participate in singing.

Hold the puppet just below your face and activate it so that it appears to be singing. Many of these troubled children have a profound distrust of people but will relate to an inanimate object such as a puppet.

II   Learning Songs

Do in sequence:
1. Go over the song phrase by phrase.
2. Say the words first in the rhythm of the song and the children repeat.
3. Sing the words and music of small section of the song and the children repeat.
4. Sing the whole song together.
5. If it is a long song, do just one or two sections the first day and the rest another time.

If you are timid about singing, you can use a record to teach the song or ask the teacher down the hall to help. She might come in and teach the song to your class or you might send a small group of four or five of your children to her room when she teaches the song. This group along with a group of her best singers could then come back and teach the song to your class. Her class can also sing songs on a cassette tape for you to play to your class.

III   Beat

Do the following in sequence:
1. Sing a song "catching the beat" by (a) clapping hands (b) snapping fingers   (c) patting knees   (d) patting stomach (e) tapping beat on ears, nose or feet (f) patting head (g) walking beat.

Body awareness
Coordination

These of course are not all done in the same session but over a period of several days or a week. By using these ideas and any others you can think of, much practice in maintaining the beat is gained and boredom does not set in.

2. Play the beat of song on hand drums, bells or other percussion instruments.

3. Play simple accompaniments on melodic instruments using the beat: *i.e.* glockenspiels, xylophones, chime bars *etc.* (See **Instruments**, page 211, and **Songs**, page 55, for examples.)

If children find it difficult to keep the beat, a word pattern taken from the song can be chanted to help hold things together. For example, from *Frère Jacques:*

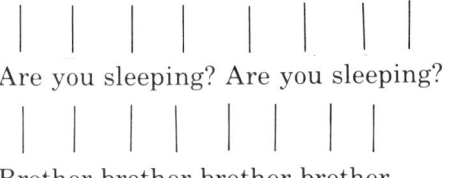

Are you sleeping? Are you sleeping?

Brother brother brother brother

Speech   Have one-half of the children chant this and clap the beat while the rest of the class sing the song. Finally, they will all be able to sing and keep the beat at the same time.

IV   Rhythmic Pattern

(This is just the rhythm of the words of the song.)

Clap the rhythmic pattern while singing the song.

Clap the rhythmic pattern with the hands while walking the steady beat with feet. This is very difficult for many children and some will take months before mastering it even if it is practised

Speech   every day.

When the children are very proficient change this and clap the beat with the hands while trying to stamp the rhythm pattern with the feet.

Have one group of children clap the beat while the other group claps the rhythmic pattern. All are singing the song at the same time.

Have the rhythmic pattern played on a simple instrument — *i.e.* sticks or wood block — while the beat is played on two notes on a xylophone or on a drum.

V   Accompaniments

Have some children play the beat (see above) on instruments while others, perhaps, use other notes to invent accompaniments. See **Instruments**, page 219, for a detailed explanation of different ideas for accompaniments.

VI   Different Rhythms

Older children can learn to clap or play other rhythms over and over while singing the song itself. These rhythms could also be taken from the words of the song.

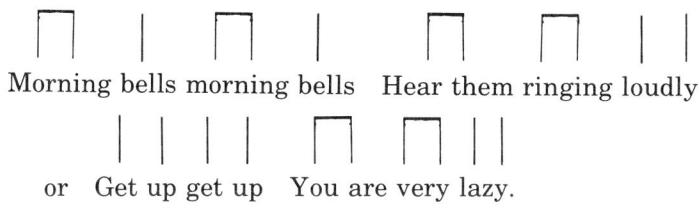

brother John   brother John   or morning bells are ringing

This is very difficult but provides excellent training in coordination and independence.

VII   Introductions, Interludes and Endings

Have some children make up introductions, interludes and endings to go with the songs using clapping or percussion instruments. This provides practice in the more difficult rhythms but is easier, as it does not require playing them at the same time as singing the song. Find word patterns from the song or related to it, to give the rhythm.

Morning bells morning bells   Hear them ringing loudly.

or   Get up get up   You are very lazy.

VIII   Draw Sound Pictures

Have the children draw a "picture" of the melody in the air with the finger or hands. This gives you a clear idea of their understanding of high and low, the rise and fall of the melody, and of phrasing.

The picture of the melody line can be drawn or painted on the chalkboard or a piece of paper. The bigger the sheet of paper the better, as this allows the children a feeling of freedom.

Have the children represent the character of the sound visually on paper:

staccato notes

flowing melodic line

Using these pictures, it is possible to distinguish one song from another by visual means only.

Visual awareness

IX   Mixed-Up Phrases

After a song has been very well learned, sing it with the phrases in the wrong order. For example *Are You Sleeping?* could be sung
a. backwards — 4th, 3rd, 2nd, 1st:
Ding dang dong, ding dang, dong,
Morning bells are ringing, morning bells are ringing,
Brother John, Brother John,
Are you sleeping? Are you sleeping?

b. 3rd, 2nd, 4th, 1st:
Morning bells are ringing, morning bells are ringing,
Brother John, Brother John,
Ding dang dong, ding dang dong,
Are you sleeping? Are you sleeping?

X   Related Activities

Discuss the subject matter of the song with the children. Have them paint or draw pictures describing the song or related topics.

Punchinello (see **Songs**, page 100, for instance) could inspire pictures not only of clowns, but also of all related circus subjects.

Lists of important words in the song can be made and these can be used as reading words. (See **Painless Learning with Songs, Poetry and Movement**, page 170, for specific ideas.)

Some songs can be dramatized. (See **Creativity**, Creative Drama, page 189.)

SONGS

CONTENTS

The songs in this section are just suggestions, but all are very popular with children. You will, no doubt, have many more that you will wish to work with.

The songs are organized into sections according to the content or type of song, and each section is graded with the easier songs at the beginning.

When using the suggestions for movement, instrumental accompaniment, *etc.*, pick the ideas that will work with your children and leave the rest. I have tried to include some very easy ideas and others that are more difficult. If you don't feel like using any of them, sing unaccompanied, or do whatever suits your particular purpose.

Note: In the accompaniments suggested for the songs, when the stems of the notes go up, play with the right hand. When the stems go down, play with the left hand.

LIST OF SONGS

A. SONGS BASED ON THREE NOTES

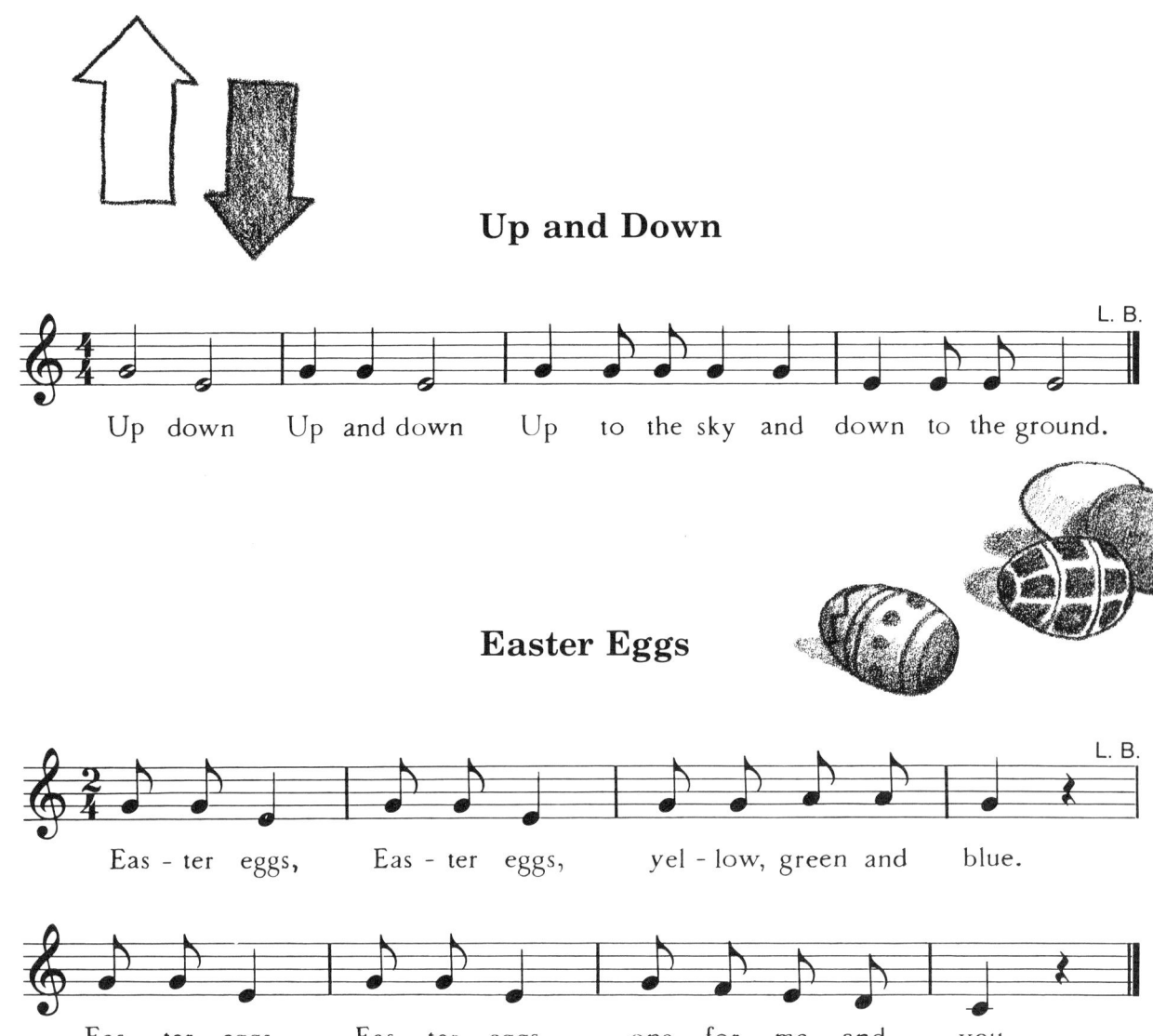

Up and Down

Up down   Up and down   Up to the sky and down to the ground.

L. B.

Easter Eggs

Eas-ter eggs,   Eas-ter eggs,   yel-low, green and   blue.

Eas-ter eggs,   Eas-ter eggs,   one for me and   you.

L. B.

Change the words.

Easter eggs, Easter eggs, yellow, blue and green.
Easter eggs, Easter eggs, the prettiest I've ever seen.

Jack Be Nimble

Nursery Rhyme

Jack be nim - ble. Jack be quick.
Jack jump ov - er the can - dle stick.

Chanukah

adapted by Flora Boxer

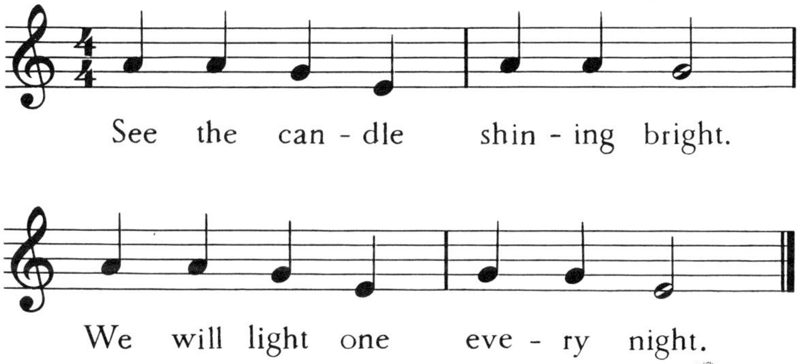

See the can - dle shin - ing bright.
We will light one eve - ry night.

PASTE
BE MY VAL-EN-TINE

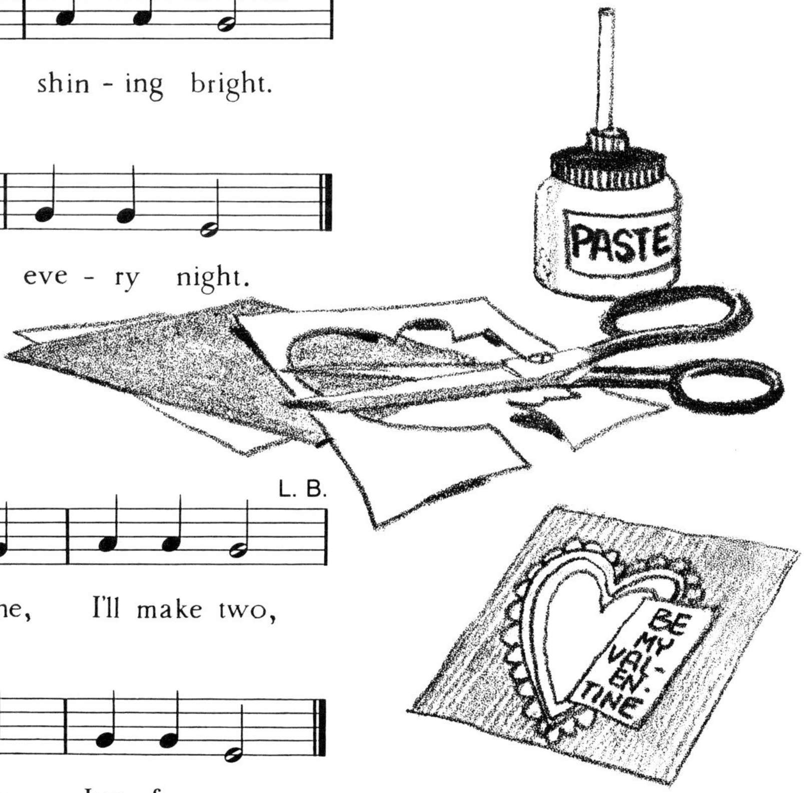

Valentines

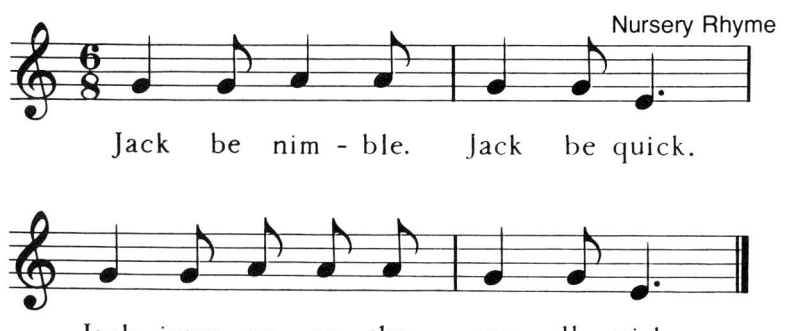

L. B.

Val-en-tine, Val-en-tine, I'll make two,
Val-en-tine, Val-en-tine, Just for you.

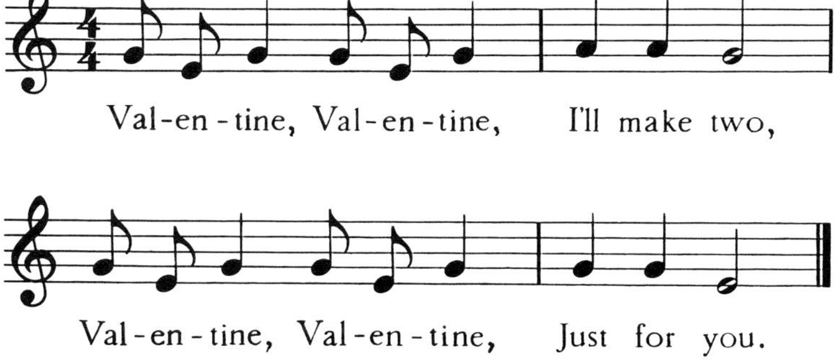

Bell Horses

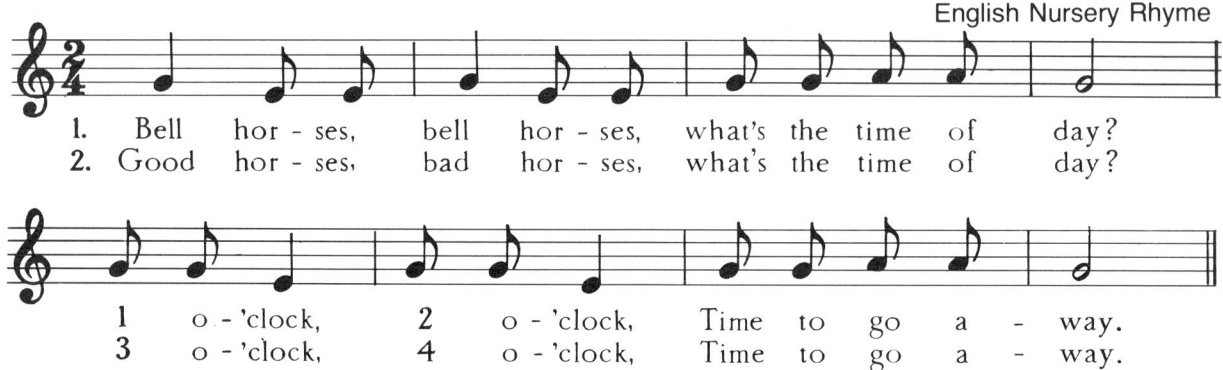

English Nursery Rhyme

1. Bell hor - ses, bell hor - ses, what's the time of day?
2. Good hor - ses, bad hor - ses, what's the time of day?

1 o - 'clock, 2 o - 'clock, Time to go a - way.
3 o - 'clock, 4 o - 'clock, Time to go a - way.

This is another favourite song with young children because it is so easy to sing and they find it interesting.

Spatial relationship
Group participation
Coordination

Activities
1. Sing, and keep the beat with any part of the body — clap, snap, sway, nod head *etc*.
2. Sing, and clap the beat.
3. Sing and walk to the beat anywhere in the room.
4. Sing, and clap the rhythm pattern of the song. One group claps the rhythm pattern, another group sings the song.

Talk about the sounds that horses make.

Use the words "clip-clop" to make a spoken accompaniment. (The word rhythm accentuates the beat.) One group starts and says "clip-clop" four times for an introduction. A second group begins to sing over the "clip-clop" accompaniment. At the end, the first group continues after the singing has stopped for four more "clip-clops", to create an ending.

Instead of the "clip-clop", children can make a sound with their mouths to imitate the sound of the horses' feet. Use this sound as above for an accompaniment.

Instruments

Wood block or sticks

Try out different instruments for the best sound describing horses. The children will probably decide on the woodblock or sticks.

Play on the beat.

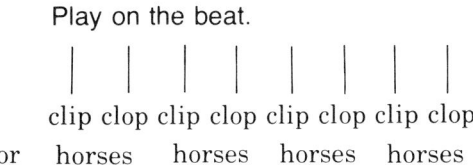

clip clop clip clop clip clop clip clop

or   horses   horses   horses   horses

Xylophone

For very young, handicapped children or slow learners, set xylophone up with just C and G:

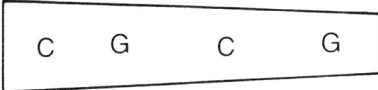

The child can play any one or two notes on the beat.

For more advanced children, set the xylophone up in the pentatonic scale. In this case, it is in C pentatonic:

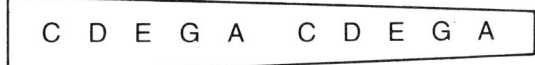

Have a child choose any four "walking" notes he likes. Some suggestions might be as follows. Play throughout:

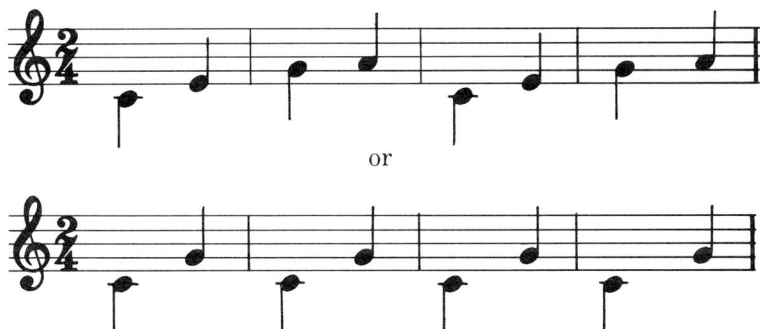

Bells

Discuss the bells on horses. If you can find some jingle bells, these are perfect; otherwise, use any bell sounds available.

Have these played every other beat.

day   day   day   day

Introduction

An introduction can consist of something as simple as playing the accompaniment four times before starting the song. Keep everybody together by chanting "horses horses horses horses" in a soft whisper while playing.

Another introduction for more advanced children could evolve from a discussion of how horses move; they walk, trot, gallop, run. Have the children show this in movement, and then play it on woodblocks and/or bells.

running running running running. See the horses run.

Movement

Have the children trot, run, gallop, *etc*. like horses — singly, in groups or in pairs — while others are playing and singing.

Related Activities

Discuss different breeds of horses, what they are used for, what they look like — race horses, farm horses, cart horses, ponies and so on.

Draw or paint pictures of these different kinds of horses.

Little Sally Water

Old English Song

Lit-tle Sal-ly Wa-ter, Sit-ting in a sau-cer, Rise Sal-ly, Rise Sal-ly, Dry your weep-ing eyes Sal-ly, Turn to the east and turn to the west and turn to the one that you like the best.

Spatial relationship
Action song
Group participation

Activities

The children walk in a circle holding hands, around one child ("Sally") who is sitting in the middle. "Sally" rises, points to the east and then to the west and then to the one she likes the best (any other child). This second child takes the place of the first in the centre and the game is repeated.

B. PENTATONIC SONGS

Rover

C Pentatonic (C D E G A)

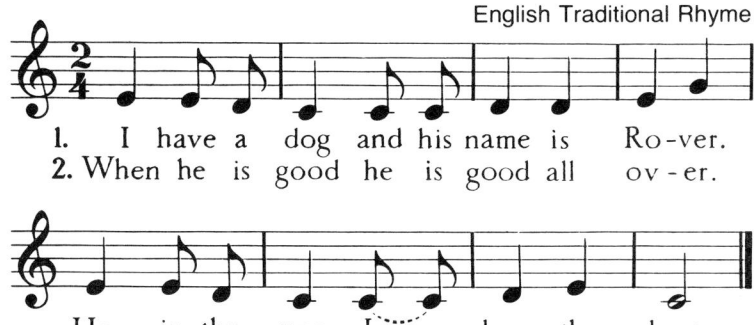

English Traditional Rhyme

1. I have a dog and his name is Ro-ver.
2. When he is good he is good all ov-er.

He is the one I love the best.
When he is bad He is just a pest.

This song is an all time favourite with children, especially very young children, who keep asking for it many years after they have been taught the song.

Activities
1. The children sing and keep the beat any way they wish: in their hands, tapping their head, patting their knees *etc*.
2. When they know the song well, have them walk the beat as they sing.
3. Clap the rhythm pattern of the words.
4. Have one group keep the beat; another clap the rhythm pattern.
5. If children are ready, have them walk the beat and clap the rhythm pattern with their hands.
6. Change the words to:
   I have a friend and his name is Billy...
   I have a friend and her name is Judy...

Instruments

Sticks, drum or wood block
After practising the beat as above, let one or two children play the beat on these percussion instruments while the rest sing.

Xylophone or chime bars
For very young children or those who are physically handicapped or retarded, set the xylophone up as follows:

C G C G (This is in the key of C.)

Tell the child to play any two notes (or one, if that is all that is possible) on the beat.

Spatial relationship
Group participation

65

For more advanced accompaniment, set the xylophone up in the pentatonic scale as follows:

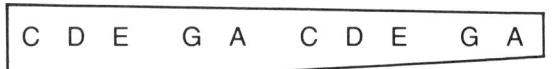

Play throughout

or

or another pattern the children have made up themselves.

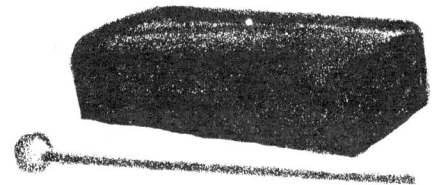

To keep the rhythm steady, have everybody chant "Rover, Rover, Rover, Rover" while the children play the xylophone and percussion instruments.

For a simple introduction this could be done four times before the song starts.

Have no more than two instruments accompany the singers at this stage. Young children will have enough trouble putting three things together (*i.e.* two instruments in the accompaniment, as well as the singing.)

Related Activities

Have the children paint or draw a picture of their dog, if they have one, or of one they would like to own.

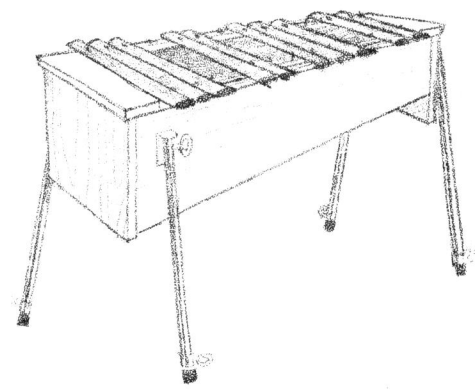

Jig Jog Jig Jog

C Pentatonic (C D E G A)

I want some-one to buy me a po - ny, Jig Jog Jig Jog

Jig - a Jog Gee. Not too fat and not too bo - ny,

Jig Jog Jig Jog Jig - a Jog Gee. For I want to

go for a ride All a - round the coun - try side, With a

Jig Jog Jig Jog Jig Jog Jig Jog Jig Jog Jig - a Jog Gee.

Activities

Have one group of children make "clucking" sounds with their tongues while the other group sings the song. Repeat, changing sides.

Spatial relationship
Group participation

Instruments   **Woodblock** $\frac{4}{4}$ | | | |

Xylophone

play throughout

If the children have trouble keeping the beat, have them re-peat over and over, "pony pony pony pony".

Movement

Have the children gallop like horses.

The Old Red Wagon

American Folk Song

G Pentatonic (G A B D E)

1. Cir - cle to the left, old red wa - gon,
Cir - cle to the left, old red wa - gon, Cir - cle to the left,
old red wa - gon, Fare you well my dar - ling.

2. Circle to the right, old red wagon . . .
3. Everybody in, old red wagon . . .
4. Everybody out, old red wagon . . .
5. Shake right hands in the air, old red wagon . . .
6. Pat your back, old red wagon . . .

Spatial relationship
Body awareness
Directionality
Coordination
Action song
Group participation

Make up your own words. If some of the children you are working with have perceptual or motor problems, try to choose concepts that will help them overcome these.

Movement Pattern

The movement is, of course, dictated by the words of the song. In the verses "circle to the left" (or right) or "everybody in", have the children join hands and caution them to take *small* steps.

Head and Shoulders Baby

F Pentatonic (F G A C D)

American Folk Song

Head and shoul-ders ba - by, yes! yes!

Head and shoul-ders ba - by, yes! yes!

Head and shoul-ders, Head and shoul-ders,

Head and shoul-ders ba - by, yes! yes!

Knees and ankles baby, yes! yes! ...
Throw a ball baby yes! yes! ...
Ride a bike baby yes! yes! ...
Milk a cow baby yes! yes! ...
Swim the pool baby yes! yes! ...

Activities

The children can make up many other verses to this song. If the children you are working with have specific problems, make up words to help correct these:
i.e. body awareness

Head and shoulders baby, yes, yes ...
Knees and ankles baby, yes, yes ...
Shoulders, back baby, yes, yes ...
Wrist and elbow baby, yes, yes ...

laterality

Shake your right hand baby, yes, yes ...
Pat your left knee baby, yes, yes ...

Body awareness
Coordination
Laterality
Midline problems
Improvising words
Action song
Group participation

69

Movement Pattern

The action of this song is performed in two's, each child facing another.

Part I: "Knees and ankles", "Throw the ball", *etc.* Each child touches the part of the body named or imitates the action described.

Part II: "Baby". Each child claps his own hands once.
"Yes, Yes". 1. With both hands, clap partner's hands twice.
or
2. Right hand crosses body to clap partner's right hand. Left hand crosses body to clap partner's left hand.

If children are fairly advanced in movement skills, have them do the whole song in partners in a circle, with an inner circle facing out, and an outer circle facing in. The last verse is:

Change your partner baby yes! yes!
Change your partner baby yes! yes!
Change your partner, change your partner,
Change your partner baby yes! yes!

Each child in the outer circle moves to the right, to the next partner, on "change your partner". He performs the clapping action with that partner on the words "baby yes! yes!" and then moves on for the next "change your partner". The trick is to change quickly three times in succession for the last two lines.

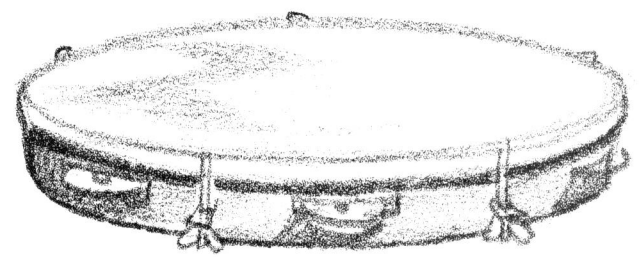

Li'l Liza Jane

C Pentatonic (C D E G A)

American Folk Song

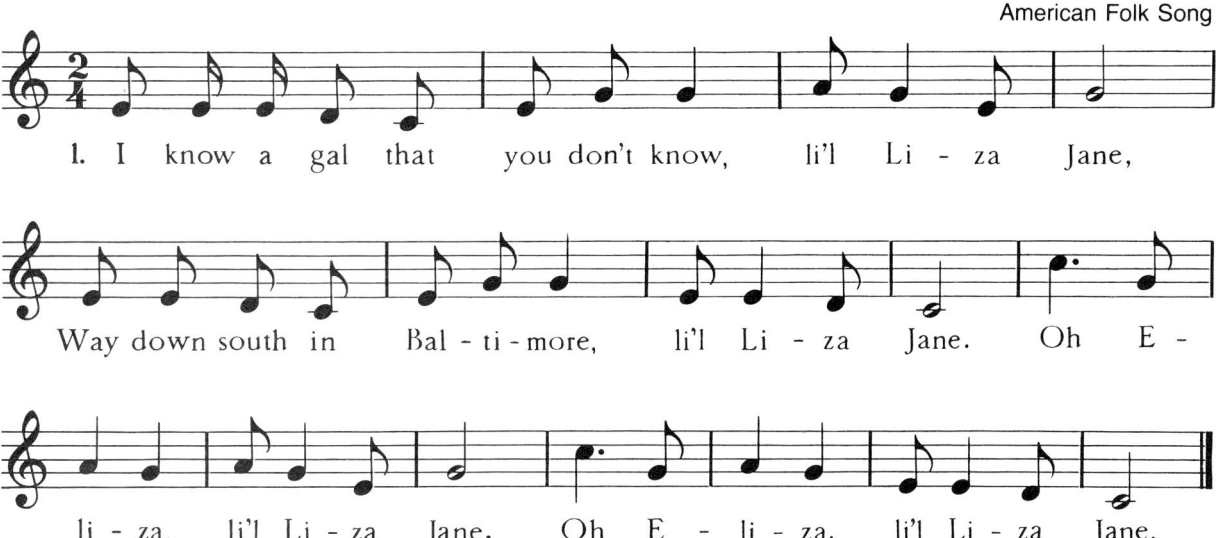

1. I know a gal that you don't know, li'l Li - za Jane,
Way down south in Bal - ti - more, li'l Li - za Jane. Oh E -
li - za, li'l Li - za Jane, Oh E - li - za, li'l Li - za Jane.

2. Liza Jane looks good to me
   Sweetest gal you'll ever see.

3. Where she lives the flowers grow
   Chickens round the kitchen door.

4. What do I care how far we roam
   Where she's at is home sweet home.

5. Liza Jane is ten feet tall
   When she sleeps her feet are in the hall.

Activities

The children can make up their own words. For example, a Grade 2 class was studying "Community Helpers" and this is what they devised.

1. The policeman helps you across the street
   And when you're bad he spanks your seat.
2. The doctor comes when you are ill
   And he gives you a big green pill.

Spatial relationship
Body awareness
Coordination
Improvisation
Action song
Group participation

Instruments

Xylophone

throughout

Glockenspiel or Chime Bars

throughout

Drums or Sticks

At chorus, "Oh Eliza", shake a tambourine.

Movement Patterns

a) Have the children pat their knees to the beat until the chorus starts.

Chorus
At "Oh Eliza" — they roll their hands in the air.
At "Li'l Liza Jane" — they clap the rhythm of the words.
Repeat.

b) The children stand in a circle holding hands.

1st line ("I know ... Liza Jane")
move by walking the beat or by sliding steps to the right.

2nd line ("Way down ... Liza Jane")
move the same way to the left and back to the original spot.

Chorus
At "Oh Eliza" — slap hands very quickly on thighs.
At "Li'l Liza Jane" — clap hands and turn around.
Repeat for last 4 bars.
Repeat whole pattern for other verses.

Jingle at the Windows

C Pentatonic (C D E G A)

Traditional American Singing Game

Pass one win-dow, ti-de-o. Pass two win-dows,

ti-de-o. Pass three win-dows, ti-de-o. Ti-de-o, ti-de-o,

Jin-gle at the win-dow, ti-de-o. Ti-de-o, ti-de-o,

Jin-gle at the win-dow ti-de-o. Ti-de-o

ti-de-o Jin-gle at the win-dow ti-de-o.

Instruments

Xylophone

Win-dow Win-dow

Sticks

(good walking beat).

play throughout

Spatial relationship
Body awareness
Coordination
Action song
Group participation

At the words, "Jingle at the window", shake a tabourine or wrist bells to make a jingling sound. This sound could also be used as an introduction and an ending to the song.

Movement Pattern

There are many different movement patterns that could be used with this song, but the following pattern is fairly easy for small children.

1. The children stand in a circle with spaces between them to make "windows". They can join jands and raise their arms to make an arch if desired.

2. One child, chosen to be "it", stands outside the circle.

> 1st phrase ("Pass one window, tideo"): the child moves to the inside of the circle through a window.

> 2nd phrase ("Pass two windows, tideo"): he goes out again.

> 3rd phrase ("Pass three windows, tideo"): the child comes to the centre again.

> 4th phrase ("Jingle at the window, tideo"): the child picks a partner and stands in front of him or her.

> 5th phrase ("Tideo, tideo"): on the word "tideo" these two children pat their own knees, clap their own hands and then pat the hands of their partner to the rhythm of the word. Repeat for the second "tideo".

> 6th phrase ("Jingle at the window, tideo"): shake own hands loosely in the air and then clap the rhythm of tideo | | | ♪.
> 7th and 8th phrases: repeat actions for the 5th and 6th.

3. The first child takes the place of his partner in the circle while the partner becomes "it" for the repeat of the song.

Cape Cod Chanty

American Sea Song

C Pentatonic (C D E G A)

1. Cape Cod girls they have no combs, Heave a - way, Heave a - way They comb their hair with cod - fish bones. We are bound for Aus - tral - lia,

CHORUS

Heave a - way my bul - ly, bul - ly boys, Heave a - way, Heave a - way. Heave a - way and don't you make a noise, We are bound for Aus - tral - ia.

2. Cape Cod boys they have no sleds,
   They slide down-hill on cod-fish heads.

3. Cape Cod men they have no sails,
   They sail their boats with cod-fish tails.

4. Cape Cod wives they have no pins,
   They pin their gowns with cod-fish fins.

5. Cape Cod doctors have no pills,
   They give their patients cod-fish gills.

6. Cape Cod cats they have no tails,
   They lost them all in southeast gales.

Improvising words

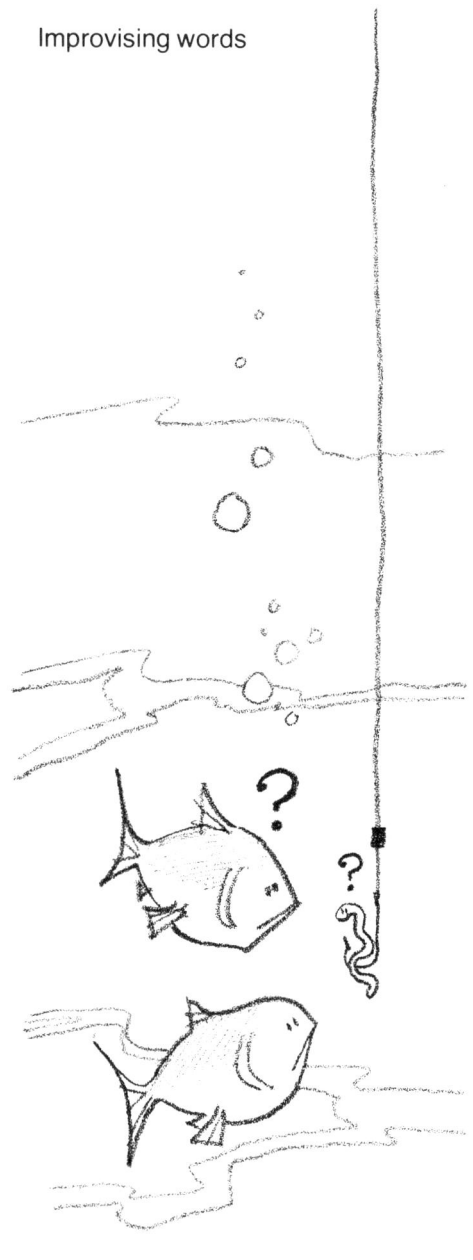

Activities
Children can make up their own words using other parts of the cod fish:

> Cape Cod boats they can't turn south
> The boats are steered with a cod-fish mouth.

The words don't have to make any sense as long as they rhyme.

Instruments

Xylophone

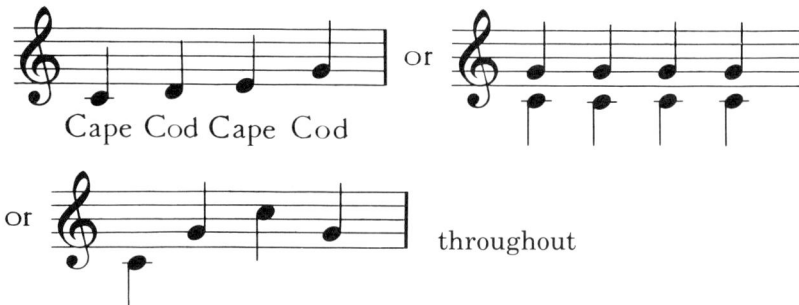

Cape Cod Cape Cod

or throughout

Glockenspiel or Chime Bars

bones   bones   or   We'll catch a fish

Metallophone

boats   boats   throughout

These words are just suggestions. Other words can be substituted. They are useful for keeping the rhythm steady.

Drum, sticks or tambourine
Use the rhythm of words from the song for an introduction and ending.

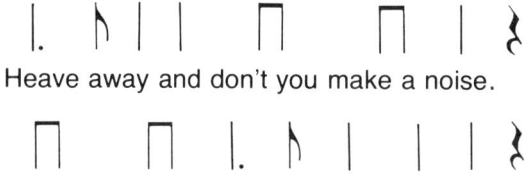

Heave away and don't you make a noise.

We are going to catch the Cape Cod fish.

C. ROUNDS

Are You Sleeping? and *Row Row Row Your Boat* are the best known rounds but there are many others as well. Several of these follow. By the time children are at Grade 3 level, they should be able to sing rounds fairly easily. Do not attempt to sing a song in rounds until it is well known. If your children are not able to attempt these songs as rounds, just sing them in unison.

Singing in rounds is very good for developing powers of concentration.

Apples Pears and Oranges

Key of C Major

Danish Round
Trans. Aksel Schiotz

This song has only four notes.

It sometimes helps to draw pictures of the objects in the order they are mentioned in the song, because they are so easily mixed up.

Auditory sequencing
Concentration

Little Tommy Tinker

Concentration

Key of C Major

Old English Round

Sing Together

Key of F Major

Old Round

Sing, sing to - geth - er; Mer - ri - ly, mer - ri - ly

sing. Sing, sing to - geth - er; Mer - ri - ly,

mer - ri - ly sing. Sing, sing, sing, sing.

Concentration

This song is a little harder than the other rounds but is a favourite of children anyway. We should make it the theme song of this book.

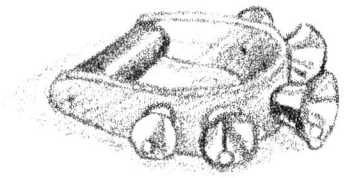

D. USING WELL-KNOWN SONGS WITH DIFFERENT WORDS

Frère Jacques
or Are You Sleeping?

This tune is so well known that it can be used with many different words.

1. I hear sleigh bells, I hear sleigh bells,
   Hark do you? Hark do you?
   Maybe it is Santa. Maybe it is Santa,
   Yes it's true. Yes it's true.

2. Posture perfect. Posture perfect. (all sit up straight)
   Do not slump. Do not slump. (slump over with hump in back)
   You must grow up handsome. You must grow up handsome. (all sit up straight)
   Do not slump. Do not slump. (slump over and then sit up straight at the end)

A group of children can chant a word accompaniment such as:

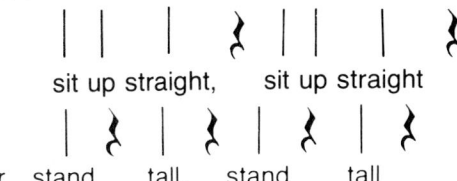

sit up straight,   sit up straight

or   stand   tall,   stand   tall

3. I hear thunder, I hear thunder.
   Hark do you? Hark do you?
   Pitter patter raindrops, pitter patter raindrops,
   I'm wet through, so are you.

Have the children make up their own words to this music.

Alligator Pie

Sing to the tune of *Skip to My Loo*.

Alligator pie, alligator pie,
If I don't get some I think I'm gonna die.
Give away the green grass, give away the sky,
But don't give away my alligator pie.

Alligator stew, alligator stew,
If I don't get some I don't know what I'll do.
Give away my furry hat, give away my shoe,
But don't give away my alligator stew.

Alligator soup, alligator soup,
If I don't get some I think I'm gonna droop.
Give away my hockey stick, give away my hoop,
But don't give away my alligator soup.

Dennis Lee

Mulberry Bush

The music to the old nursery rhyme *Here We Go Round the Mulberry Bush* can be used for many action songs.

Here we go round the mulberry bush
The mulberry bush, the mulberry bush
Here we go round the mulberry bush
On a cold and frosty morning.

This is the way we brush our teeth . . .
This is the way we sweep the room . . .
This is the way we dig the road . . .
This is the way we drive a truck . . .
This is the way we fly our rocket . . .
This is the way we walk on the moon . . .

Spatial relationship
Coordination
Language development
Improvising words

79

E. SONGS FOR IMPROVISING WORDS OR SOUNDS

At the Farm

Key of C Major

Pigs at the farm go, "oink oink oink".

Pigs at the farm go, "oink oink oink".

Pigs at the farm go, "oink oink oink".

The pigs go, "oink oink oink".

Cows at the farm go, "moo moo moo"...
Horses at the farm go, "neigh neigh neigh"...
Ducks at the farm go, "quack quack quack"...

The list is endless!

This song is a favourite with young children because all of them love to make animal sounds. It is also an excellent song for children with learning difficulties. It falls within an easy singing range, there is lots of repetition and it also teaches the name of the animal and its related sound.

Activities

If you are studying the jungle or the zoo, identify animals from these places and change the words around:

Tigers in the jungle go, "growl growl growl"...
Monkeys in the zoo go, "chee chee chee"...

Improvising words
Reading

*"At the Farm" from *Lucile Panabaker's Song Book* by Lucile Panabaker. Copyright © 1968 by Peter Martin Associates Limited. Used by permission of Peter Martin Associates Limited.

Instruments

Guitar, ukelele or autoharp: use the chords suggested in the song.

Drums, sticks, other hand percussion: play on the beat.

Movement

Have children move like the animals in the song.

Related Activities

This is primarily a fun song but you could print the names of the different animals on cards and use it as a reading exercise. Hold the card up before each verse. The children have to read it to find what animal to sing about.

Old House

American Folk-Game Song
Collected by John W. Work
Adapted by L.B.

Key of E Minor

1. Old house. Tear it down! Who's going to help me?

Tear it down! Bring me a ham-mer. Tear it down!

Bring me a saw. Tear it down! Next thing you bring me.

Tear it down! Is a wreck-ing ma-chine. Tear it down!

Old house. Tear it down! Who's going to help me? Tear it down!

2. New house. Build it up!
Who's going to help me? Build it up!
Bring me a hammer. Build it up!
Bring me a saw. Build it up!
Next thing you bring me. Build it up!
Is a carpenter man. Build it up!
New house. Build it up!
Who's going to help me? Build it up!

Language development
Reading
Improvising words

Activities

Instead of going on with the fifth line, "Next thing you bring me", have children repeat the third and fourth lines, substituting their own ideas for things needed to tear a house down: "Bring me a dump truck. Tear it down. Bring me a drill . . . a screwdriver . . . a shovel . . . a bulldozer" *etc*.

The same can apply to building the house up. The list here is limitless: lights, windows, bricks, wood, wires, pipes, tiles, nails *etc*.

Instruments

The sound of many of the items suggested can be described by instruments: *e.g.* the hammer — a woodblock or sticks; the saw — sandblocks rubbed together or a hand rubbed across a drumhead.

Guitar or ukelele accompaniment would be excellent here.

Related Activities

A trip could be organized to the site of a house being wrecked and one to where a house is being built. Have the children draw or paint a picture of these field trips.

After the children have thought up different things to use for tearing down or building up a house, put the names of these things on cards. When singing the song, hold up the cards one by one: "Bring me a . . . ". The children have to read the word on the card before singing the next verse.

Down by the Bay

Key of F Major
CHORUS

Old English Song

Down by the bay (Down by the bay) Where the
wat - er - mel - ons grow (Where the wat - er - mel - ons grow)
Back to my home (Back to my home) I dare not
go (I dare not go). For if I do (For if I
do) My moth -er will say, (My moth - er will say,) "Did you
ev - er see a cow with a green eye - brow, Down by the bay?"

Activities

Repeat the song over and over, asking each child to make up a verse. This activity provides good practice in using rhyming words. The following are some ideas that might be used:

Did you ever see a horse, on a golf course?
Did you ever see a mouse, sitting on a house?
Did you ever see a snake, baking a cake?
Did you ever see a carp, playing the harp?
Did you ever see a loon, digging with a spoon?

Improvising words
Rhyming words
Group participation

This can be sung as a response song, where the leader or one group sings the first part while the rest come in on the repeated (bracketed) words.

Instruments

Use guitar, ukelele, autoharp or piano as an accompaniment, using the chords marked above the music.

Going Over the Sea

Key of G Major

1. When I was one I ate a bun Go-ing o-ver the sea. I jumped a-board a pi-rate's ship and the pi-rate said to me, Go-ing o-ver, go-ing un-der, Stand at at-ten-tion Like a sol-dier with a 1 - 2 - 3.

When I was two I buckled my shoe...
When I was three I climbed a tree...
When I was four I shut the door...
When I was five I took a dive...
When I was six I picked up sticks...
When I was seven I went to heaven...
When I was eight I shut the gate...
When I was nine I scratched my spine...
When I was ten I began again...

Have the children make up their own words.

84

Group participation
Spatial relationship
Coordination
Left and right
Rhyming words
Action song

Instruments

Guitar, ukelele, autoharp. Use the chords suggested in the song. Drums, sticks and other percussion. Play on the beat.

Movement Pattern

The children stand in a circle, holding hands.

1st four bars ("When I . . . over the sea"):
walk or slide step or skip 8 counts to the right.

2nd four bars ("I jumped . . . said to me"):
repeat movement pattern of 1st four bars, 8 counts to the left.

Final bars
("Going over"): hands up.
("Going under"): hands down under.
("Stand at attention like a soldier"): salute.
("With a 1, 2, 3"): clap three times

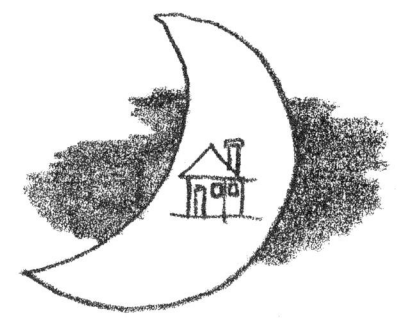

Aiken Drum

Key of G Major

Old Scottish Folk Song

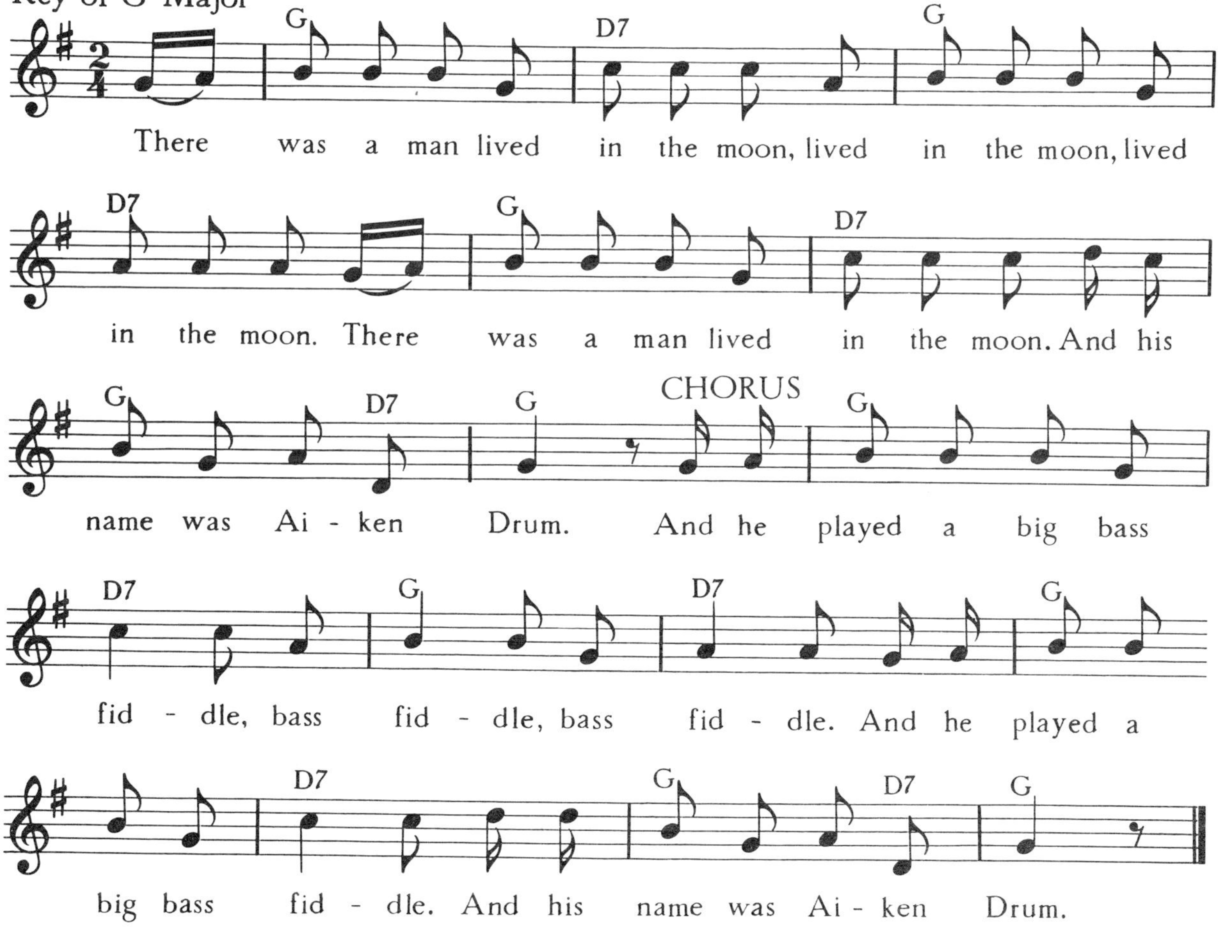
G D7 G
There was a man lived in the moon, lived in the moon, lived
D7 G D7
in the moon. There was a man lived in the moon. And his
G D7 G CHORUS G
name was Ai - ken Drum. And he played a big bass
D7 G D7 G
fid - dle, bass fid - dle, bass fid - dle. And he played a
D7 G D7 G
big bass fid - dle. And his name was Ai - ken Drum.

and his hat was made of chocolate cake . . .
and his pants were made of spaghetti . . .
and his shoes were made of bananas . . .
and his shirt was made of hamburgers . . .

This is a good song, especially for boys.

Body awareness
Language development
Reading
Improvising words

Activities

Have the children make up different things from which Mr. Aiken Drum's clothing could be made — the funnier the better.

The song could be sung using parts of the body instead of clothing:

and his arms were made of pretzels . . .
and his head was made of fried eggs . . .
and his feet were made of bananas . . .

This is good for body awareness, especially if the children draw a picture of their Aiken Drum.

Instruments

Guitar, ukelele, autoharp. Use chords suggested in the song.

Related Activities

Have each child draw a picture of Mr. Aiken Drum in his weird costume.

Dress up one person, a verse at a time, by having the other children give him a hat made from cardboard "chocolate cake", pants made from paper "spaghetti", shoes made from cardboard "bananas" *etc*.

Make word cards of the different parts of Mr. Aiken Drum and use them for reading.

F. SONGS WITH ACTIONS

Paw Paw Patch

Key of F Major

Traditional American Singing Game

1. Where oh where is good old Tom - my?
(Ma - ry)

Where oh where is good old Tom-my?

Where oh where is good old Tom - my?

Way down yon-der in the Paw Paw Patch.

2. Come on boys (girls) let's go find him (her) (sing 3 times)

Way down yonder in the paw paw patch.

3. Come back Tommy (Mary) now we've found you (sing 3 times)

Way down yonder in the paw paw patch.

4. Picking up paw paws, put them in your pocket (sing 3 times)
Way down yonder in the paw paw patch.

Instruments

Ukelele, guitar, autoharp: use the chords suggested in the song.
Drums, sticks and other hand percussion: play on the beat or use at certain places for effect.

Names
Spatial relationship
Coordination
Action song
Speech ("p")
Group participation

Movement Pattern

The child whose name is used, hides; the others stand in a circle.

Verse 1.

Everyone makes "looking" motions.

Verse 2.

Boys or girls go and search for the first child.

Verse 3.

All return to the circle (standing).

Verse 4.

The children make believe they are picking paw paws from the ground and putting them in their pockets.

Repeat the song with another child as "it".

Go In and Out the Windows

Old English Singing Game

Key of F Major

Go in and out the win-dows, Go in and out the win-dows,

Go in and out the win-dows, as you have done be-fore.

2. Now stand and face a partner...

If children cannot understand this have them say —

Now stand before a good friend...

3. Now follow me to London...

Instruments

Guitar, ukelele, autoharp, piano. Use the chords suggested in the song.

Movement Patterns

There are two good movement patterns!

(a) The children stand behind chairs in a circle.

Verse 1. One child goes in and out between the chairs, without touching them.

Verse 2. The child stands and faces a partner — these words can be changed to "stand before a good friend" if this instruction is easier.

Verse 3. The first child and partner skip around the outside of the circle.

The first child takes the place of the second in the circle and the second child repeats the action.

(b) The children join hands in a circle, raising their arms to make the "windows".

The action is the same as in (a).

Spatial relationship
Coordination
Action song
Group participation

Horses Horses

Key of F Major

Hor-ses, hor-ses, I've got hor-ses, white and dap-ple gray.

Hor-ses, hor-ses, I've got hor-ses, white and dap-ple gray.

verse 1. If I give them oats to eat, they jump five and twen-ty feet.
verse 2. If I give them su-gar sweet, they jump five and thir-ty feet.

Hor-ses, hor-ses, I've got hor-ses, white and dap-ple gray.

If the word "dapple" is too difficult for the children you are working with, change the words to "white and black and gray".

Instruments

Woodblock, sticks

Play on each beat to make the sound of horses' hooves.

horses horses horses horses *etc*.

Children can also make a "clucking" sound with tongue on the beat to imitate the horses' hooves.

Xylophone

throughout

Movement

The children can run, gallop, and trot like horses.

Related Activities

Discuss horses, how they eat, the different breeds, how they move — fast, slow trot, gallop *etc*.

Draw or paint pictures of horses.

Coordination
Spatial relationship

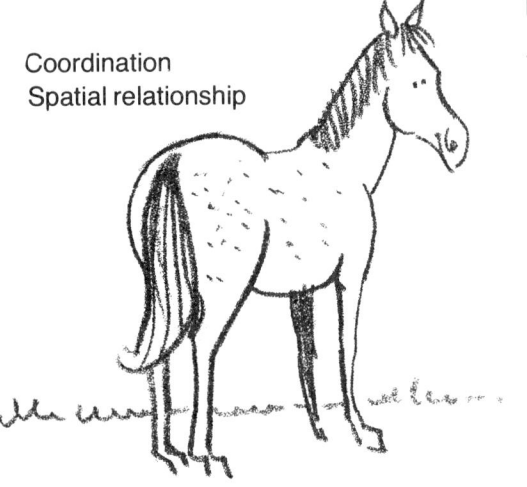

One Finger One Thumb

Key of F Major

Traditional Children's Game

1. One fin - ger, one thumb, keep mov - ing. One fin - ger, one thumb, keep mov - ing. One fin - ger, one thumb, keep mov - ing. We'll all be hap - py and bright.__

2. One finger, one thumb, one foot, keep moving...
3. One finger, one thumb, one foot, one elbow, keep moving...
4. One finger, one thumb, one foot, one elbow, one head, keep moving...

Keep adding parts of the body until the song becomes impossible.

Body awareness
Coordination
Sequencing

Shoo Fly

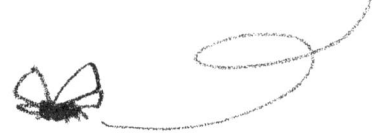

Old American Singing Game

Key of F Major

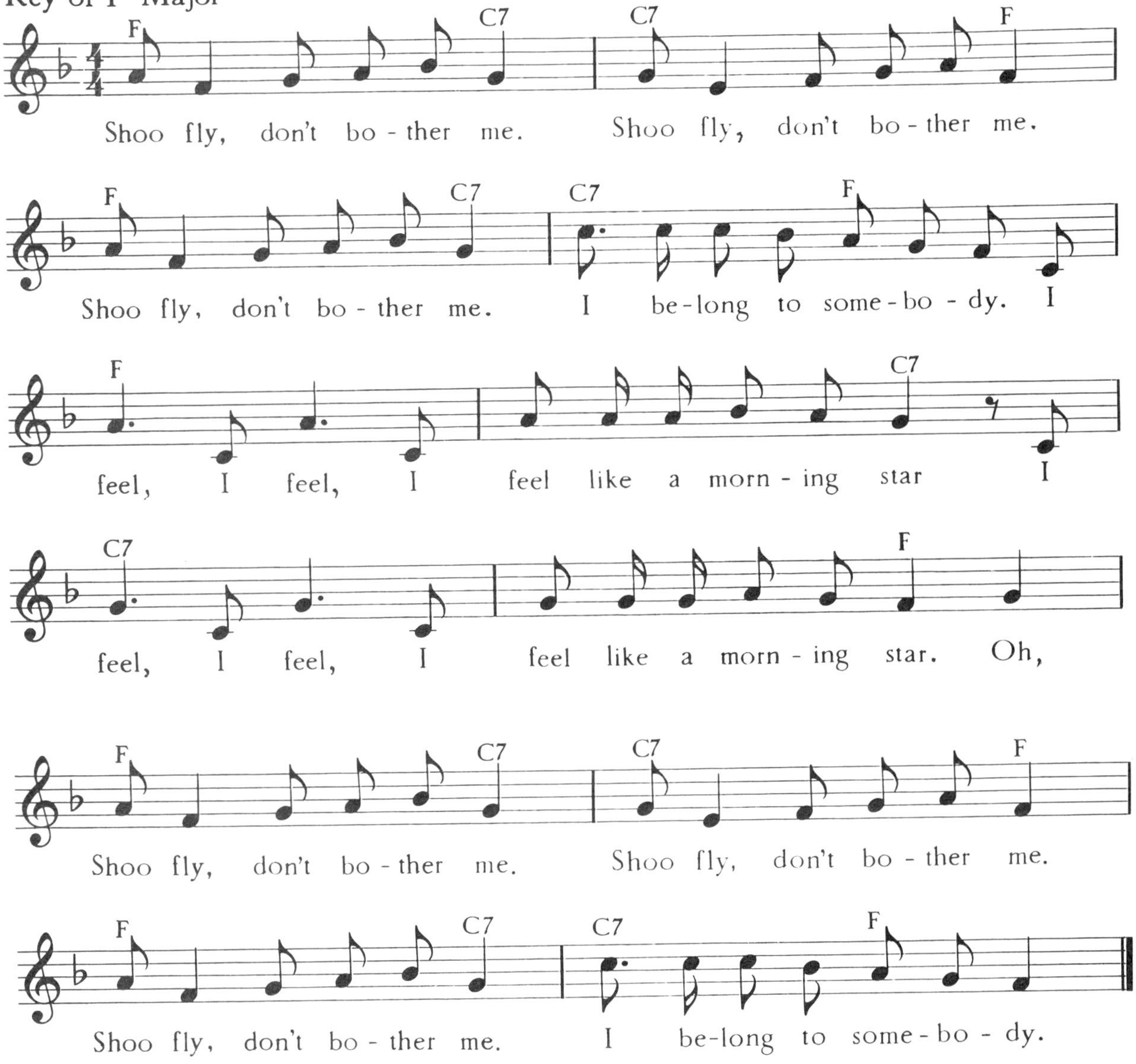
F C7 C7 F
Shoo fly, don't bo - ther me. Shoo fly, don't bo - ther me.
F C7 C7 F
Shoo fly, don't bo - ther me. I be-long to some - bo - dy. I
F C7
feel, I feel, I feel like a morn - ing star I
C7 F
feel, I feel, I feel like a morn - ing star. Oh,
F C7 C7 F
Shoo fly, don't bo - ther me. Shoo fly, don't bo - ther me.
F C7 C7 F
Shoo fly, don't bo - ther me. I be-long to some - bo - dy.

This is a favourite singing game with children

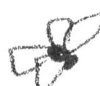

Activities

There are various activities that can be attempted with this song depending on the abilities of your children.

Instruments

Guitar, ukelele, percussion, or piano. Use the chords suggested in the song.

The following simple accompaniment would also be effective.

Xylophone

 throughout

Drum

Brush with fingers on words "shoo fly".

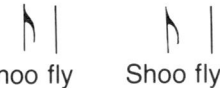

Shoo fly   Shoo fly

Finger Cymbals

Have one child play the cymbals, only in the second part, on the words "feel" and "star".

Add the following pattern played, perhaps, on a drum, for an introduction and ending.

Shoo fly don't bother me   Shoo fly don't bother me

Movement Patterns

a) Have the children sing the song, pretending they are brushing away a fly on the words "shoo fly".
   In the middle section ("I feel, I feel"), have children keep the beat by clapping, patting knees *etc*.

b) Have the children stand in a circle holding hands.
   In the first section, beginning "shoo fly", circle to the left walking.
   In the second section, beginning "I feel, I feel", stand still and clap hands.
   Repeat the first movement when the first section is sung again.

The above two movement patterns are suitable for very young children. They may also be used for slow learners, or even retarded children, as they are easy enough.

c) This movement pattern is quite complicated and should not be attempted with children who are not ready.

Call the first part ("Shoo fly"), Part A.
Call the second part ("I feel, I feel"), Part B.

The pattern calls for A and B to be repeated so that the form is A B A B A:

A. The children stand in a circle holding hands. They take four steps or skips into the centre, raising their hands, then four steps or skips back, lowering their hands.

Repeat.

B. One couple holds up their hands to form an arch. Still holding hands, one person on the other side of the circle leads the rest through the upraised hands to form another circle but this time children are back to back. When this is attempted, stress that no one can let go of hands and that the couple with the upraised arms have to turn under their own arms at the end.

A. The children take four steps backwards to centre of circle, then forward to original place.

Repeat.

B. The couple who raised their arms in first place do so again. The same person who led the rest through does so again. The circle should be back to where it was, with the children facing in at the completion of this movement.

A. Repeat the first "A" pattern, taking four steps into the circle and back.

Ha, Ha Thisaway

Key of F Major

Huddie Ledbetter

Ha, Ha, this - a - way, Ha, Ha, that - a - way, Ha, Ha,

this - a - way, All day long. Now we go march - ing,

march - ing, march - ing, Now we go march - ing, all day long.

Movement Pattern

For the "this-a-way, that-a-way" part, decide on a set action and do the same thing every time it repeats.

For the "Now we go" part, walk, skip, hop, run *etc*.

This exercise provides excellent practice for coordination and movement skills.

Spatial relationship
Body awareness
Coordination
Improvising words
Action song
Group participation

Ha, Ha Thisaway: Words and music by Huddie Ledbetter. Collected and adapted by John M. Lomax and Alan Lomax. TRO- © Copyright 1936 and renewed 1964 FOLKWAYS MUSIC PUBLISHERS, INC., New York, N.Y. Used by permission.

Shoe Game

Key of F Major

Netherlands Singing Game

You must pass this shoe from me to you, to you.

You must pass this shoe and do just what I do.

Body awareness
Coordination
Left and right
Action song
Group participation

Movement Pattern

1. The children kneel in a circle, each holding one shoe in the right hand.
2. Tap eight times for the beats of the first 2 bars.
3. Change the shoe to the left hand and tap 4 times (3rd bar).
4. Each child passes his shoe to the person on the left and picks up the shoe which the person on the right has passed to him (4th bar).
5. Repeat.

When the children become proficient do the movement more quickly.

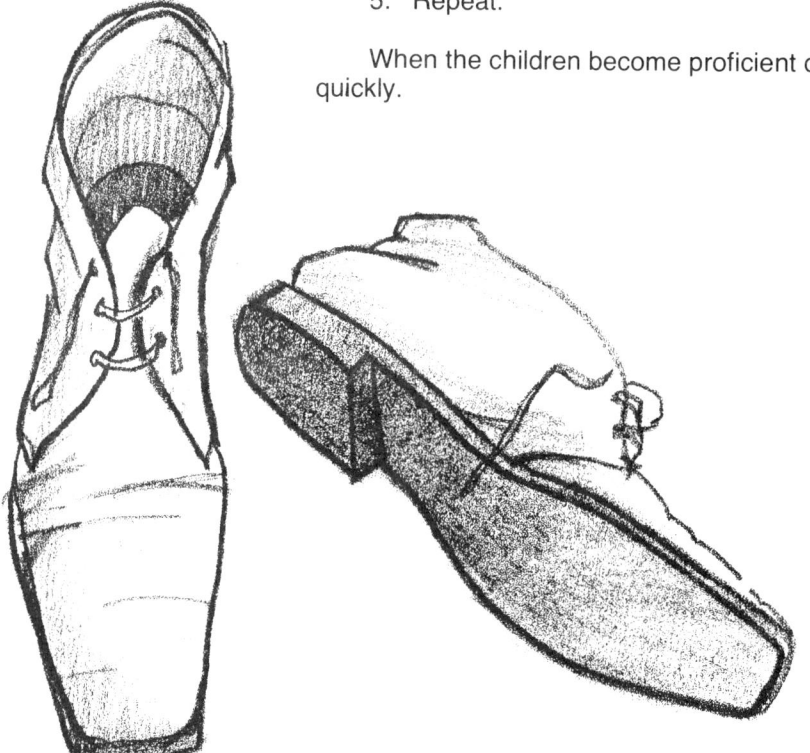

Looby Loo

Old English Singing Game

Key of F Major

Here we go loo - by loo___ Here we go loo - by light___

Here we go loo - by loo___ All on a Sat-ur-day night. You

put your left hand in. You put your left hand out. You

give your hand a shake shake shake and turn your-self a - bout.___

Repeat the song for right hand, left leg, right leg, whole head and finally whole self.

Instruments

Ukelele, guitar, autoharp: use the chords suggested in the song.

Movement Pattern

The children stand in a circle and perform the actions of the song.

Spatial relationship
Body awareness
Coordination
Left and right
Action song
Group participation

Head and Shoulders

Sing to the tune of *London Bridge*.

Head and shoulders, knees and toes,
Knees and toes, knees and toes,
Head and shoulders, knees and toes,
Eyes, ears, mouth and nose.

Traditional Singing Game

Body awareness
Action song

Activities

The children face the teacher or stand in a circle and touch the part of the body mentioned in the song.

When the children are able to follow at a slow tempo, sing faster and faster.

Do the actions facing different directions, sitting down, and (very slowly) lying down.

If You're Happy

Key of F Major

If you're hap-py and you know it, clap your hands. *(clap clap)* If you're
hap-py and you know it, clap your hands. *(clap clap)* If you're
hap-py and you know it, and you real-ly want to show it,
If you're hap-py and you know it, clap your hands. *(clap clap.)*

If you're happy and you know it touch your head . . .
If you're happy and you know it touch your eyes . . .
If you're happy and you know it do all four . . .

Activities

The list of things to do is unlimited — whistle a tune, wink an eye, rub your stomach, *etc.*

Change the character of the song completely by saying:

If you're sad and you know it cry a tear . . .
If you're mad and you know it stamp your feet . . .
If you're mad and you know it shake a fist . . .

Do the song in different positions; standing, sitting, lying down, kneeling, facing different directions, for even greater practice in body awareness.

Body awareness
Coordination
Auditory sequencing
Action song
Group participation

Instruments

Ukelele, guitar, autoharp, piano. Use the chords suggested in the song. Drums, sticks, other hand percussion. Use sparingly, playing on the beat.

Related Activities

Have the children follow the melodic line with a hand in the air and draw a "map" of the melody on the chalkboard or a piece of paper.

Punchinello

Key of F Major

Look who is here, Pun-chin - el - lo, fun - ny fel - low

Look who is here, Pun - chin - el - lo, fun - ny boy.

2. What can you do
Punchinello funny fellow?
What can you do
Punchinello funny boy?

3. We'll do it too
Punchinello funny fellow
We'll do it too
Punchinello funny boy.

4. Who do you choose
Punchinello funny fellow?
Who do you choose
Punchinello funny boy?

Spatial relationship
Body awareness
Coordination
Action song
Improvising movement

Instruments

Xylophone

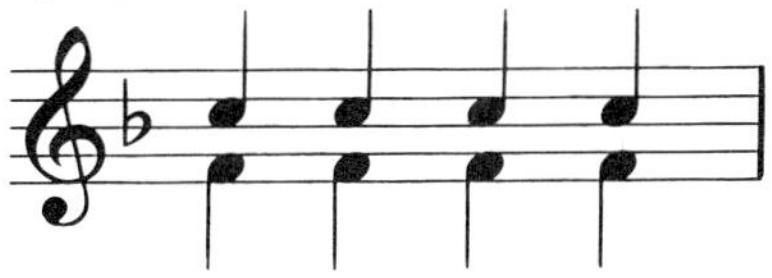 throughout

Glockenspiel

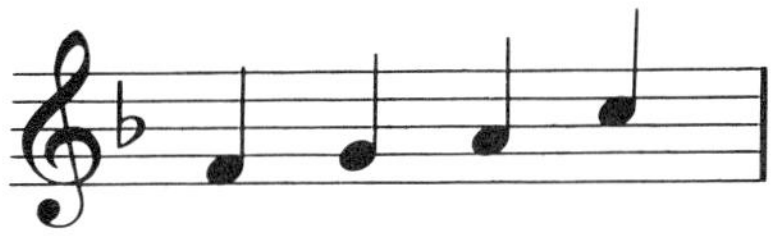 throughout

Metallophone

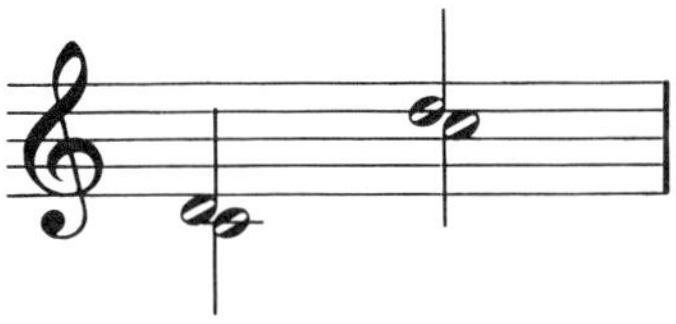 throughout

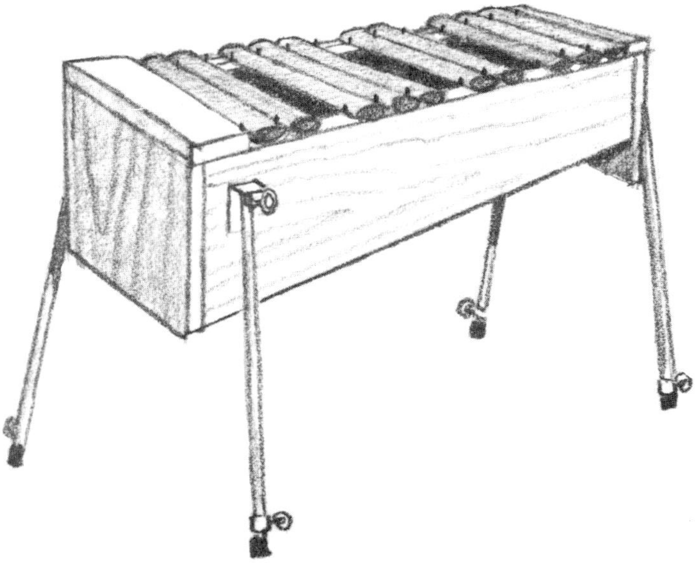

Sticks

Introduction

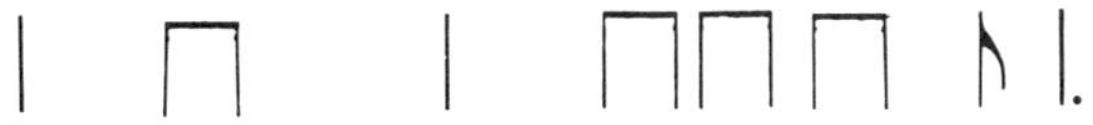

Look who comes here Punchinello funny fellow

Movement Pattern

The children stand in a circle with one child in the middle.

Verse 1. The child in the middle skips around the circle; the others sing and clap.

Verse 2. The children in the circle stand, hands on hips, in a "show me" attitude while the one in the middle makes up an action.

Verse 3. All copy the motion of the child in the middle.

Verse 4. The children in the circle join hands and walk to the right.
The child in the middle shuts his eyes and points as he turns around.
The person he is pointing to at the end of the verse takes his place in the centre of the circle.

Repeat the song.

Related Activities

Discuss clowns like *Punchinello*.
Draw pictures of clowns and other related circus objects.

Rig a Jig Jig

Key of C Major   Old English Folk Song

As I was walk - ing down the street, down the street,

down the street, A pret - ty girl I chanced to meet, Hi -

ho Hi - ho Hi - ho_____ Rig - a - jig jig and a -

way we go and a - way we go and a - way we go.

Rig - a - jig jig and a - way we go, Hi - ho Hi - ho Hi - ho._____

Spatial relationship
Names
Coordination
Action song

Activities

Substitute each child's name in turn for "I" to make a name song.

Have each child decide how to come down the street: *i.e.* walk, run, skip, jump *etc*.

Depending on whether a boy or girl is chosen, use "pretty girl" or "handsome boy".

Instruments

Guitar, ukelele: use the chords suggested in the song.
Drums, sticks, bells: use sparingly, playing on the beat.

Movement Pattern

1. The children stand in a circle. One who is "it" stands outside the circle.
2. As the children in the circle sing and clap beat to first half of the song, the child on the outside skips, walks, or runs, *etc.* around the outside of the circle.
3. At the words "a pretty girl" or "handsome boy" the one outside the circle picks a partner and together they skip around until the end of the song.
4. The first child comes back to the circle and the game repeats with the first child's partner on the outside of the circle.

Related Activities

Discuss the different ways to come down the street (walk, run, skip, drive, *etc.*). Write a list of these and use them for reading words.

Discuss the different things seen on the street. Write a list of them also.

Draw or paint a picture of a street using the ideas discussed above.

Hot Potato

Key of C Major

Hot po-ta-to pass it on. Hot po-ta-to pass it on.

Hot po-ta-to pass it on. Get rid of the hot po-ta-to.

Activities

1. The children sit in a circle and one child holds a ball.
2. As the children start to sing, they pass the ball in one direction. (Decide before beginning whether to the left or right.)
3. The child holding the ball at the end of the song is "out".
4. The game repeats until only one person is left.

Start with a large ball and slowly pass it.

As the children grow more proficient, sing faster and use a smaller and smaller ball.

Do the movements standing or kneeling in a circle, for variation and extra practice in coordination.

Body awareness
Coordination
Left and Right
Action song

Deep and Wide

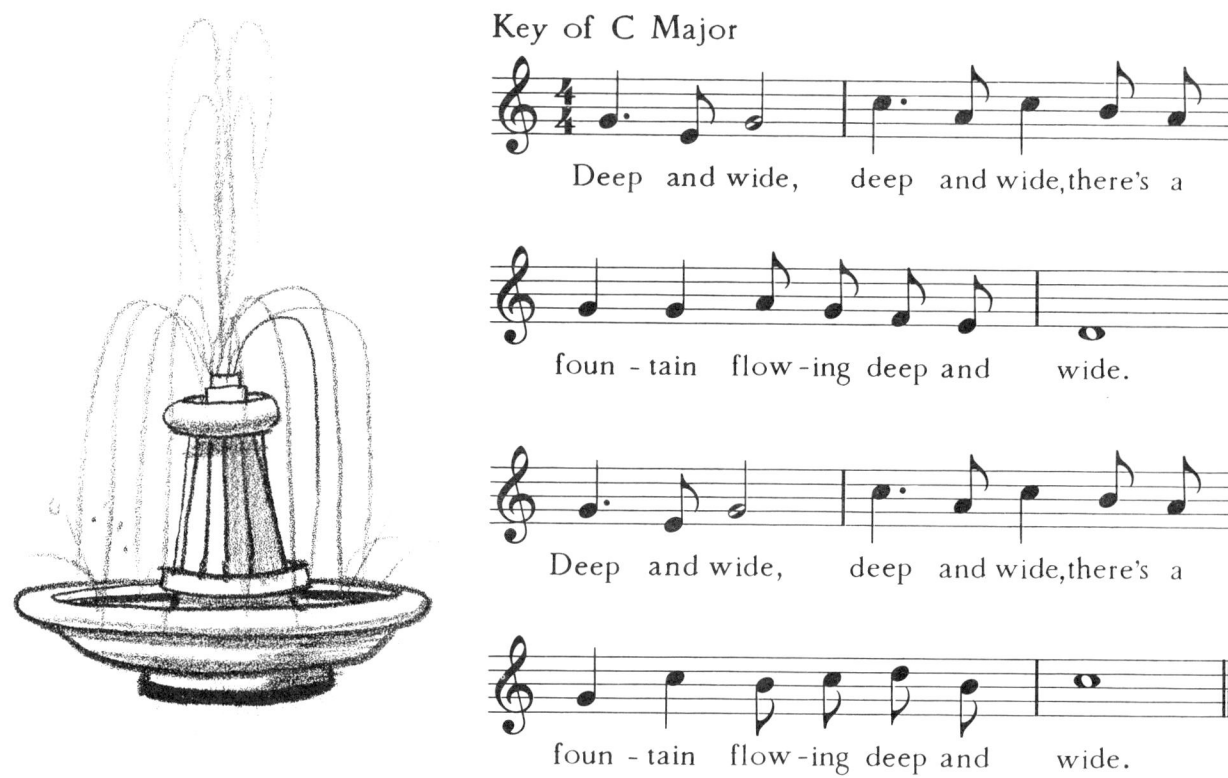

Key of C Major

Deep and wide,　deep and wide, there's a foun - tain flow - ing deep and　wide.

Deep and wide,　deep and wide, there's a foun - tain flow - ing deep and　wide.

Spatial relationship
Body awareness
Coordination
Sub-vocalization
Action song

Activities

Have the children do the following:
1. Stand or sit, arms out in front.
2. Palms facing each other, show "deep", with hands horizontal. ＝
3. Palms facing each other, show "wide", hands held vertically. ‖
4. Show "fountain" by moving arms and hands up, then out. ⌐⌐
5. Show "flowing" by fingers wiggling as arms move from right to left across the front of body.

As the song is repeated, omit the singing of the action words (still performing the action) one at a time until the song is all rhythmic action.

G. SONGS JUST FOR FUN

The Crooked Man

Key of C Major

Old Nursery Song

There was a crook-ed man who walked a crook-ed mile. He

found a crook-ed six-pence up - on a crook-ed stile. He

bought a crook-ed cat who caught a crook-ed mouse And they

all lived to-geth-er in a lit-tle crook-ed house.

This is a song "just for fun".

Several of the words such as "stile" and "sixpence" will have to be explained to North American children, but they accept these very easily.

Activities

Children enjoy making pictures of the story in this song and they will also act out the story with great enthusiasm.

105

Donkey Riding

Key of F Major

Lancashire Sea Song

Were you ev - er in Que-bec Stow-ing tim - ber on a deck

Where there's a King with a gold - en crown Rid -ing on a don- key?

CHORUS

Hey, ho! A - way we go Don-key rid - ing, don-key rid - ing.

Hey, ho! A - way we go Rid - ing on a don - key.

2. Were you ever off the Horn
Where it's always fine and warm
See the lion and the unicorn
Riding on a donkey.

Hey ho away we go . . .

3. Were you ever in Cardiff Bay
Where the folks all shout hurray
Here comes John with six months pay
Riding on a donkey.

Hey ho away we go . . .

Instruments

Guitar, ukelele, autoharp, piano: use the chords suggested in the song.

Movement Pattern

There are two very simple but very effective movement patterns for this song, based on two formations, the line and the circle.

a)   Line — the children make two lines, facing each other.

Verse   The head couple join both hands and skip sideways for eight steps down the middle to the end. The couple skip eight steps back to the head of the line.

Chorus   The couple drop hands and each child skips down the outside of his line to the bottom, in eight steps. The couple then link right arms and skip around for eight steps in place at the bottom of the two lines. When finished they stand at the ends of the lines. This makes a new head couple. Repeat with a new head couple.

b)   Circle — the children join hands in a circle.

Verse   Everyone skips sideways to the left for eight counts and back to the right for eight counts.

Chorus   Each child links arms with a partner and skips around him for the count of eight. The children change arms and skip around for eight counts in the other direction. Repeat as often as you wish.

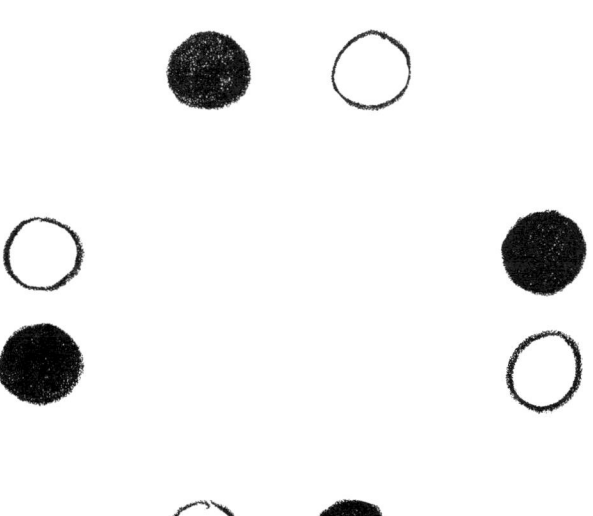

Land of the Silver Birch

Key of D Minor

Canadian Folk Song

2. Down in the forest, deep in the lowlands,
   My heart cries out for thee, hills of the north.
   Blue lake and rocky shore, I will return once more.
   Boom diddy boom boom, boom diddy boom boom,
   boom diddy boom boom. Boom!

3. High on a rocky ledge, I'll build my wigwam,
   Close by the water's edge, silent and still.
   Blue lake and rocky shore, I will return once more.
   Boom diddy boom boom, boom diddy boom boom,
   boom diddy boom boom. Boom!

This is a lovely Canadian folk song which has a rather Indian "flavour", although it is not thought to be a true Indian song.
The singing and the instrumental accompaniment should be
quiet and simple to reflect the peace of the north woods.

108

Instruments

Metallophone

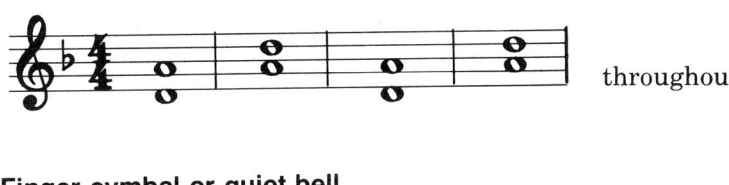

throughout

Finger cymbal or quiet bell

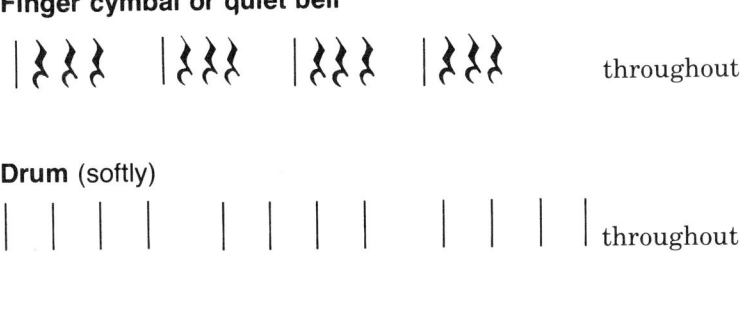

throughout

Drum (softly)

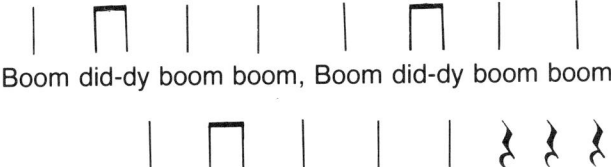throughout

In the chorus the drums can play the rhythm pattern of the words.

Boom did-dy boom boom, Boom did-dy boom boom

Boom did-dy boom boom Boom.

This same rhythm pattern of the chorus can be played along with the metallophone part for an introduction.

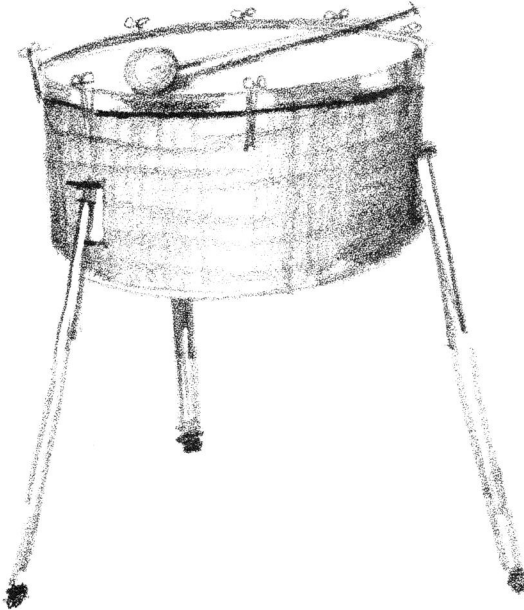

C-C-C-C-Cold

Danish Song
Words by John Wood

Key of G Major

1. There was a man and he did sing, "C-C-C-C-C-C - cold!"

A - cross the north land it would ring, "C-C-C-C-C - C - cold!"

No mat-ter what he tried to say, "C-C-C-C-C-C-C-C-"night or day,

His words kept com-ing out this way, "C-C-C-C-C - C - cold!"

2. This little man was very thin
"C-C-C-C-C-C-C-cold."
With icy whiskers on his chin
"C-C-C-C-C-C-C-cold."
One night he had an awful dream,
"C-C-C-C-C-C-C-C-" he did scream,
"For my dessert don't serve ice-cream
C-C-C-C-C-C- cold."

If the children you are working with have speech problems, do not use this song.

Instruments

Xylophone or Glockenspiel or Chime Bars.

Metallophone

110

Triangle

played quietly throughout

Tambourine

Shake on the words "C-C-C-C-C-C-Cold"

This song might be divided so that one group sings the verses while another sings only the "C-C-C-C-C-C-Cold".

Mister Banjo

Key of G Major

Creole Song

1. See Mis-ter Ban-jo, See Mis-ter Ban-jo

Strut-ting a-long the street.

Hat cocked on one side, Mis-ter Ban-jo

Gold tipped cane in hand, Mis-ter Ban-jo

See Mis-ter Ban-jo, See Mis-ter Ban-jo

Strut-ting a-long the street.

2. See Mr. Banjo. See Mr. Banjo
                walk like a millionaire.
    See Mr. Banjo. See Mr. Banjo
                walk like a millionaire.
    Boots that glow and shine, Mister Banjo,
            yellow gloves so fine, Mister Banjo.
    See Mister Banjo. See Mister Banjo
                walk like a millionaire.

Activities

Have one or more children imitate the pompous, stuck-up Mr. Banjo as he struts along the street or walks like a millionaire. Everyone will want a turn. If possible, equip Mr. Banjo with props such as a hat, a cane and some gloves.

Instruments

Guitar, ukelele, autoharp, piano: use the chords suggested in the song.

Woodblock or sticks: play a steady beat to give an accompaniment of "walking" music.

H. SONGS FOR SPECIAL DAYS

I Hallowe'en

Witches in the Dark

This is sung to the tune of *The Farmer in the Dell*. Have children form a circle with one child in the middle. Instead of using "farmer, wife, nurse" *etc*. pick names that have Hallowe'en meanings. The children are called one by one into the centre as the rest of the circle walks around.

Witches in the dark, Witches in the dark,
Hi ho for Hallowe'en, Witches in the dark.

The witch takes a bat, The witch takes a bat,
Hi ho for Hallowe'en, The witch takes a bat.

The bat takes a black cat, The bat takes a black cat,
Hi ho for Hallowe'en the bat takes a black cat.

Continue until there is only one child left. Call this child the ghost.

The ghost says BOO! The ghost says BOO!
Hi ho for Hallowe'en, The ghost says BOO!

They all run away, They all run away,
Hi ho for Hallowe'en, They all run away.(Everyone scatters.)

Brownies and Witches

Words by Mayme Christenson
Music by J. Wolverton

Key of E Minor

Brow - nies   and   wit - ches   and   gob - lins   and   such

Folks   can't   see   and   folks_   can't   touch.   BOO!

The Witches' Brew

Key of E Minor

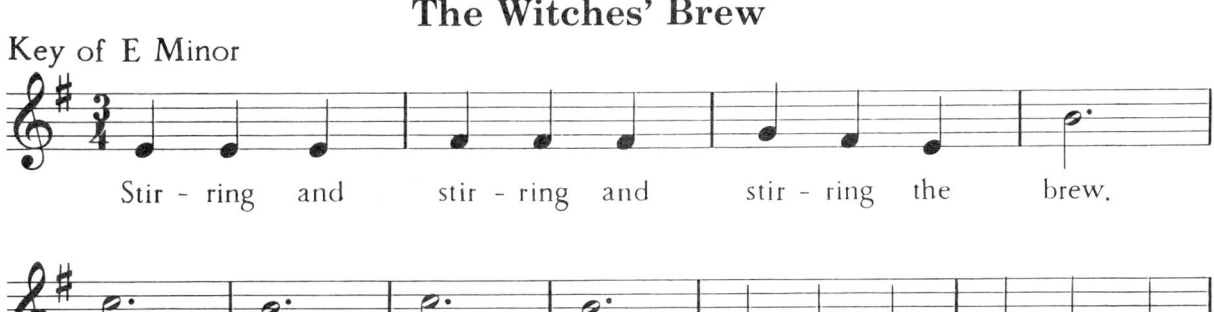

Stir - ring   and   stir - ring   and   stir - ring   the   brew.

Whoo - oo   Whoo - oo   Stir - ring   and   stir - ring   and

stir - ring   the   brew.   Whoo - oo   Whoo - oo.   BOO!

These two Hallowe'en songs are very popular with children. They must be sung slowly, very quietly and very mysteriously so that the final "BOO!" is startling.

Activities

Instruments can be used to provide sound effects: *e.g.* a drum rubbed with the flat of the hand will suggest a wind sound, sticks rattled together will suggest skeletons, a drum scratched with fingernails might be mice scratching, a cymbal played softly and slowly might suggest a far-off church bell. The children will be quick to suggest others.

If you are working with emotionally disturbed or easily excited children, I would suggest that you omit the "BOO" or perhaps use other songs which are less upsetting. The following two are good examples of quieter songs.

The Witch Rides

Key of D Minor

Words and music by Grace M. Meserve

The witch is on her broom - stick Rid - ing ve - ry fast___ Oo - oo Oo - oo Hal - low - e'en at last.___

2. See the ghosts come floating
   White against the sky,
   Oo . . . oo Oo . . . oo
   They go drifting by.

3. The skeleton is dancing
   On his bony toes,
   Tipping, tapping
   On and on he goes.

4. See the funny goblins
   Dancing down the street,
   Knocking, knocking
   Crying "trick or treat."

There Was an Old Witch

Key of E Minor

Traditional Song

There was an old witch, Be - lieve it if you can. She
tapped on the win-dow and she ran ran— ran. She
ran hel - ter skel - ter with her toes in the air,
Corn - stalks fly - ing from the old witch's hair. "Swish," goes the
broom - stick, "Me - ow," goes the cat, "Plop," goes the hop - toad,
sit - ting on her hat. "Wee," chuck - led I, "What
fun fun fun!" Hal - low - een night when the wit - ches run.

This is a great Hallowe'en song which all children love.

Percussion Instruments

Woodblock

Play the rhythm pattern of the words, "she tapped at the window".

Drum I

Play a fast eighth note pattern (running pattern) for "ran ran ran" and "ran helter skelter".

Drum II

Create a spooky sound effect throughout by scratching fingernails on the drumhead or swishing the palm of the hand across it.

Xylophone

a. Play the following softly all the way through. Wooden mallets could be used.

b. Use wooden mallets on wooden xylophone (for a spooky sound) for an introduction and ending. Play a *glissando* up and down the xylophone twice.

Metallophone

Imitate the sound of the church bell with the metallophone.

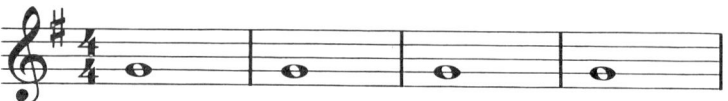

Have the children sing, using as much expression as possible when imitating the sounds "swish", "meow", "plop" and "whee".

Rocking Horse

Key of F Major

I'm a Christ-mas rock-ing horse. See me rock, see me rock.

San - ta brought me here last night, Just at 12 o - 'clock.

Many of the songs we sing at Christmas are too difficult for very young children and slow learners because of their words. This song about a rocking horse is just right.

Instruments

Guitar, ukelele or autoharp: use the chords suggested in the song.

Tiny bells or finger cymbals could be used to play the rhythm of the words. The beat is too slow for small children to play accurately.

Movement

Have the children kneel with hands on the floor and rock like a rocking horse.

Christmas Is Here

Key of F Major

Swedish Carol

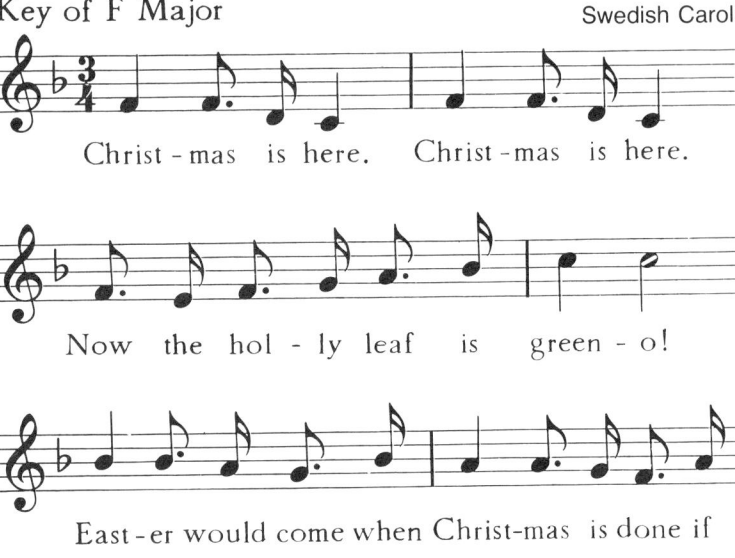

Christ - mas is here. Christ - mas is here.

Now the hol - ly leaf is green - o!

East - er would come when Christ - mas is done if

Lent did - n't fall be - tween - o!

Instruments

This tune is obviously made for dancing and so the accompaniment should be kept fairly simple throughout.

Tambourine and bells

These instruments can play on the beat with a good strong accent on the first note of the bar.

Be careful that overzealous playing does not drown out the singing.

If you have children who are advanced enough, the following could be tried.

Glockenspiel, metallophone or chime bars

throughout

Have a singing introduction of four bars.

La la la la   La la la la   La la la la   La la la la

Movement Pattern

The children join hands in a long chain, holding their hands up. For the introduction, the children sway in their places. Then, when the song starts, they walk the beat, following the leader, bending alternate knees on successive strong beats, and turning the body slightly each time. The song can be repeated as many times as you wish.

Uneven metres such as threes are difficult for all children at first because they are so used to $\frac{2}{4}$ $\frac{4}{4}$ and $\frac{6}{8}$ metres, all of which have the strong beat falling on the same side of the body every time. In threes the strong beat comes on alternate sides of the body if the beats are walked or clapped.

Christmas Is Coming

Key of C Major

Old English Carol

Christ - mas is com - ing, the goose is get - ting fat.

Please put a pen - ny in the old man's hat. If you

have - n't got a pen - ny, a ha' pen - ny will do. If you

have - n't got a ha' pen - ny, well God bless you.

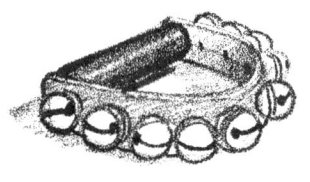

This is a very old English carol which appears in several versions. Children like this one because it has a longer story line.

Explain that the old beggar man is going from door to door with his hat in his hand looking for money as it is Christmas time and he expects that people might be more generous. The terms "penny" and "ha'penny" will have to be explained also.

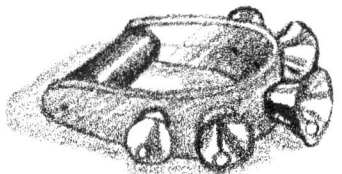

Instruments

Bells, finger cymbals, small triangle.

One of the best sounds to describe Christmas is the chiming of bells. You can find objects to create beautiful bell sounds in antique stores, in the house and even in the school. Have the children hunt for these.

Play the finger cymbals, or some other instrument with a similar sound, to imitate the sound of money dropping into the hat.

Xylophone

throughout

or   throughout

Glockenspiel

This instrument is a good choice for Christmas songs because of its bell-like quality. The following suggestion is taken from one of the best known church bell peals.

Metallophone

This is another good bell sound!

throughout

120

Deck the Hall

Key of C Major

Old Welsh Carol

1. Deck the hall with boughs of hol - ly, Fa la la la la la la la la;

'Tis the sea - son to be jol - ly, Fa la la la la la la la la.

Don we now our gay ap - par - el, Fa la la la la la la la la;

Troll the an - cient Yule-tide car - ol, Fa la la la la la la la la.

2. See the blazing yule before us, fa la la ...
   Strike the harp and join the chorus, fa la la ...
   Follow me in merry measure, fa la la ...
   While I tell of Yuletide treasure, fa la la ...

3. Fast away the old year passes, fa la la ...
   Hail the new ye lads and lasses, fa la la ...
   Sing we joyous all together, fa la la ...
   Heedless of the wind and weather, fa la la ..

Deck the Hall is a song suitable for older children as the words are quite difficult. If the old English sayings are not familiar, they can be explained and children accept them readily.

Young children also like this song. It can be managed if the leader sings the verses and the children do just the "fa la la's".

Instruments

Tambourines, bells, triangles

Use percussion instruments such as tambourines, light sounding bells, and the delicate sound of a triangle for the "fa la la" section.

The form of this music is A A B A. That is, the first, second and last lines are the same musically, while the third line is different. When using a melodic accompaniment, it is necessary to change the accompaniment on the third line. This can be done by having the same group play something different or by having two groups — one playing for lines 1, 2, and 4, while another plays something different for line 3. Of course, it is easier to have the two groups.

Xylophone or glockenspiel

lines 1, 2, and 4.

line 3.

Metallophone

lines 1, 2, and 4.

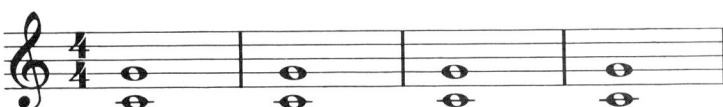

line 3.

This accompaniment imitates the sound of Christmas bells.

Related Activities

Discuss the celebration of an old English Christmas, with the decorating of the great hall with holly boughs, the bringing in of the Yule log to burn in the huge fireplace, the dancing and singing in which everyone participated in those long ago days before television.

The children might illustrate such a scene.

III   Chanukah

Chanukah

Chanukah

Key of G Major   Collected by June Barber

Cha - nu - kah.   Cha - nu - kah   So   much light and   joy

Sing and play   all   the day   Ev - ery girl and   boy.

This is a very easy song for children to sing at Chanukah time. Repeat as many times as you wish.

Activities

Use this short song for the "A" section of a rondo.

A Everyone sings, with a few people playing either the accompaniment suggested below or one that the children have devised themselves.
B One child improvises for eight bars on woodblock or drums.
A All sing the song with accompaniment.
C Another child improvises, on another percussion instrument.
A All sing the song with accompaniment.

See **Creativity**, page 181, for a more detailed description of the rondo form.

Xylophone

   throughout

Finger cymbals

Play only on
the words:
                Cha-nu-kah Cha-nu-kah;

      and: Sing and play all the day.

My Dreydel

Words by S. S. Grossman
Music by S.E. Goldfarb

Key of C Major

1. I have a lit - tle drey-del. I made it out of clay And
when it's dry and read - y Then drey - del I shall play.

CHORUS

Oh drey-del drey-del drey-del I made it out of clay. Oh
drey - del drey - del drey - del Now drey - del I shall play.

2. My dreydel's always playful,
   It loves to dance and spin.
   A happy game of dreydel
   Come play, now let's begin.
   Oh, dreydel, dreydel, dreydel,
   It loves to dance and spin.
   Oh, dreydel, dreydel, dreydel,
   Come play, now let's begin.

Activities
During Chanukah children play with a small top called a dreydel. Imitate the spinning action of the top in movement and with instruments.

Instruments

Drum
With the flat of the palm, make a circular motion on the drumhead to give a swishing sound.

Xylophone

A pattern which turns back on itself is good for imitating the round and round motion of the top.

or   throughout

Alternate left and right hands.

If these accompaniments are too difficult, play the pattern half as fast in quarter notes.

play throughout

or

Movement Pattern

The children join hands in a circle.

First two lines
   —8 slide steps to the left, then 8 back again to the right.

Chorus
   —Everyone drops hands and each child spins around like a top.
Join hands again in a circle for the second verse.

Making Valentines

Words and Music by J. Wolverton

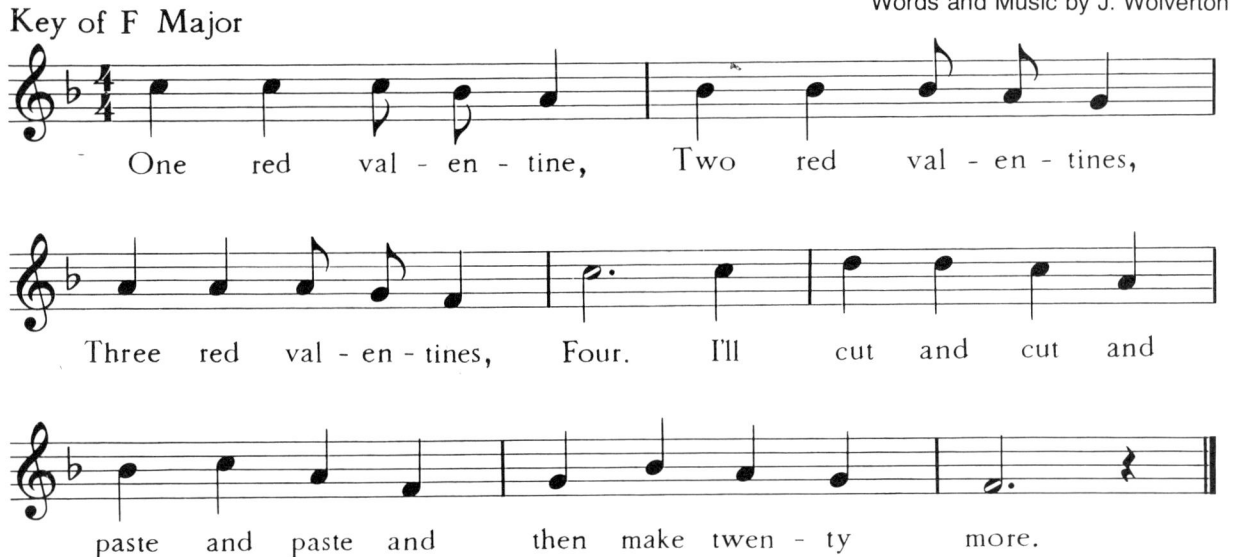

Key of F Major

One red val - en - tine, Two red val - en - tines,

Three red val - en - tines, Four. I'll cut and cut and

paste and paste and then make twen - ty more.

Activities

Counting
Finger play
Reading
Action song

Action
    "One, two, three, four" — hold up the correct number of fingers on each count.
    "Cut and cut" — make second and third fingers into scissors and "cut".
    "Paste and paste" — make an action like pasting.
    "Twenty more" — hold up all ten fingers twice.

Reading Skills
    Cut valentines out of red paper. Put "1", "2", "3", and "4" on them or "one", "two", "three", and "four", depending on the abilities of the children. Hold these up. The children then have to read them as they sing.

I. EXTRA SONGS

Don't forget these well-known songs. They are fun to do and have stood the test of time. Children love them.

A-Hunting We Will Go
Ants Come Marching One by One
Are You Sleeping? (Frère Jacques)
Baa Baa Black Sheep
Barnyard Song (I bought a cat and the cat pleased me)
Bingo (Farmer Brown's Dog)
(The) Bus (The people on the bus go up and down)
Canoe Song (My paddle's keen and bright)
Christmas Carols
Clementine
Come All You Playmates
Did You Ever See a Lassie? (Laddie)
Eensy Weensy Spider (see **Poems**, page 152, for words)
also known as *Inky Pinky Spider*
Everybody Loves Saturday Night
(The) Farmer in the Dell
Here We Go Round the Mulberry Bush
He's Got the Whole World in His Hands
Hush Little Baby (Don't say a word)
I Know an Old Woman Who Swallowed a Fly
I'se the B'y (That Builds the Boat)
I've Been Working on the Railroad
I Went to the Animal Fair
Jack Was Every Inch a Sailor
Jimmy Crack Corn (Bluetailed Fly)
Jingle Bells (and other well-known Christmas songs)
John Brown's Body
Kookaburra
Kum Ba Yah
London Bridge
Looby Loo
Lukey's Boat
Michael Finnegan
Michael Row the Boat Ashore
Miss Polly Had a Dolly
Monkey See Monkey Do
Oh Susanna
Old MacDonald Had a Farm
Old Texas
Over in the Meadow
Polly Wolly Doodle
Pop Goes the Weasel
Row Row Row Your Boat
She'll Be Coming Round the Mountain
Skip to My Loo
Sweetly Sings the Donkey
This Old Man

Three Blind Mice (can be sung with *Are You Sleeping*, as a partner song)
Twinkle, Twinkle Little Star
We Wish You a Merry Christmas
Waltzing Matilda

Many of the above suggestions can be found in the folk song or camp song books listed in **Books**, pages 233-235.

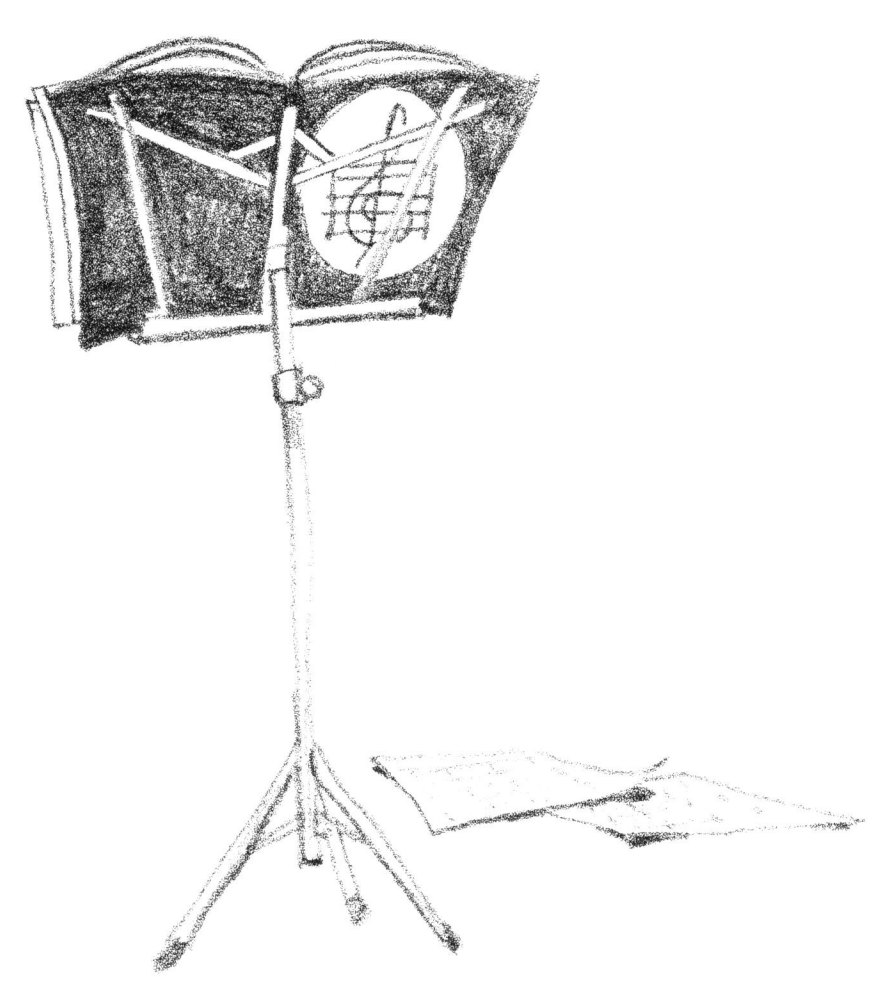

SPEECH AND POETRY

CONTENTS

It is difficult to separate songs and poetry as a song is poetry set to music. Many of the games and ideas are similar for both but there are some peculiar to speech alone.

Speech is an important source of rhythm. Any rhythm in music can be expressed in a word pattern and of course rhythm is one of the most important components of speech. Often, if you cannot fully hear the words someone has spoken to you, it is possible to grasp the meaning because of the powerful clue of rhythm.

The early babbling of babies takes shape into a rhythmic babble. Often the flow of whole sentences is present but of course there is no meaning to the babble at this stage. This comes later. If this rhythmic development does not take place it is sometimes the first symptom of trouble — deafness, learning disability, etc.

Nursery rhymes and songs and all the little finger games which should be part of the very young child's life are of prime importance in establishing the inner rhythmic sureness everyone needs in order to have a healthy rapport with the rest of the world. Many speech therapists and speech teachers are using more and more poetry and rhythmic nonsense rhymes to help youngsters, because they know that rhythm can be the magic carpet which carries other learning along with it.

Children with poor oral language are often poor readers as well. If a child has a lot of experience chanting poems and nursery rhymes, his vocabulary will be enriched and he will find reading easier and more meaningful.

Occasionally use puppets to "say" the poem for you. All children find this fun and withdrawn, emotionally disturbed and autistic children will sometimes respond to a puppet when they will not to a person.

We will start by discussing word rhythms and then, poetry.

A. WORD RHYTHMS

I Individual Words

Speech training

Have the children say and clap the rhythm (syllables) of many words. Start with their names, as names are of prime importance to all children. Objects in the room can be clapped: vegetables, toys, animals, the list is endless.

Body awareness

Later, instead of clapping, have children play these rhythm patterns on their knees, heads, and shoulders, or walk or stamp them.

Next, use drums and other percussion instruments to play the rhythm. Make sure that the word is spoken each time.

I Hear with My Little Ear

Auditory awareness

Play a guessing game. Say "I hear with my little ear the name of something that sounds like . . ." and clap or play the rhythm of the name of the object. If this is too difficult, you can qualify it by saying "It is green," or "It is near the window," at first.

Draw the Sound

Visual awareness

Older children can "draw the sound". Tell them to pretend they are holding a piece of chalk in their hand and draw in the air. Next, actually write the rhythm on chalkboard or paper. (See **Notation**, page 196, for further explanation.

This visual representation of the auditory is a great aid to learning. Here are a few examples:

Teddy Bear   Mary   cauliflower

With plenty of this kind of preparation, dividing words into syllables later on presents no problems.

II Combining Words

After children have become proficient in clapping words individually, combine these in pairs.

A good place to start is with the children's names.

Add accents if you want a visual picture of the stress syllables.

Mary Peter   Christopher John   Antonio Carlos

Have the children walk these rhythms, clap them, play them on percussion instruments, just the same as they did with the individual words.

When the children are able, combine four or more words to give a longer pattern.

Names of cars are always favourites with children.

Cadillac   Volkswagen   Pinto   Ford

Endings are important. After saying the sequence a set number of times strike a cymbal or drum or have the children recite a suitable ending, such as "yum yum yum", "our toys", or "sports cars". This helps to give the exercise form and also makes the endings definite. Here is an example.

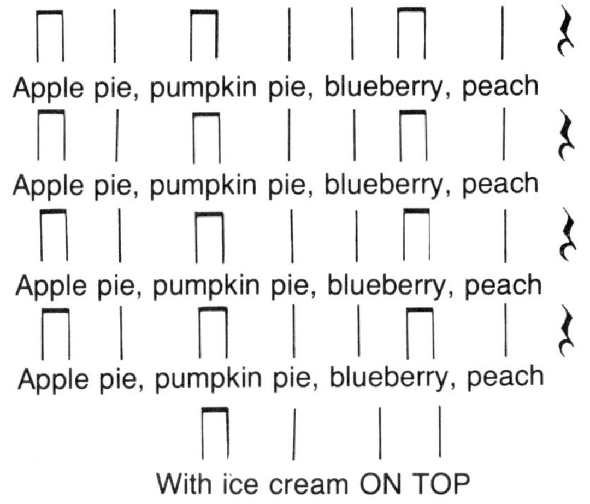

Apple pie, pumpkin pie, blueberry, peach

Apple pie, pumpkin pie, blueberry, peach

Apple pie, pumpkin pie, blueberry, peach

Apple pie, pumpkin pie, blueberry, peach

With ice cream ON TOP

Small compositions result if word rhythms are put together. Pick topics which interest the children.

Accompany the Word Rhythms with Body Sounds

Insects

Start one group saying "inchworm" very slowly, accompanied by walking the rhythm softly:

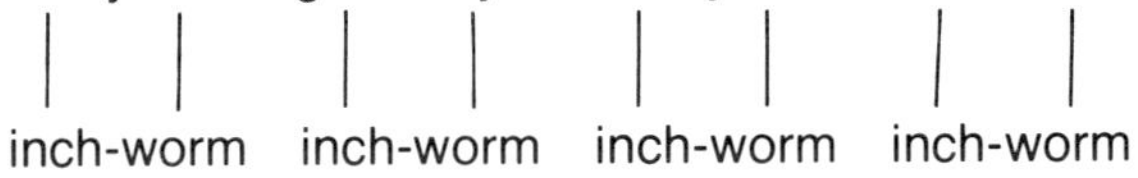

inch-worm   inch-worm   inch-worm   inch-worm

This group continues to the end.

After the first group has said "inchworm" four times, the next group joins the first, saying "caterpillar" and patting knees on the beat:

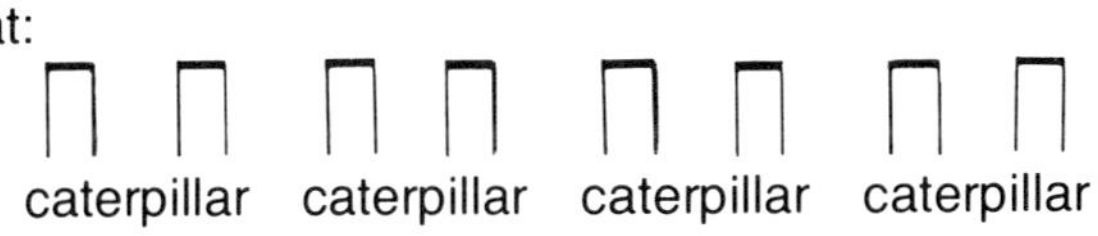

caterpillar   caterpillar   caterpillar   caterpillar

This group also keeps going.

After four more times the next two groups start. One group says "big fat bumble bee" and accompanies this by clapping and the other group says "mosquito mosquito" in a very high voice:

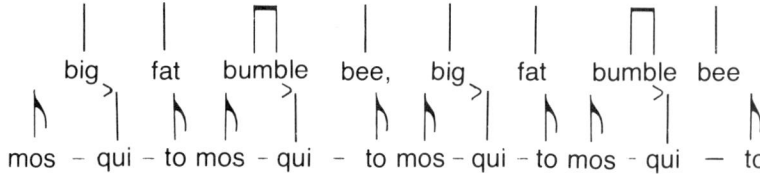

All four parts continue getting louder and louder then gradually softer, stopping one by one, until only "inchworm inchworm" is left. This part finally stops too.

Accompany the Word Rhythms with Percussion Instruments

Food

Start with one group saying "hamburgers". One member of the group plays the rhythm pattern on a drum:

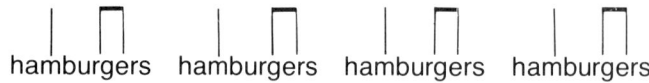

After the first group has said this four times, the second group starts saying "french fries" with the rhythm pattern played on woodblocks:

After the first two groups have said their two patterns together four more times, add the third group saying "wieners in a bun" with the rhythm pattern played on sticks:

wieners in a bun, wieners in a bun

All three parts grow louder and louder together, then everybody stops. One voice then says, "Look out, here comes the ketchup!"

Everyone says "Splot!" in a loud voice and at the same time a child plays one big crash on the drums, cymbals, or woodblocks, *etc.*

These are just ideas and you can take it from here. The scope is unlimited.

III   Phrases

Phrases can be treated in the same way as individual words or groups of words. That is, by accompanying them with body sound, playing the rhythms on percussion instruments, walking the rhythm, saying several together, *etc.*

Have the children invent their own phrases.

A few suggestions follow.

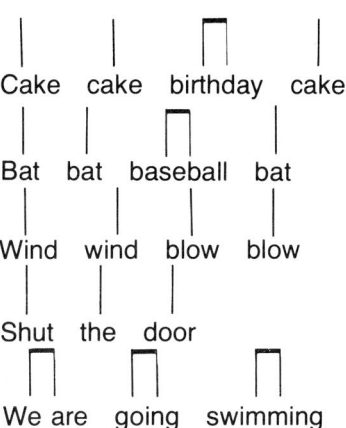

Cake cake birthday cake

Bat bat baseball bat

Wind wind blow blow

Shut the door

We are going swimming

B. POETRY

The choice of poetry is as unlimited as the choice of songs. Everyone has favourites which have been found to interest and excite the children. Some suggestions will be found in **Poems**, but of course these are only suggestions.

Some poems are best read to the class by the teacher because of their length or the involvement of the story.

Some poems can be acted out.

Some poems can be used as the "A" section of rondos. (See **Creativity**, page 181.)

Some poems are primarily rhythmic and others create a mood.

The following are ideas and games which can be used to heighten interest and increase awareness.

I   Rhythmic Poems

Say the poem and have the children move any way they wish. Pick one child who is doing the beat and say: "Let's all do what David is doing."

Say the poem and clap, stamp or walk the beat.

Say the poem and clap the rhythmic pattern of the words.

Say the poem, walk the beat and clap the rhythmic pattern of the words at the same time or have one-half of the class walk the beat while the other half claps the rhythmic pattern.

Say the poem and play the beat on a drum and the rhythmic pattern on woodblocks or sticks. (The choice of instrument is up to the children.)

Take a phrase from the poem and have a group of children say it over and over as an accompaniment. For an example of this, see *The Train*, **Poems**, page 155.

Play the accompaniment rhythm on instruments.

Start the accompaniment a set number of times before the poem and have it go on a set number of times after the poem is finished for a good introduction and ending.

Try the following:

Sub-vocalization

1. Clap the rhythmic pattern of the first line, saying the words out loud.
2. Clap the rhythmic pattern of the second line while the class thinks the words.
3. Repeat this to the end of the poem, alternating lines.

Think the pauses. They can sometimes be filled in with one note or a rhythm clapped or played on an instrument (triangle, drum, sticks).

Bow wow wow (pause)	Bow wow wow. ♩
Whose dog art thou? (pause)	Whose dog art thou? ♩
Little Tommy Tinker's dog	Little Tommy Tinker's dog
Bow wow wow (pause)	Bow wow wow. ♩

All the rhythmic elements of music can be taught through poetry — beat, rhythmic pattern, note values, *etc.* Using poetry is sometimes easier for a teacher who feels unsure in singing. Some means, of course (records, tapes, or that teacher down the hall) must be found for letting the children experience the joy of singing as well.

II   Poems Which Create a Mood

Sound effects and instrumentation can be used to heighten the mood of many poems either as background or to highlight certain words. Care must be taken that the result is artistic and not cluttered. The children themselves will usually decide when something does not sound right. Some ideas follow:

Wind sound
   — made with voice only or by running the flat of the hand lightly over a drumhead.

Horses walking, clocks ticking or cobbler hammering
   — "cluck" with tongue or use woodblocks or sticks.

Scratching sound
   — scratch fingernails on a drumhead.

Spooky hallowe'en ghost sounds
   — metallophone: 2 notes (G & A) side by side, played softly and slowly, or very soft cymbal sound (play cymbal with mallet).

Skating or flying
   — running mallet lightly back and forth over xylophone keys.

These, of course, are just a few ideas but perhaps they will be a start. Some more specific ideas are found in **Poems**.

III   Poems To Help Reading

Poems can be used to develop reading and language skills.   Language development

1. Have the children learn a poem well and experiment with rhythmic ideas and sound effects.
2. Make charts of the key words in the poem. Hold these up at the appropriate time as the children are saying the poem.   Reading skills
3. Make a chart of the whole poem so that the children can read it while reciting.
4. Use words from the poem for language skills.

IV   Poems To Help Speech

Saying poems out loud is a particularly good way of helping children overcome speech problems. Children (and adults, too, for that matter) seem to be carried along with the rhythm of the words and will often use correct speech unwittingly. We are all familiar with the person who stutters badly when speaking but can sing whole songs without a trace of hesitation. Speech therapists use techniques involving poetry and rhythmic speech in their work.

If the poem is accompanied by body sounds or percussion instruments, the whole exercise is more effective.

Here is an example (Letter "B"):

Billy Boy's Boots

Billy boy's boots are big
And Billy boy likes to jump
So Billy boy's boots go
Bumpety bumpety bumpety bumpety
          BUMP!

An accompaniment of just "pat, clap, pat, clap", *etc.* would work well.

When the last line ("bumpety", *etc.*) is reached, have the children change to the stamping rhythm of the words with their feet, accenting the last "BUMP!"

Woodblocks, sticks or drums could make the beat to accompany this poem. All, of course, play very loudly on the last "BUMP!"

See **Poems**, page 157, for other good speech poems.

POEMS

CONTENTS

These poems provide just a few suggestions which have proven popular with children. You will have your own favourites and so will the children. I have not included the more common nursery rhymes, but don't forget to use them.

All work with poetry will help children in many areas of their development, particularly those of language and speech. Some poems are also good for fostering creativity, spatial relationship or coordination.

The suggestions for accompaniments, sound effects and so on are only that — suggestions. Use them to give you ideas and then create your own. Often some of the suggestions for one poem can be used for others.

LIST OF POEMS

A. SPECIFIC IDEAS FOR USE WITH POEMS

The two poems which follow have been chosen to demonstrate possible ideas and treatments. Try these ideas with other poems.

In **Speech and Poetry**, page 135, it was noted that many poems could be treated in a similar fashion to songs, and that it was possible to learn the beat, and the rhythm pattern, to make a movement pattern or to devise an accompaniment for them. These short poems are excellent for demonstrating many of the possibilities.

If some of the ideas are a bit beyond your children, pick those which are suitable. Perhaps later they will be ready for some of the others.

Mary at the Door	**Mary at the Door**
	(modern version)

One, two, three, four,
Mary at the cottage door
Eating cherries off a plate
Five, six, seven, eight.

Old nursery rhyme

Mary at the Door
(modern version)

One, two, three, four,
Mary at the cottage door
Eating hot dogs from a plate
Five, six, seven, eight.

L.B.

Change the name in these poems to those of the children you are working with.

Beat

Have the children say the poem and walk anywhere in the room on the beat.

Have them say the poem several times, walking the beat in several ways: forwards, backwards, diagonally, reaching up high, crouching down low, on all fours, *etc*.

Have one or two children play the beat on a drum or other percussion instrument while walking.

Spatial relationship
Coordination

Rhythm Pattern

Have the children clap the rhythm of the words while saying the poem.

This rhythmic pattern can be clapped, tapped on head, snapped, played on knees, or patted on the stomach.

Body awareness

Play the rhythm pattern on percussion instruments.

Combine Beat and Rhythm Pattern.

Say the poem and have half the class mark the beat while the other half marks the rhythm pattern.

Later, when the children are more secure, they can walk the beat and clap or play the rhythm pattern at the same time. It is sometimes best at that stage to walk in a circle rather than at random through the room.

Coordination

Movement Pattern

There are many movement ideas. The following progression is simple, but effective.

Spatial relationship

1. Have the children walk 4 steps forward ("1, 2, 3, 4").
2. Clap the rhythm pattern of the next line.

    Mary at the cottage door.

3. Hold one hand out, palm up (for the plate), and pretend to eat cherries (or hot dogs) with the other hand.
4. Walk back 4 steps ("5, 6, 7, 8").

Rounds

These four-line poems work very well as rounds, either two- or four-part.

Concentration

For a two-part round, the first group says the first two lines before the second group comes in.

Sub-vocalization

For a four-part round, the first group says only one line before the second group comes in, and so on.

Do this several times in succession.

It is sometimes fun to do a round without words. Just clap the rhythm pattern and think the words.

Make a percussion round. Have the children play two or four (depending on whether it is a two- or four-part round) percussion instruments with different sounds: *i.e.*, a drum, sticks, a triangle and maracas. Have them play the rhythmic pattern in turn.

A movement round can be done also. Use the movement pattern discussed above and divide the children up into two or four lines. Have them move forward and back in these lines during a round.

Instruments

Not only the percussion instruments, but also melody instruments can be used for accompaniment. The following are just a few ideas.

A "walking" pattern can be devised on the xylophone as follows:

You can also set the instrument up in the pentatonic scale (in C: C, D, E, G, A.) and let a child create his own four-note accompaniment, playing any four notes over and over.

The metallophone has such a ringing tone that it should have a slower accompaniment.

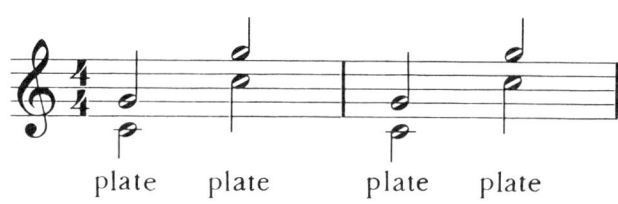

If one child is very proficient, a glockenspiel accompaniment, using the rhythm of the words, could be added.

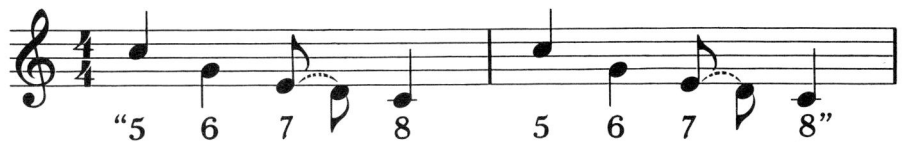

"5 6 7   8   5 6 7   8"

These accompaniments could start one at a time, before the poem is said, and continue on after it is finished, to make an introduction and ending. A woodblock or drum could also be used to create an introduction and ending.

Eat-ing cher-ries off a plate. Greed-y Mar-y
(hot dogs)

Play this twice before the poem starts and twice after.

Rondo

Rondo form is fully described in **Creativity**, page 181, number 1. This section, which describes using a short poem as the "A" section, is a model of what is possible.

The poems about "Mary at the Cottage Door" are especially good as "A" sections, or the repeated part of a rondo as they are short and rhythmic. In between, make up rhythmic or melodic patterns by clapping or playing on instruments or invent a movement pattern.

Creativity

B. VERY EASY POEMS WITH VERY EASY LANGUAGE

The Fireman

The fireman has a hose,
The fireman has a truck,
The fireman has a ladder,
That goes up, up, up.

L.B.

Spatial relationship

Spring

Sun is hot,
Wind blows,
Rain falls,
Flowers grow.

L.B.

Activities

Spatial relationship

Have different children imitate:
— the sun (with the arms in a circle over the head)
— the wind ("blow" and move like the wind)
— the rain falling (with the hands and fingers)
— the flowers (growing up from the ground)

Balloons

Language development

Red and yellow, green and blue,
Here is something nice for you,
Choose the one that you like best,
Pick it out from all the rest.

Activities
Have the children imitate floating balloons.

Houses

Houses high, houses low,
Houses everywhere I go.
But from my window I can see,
Between two houses, one green tree.

Find a drum to accompany these poems. The children enjoy playing on drums they make themselves.

The Drum

Drum, drum,
Play the drum,
BOOM, boom, boom, boom,
Boom, boom, boom.
L.B.

More Very Easy Poems

Use poems such as these to teach the alphabet. You can make up endless numbers of them.

"T"

Turtle and tick tock and table and tree
All are words that start with "T".
L.B.

"B"

Billy and Bobby and bed and bee
All are words that start with "B".
L.B.

The Snowman

Snowman, snowman,
Round and white and fat.
With your scarf of yellow
And a tall black hat.
L.B.

C. POEMS FOR MOVEMENT

Skipping

Skipping is fun, skipping is fun,
Skipping is fun for everyone.
The more you skip, the better you skip,
So skip, skip, skip.

Coordination

Jump Jim Joe

Jump, jump, jump Jim Joe,
Around and around and around you go.
Slide, slide and point your toe,
You will have fun when you jump Jim Joe.

Spatial relationship
Coordination

Hinges

I'm all made of hinges,
'Cause everything bends;
From the top of my neck,
Way down to my ends.

I've hinges in front
And I've hinges in back,
But I have to have hinges
Or else I would crack.
Helen Fisher

Relaxation
Body awareness

Cat

The black cat yawns.
Opens her jaws,
Stretches her legs,
And shows her claws.

Then she gets up
And stands on four
Long stiff legs
And yawns some more.

She shows her sharp teeth,
She stretches her lip,
Her slice of a tongue
Turns up at the tip.

Lifting herself
On her delicate toes,
She arches her back
As high as it goes.

She lets herself down
With particular care,
And pads away
With her tail in the air.

Mary Britton Miller

Hop, Hop, Hop

Coordination

Hop, hop, hop,
Go and do not stop.

Boys and Girls

Coordination

Boys and girls, walk and run,
Walk and run, walk and run.
Boys and girls, walk and run,
Skip, jump and bow.

L.B.

More Movement Poems

Teddy Bear

(action poem)

Teddy Bear, Teddy Bear, turn around;
Teddy Bear, Teddy Bear, touch the ground.
Teddy Bear, Teddy Bear, shine your shoe;
Teddy Bear, Teddy Bear, that will do.

Teddy Bear, Teddy Bear, walk upstairs;
Teddy Bear, Teddy Bear, say your prayers.
Teddy Bear, Teddy Bear, switch off the light;
Teddy Bear, Teddy Bear, say good-night!

Activities

1. Have the children perform the actions in the poem.
2. Have the children do an accompaniment of pat knees, clap hands, pat knees, clap hands.

    Introduction — pat clap pat clap.
    Poem — say it, with an accompaniment (pat, clap . . .) all the way through.
    Ending — pat clap pat clap.

Spatial relationship
Coordination

Rhythmic speech

Jelly in the Bowl

Jelly in the bowl,
Jelly in the bowl,
Wibble wobble wibble wobble,
Jelly in the bowl.

Activity

Have the children wiggle like jelly.

Relaxation

One is a Giant

One is a giant who stomps his feet,
Two is a fairy so light and neat,
Three is a mouse that crouches small,
Four is a great big bouncing ball.

Activities

Have the children stamp feet like a giant, twirl around lightly like a fairy, crouch down small like a mouse, bounce up and down like a ball.

Coordination

There was a Man in Our Town

There was a man in our town
Went for a walk one day.
The wind it blew so very hard
It turned him the other way.

Good for the beat!

Activities

1. Have one group of children walk one direction.
2. Another group of children represents the wind and blows hard on the third line.
3. The first group of "walkers" turns around and walks the other way.

Coordination

Directionality

D. POEMS ABOUT FOOD

Gravy and Potatoes

Gravy and potatoes
In a good brown pot.
Put them in the oven
And serve them hot.

This poem can be used as the "A" section of a rondo. (See **Creativity**, page 181.)

Mix a Pancake

(action)

Mix a pancake,
Stir a pancake,
Pop it in the pan;
Fry the pancake,
Toss the pancake
Catch it if you can.

Christina Rossetti

Dairy Charm

Come, butter come, come, butter come.
Peter's standing at the gate
Waiting for his buttered cake,
Come, butter come.

Traditional English Nursery Rhyme

Activities
Have the children imitate the motions of churning butter.
Do the poem as a round: one group starts and a second group comes in after the first group has said the first line.

Concentration

Maple Syrup

Bubbly, bubbly, swimming hot,
The sap is boiling in the pot.
The thickening syrup we shall make
Into a maple sugar cake.

E. FINGER PLAYS AND ACTION RHYMES

A list of old favourites:

Grandma's Glasses   (Here are Grandma's glasses . . .)   Body awareness
Here is the Church   (Here is the Steeple)
Knock on the Door   (Ring the Bell)
There was a Little Turtle (who lived in a box)
Tommy Thumb   (also a song)
I'm a Little Teapot   (also a song)

Hands on Shoulders

Hands on shoulders, hands on knees,   Body awareness
Hands behind you, if you please;
Touch your shoulders, now your nose,
Now your hair and now your toes;
Hands up high in the air,
Down at your sides and touch your hair;
Hands up high as before,
Now clap your hands, one, two, three, four.

Unknown

My Hands

My hands upon my head I place   Body awareness
On my shoulders, on my face;
On my hips I place them, so.
Now I raise them up so high,
Make my fingers fairly fly.
Now I clap them, one, two, three,
Then I fold them silently.

Unknown

Eensy Weensy Spider

Body awareness

Eensy weensy spider Went up the waterspout.	("climb" up, putting little finger of one hand on thumb of other)
Down came the rain And washed the spider out.	(bring hands down and out to sides)
Out came the sun And dried up all the rain.	(make big circle over head with arms)
Eensy weensy spider Climbed up the spout again.	("climb" up again)

Nursery rhyme

Up the Steps We Go

Up the steps we will go,
Sometimes fast and sometimes slow,
Until we reach the top.
S—l—i—d—e— down.

Activities

Coordination

Have the children make believe they are walking up the steps quickly first, then slowly.

Have them imitate the movement of sliding down with their hands and body.

F. HALLOWE'EN POEMS

Hallowe'en

Witches ride on Hallowe'en
Ho ho ho!
Their cloaks are black and their eyes are green
Ho ho ho!
And every witch has a big black hat
Ho ho ho!
And every witch has a big black cat.
Ho ho ho!

Activities

1. Try to have the children recite this slowly in low spooky voices. The "Ho ho ho!" can be done by a group with very low voices.
2. An accompaniment of spooky sounds goes very well.
   Drumheads are scratched with finger nails.
   A large cymbal is played very softly.
   A metallophone or other ringing instrument is played slowly and softly, two notes beside each other, *i.e.*, G and A.
   (Skeleton rattles — this effect can be made by shaking a tambourine.)
3. An introduction can be created from the "ho ho's" to set the mood. The children say this very softly and mysteriously.

| | | 𝄾 | | | | 𝄾 | | | | | | | | 𝄾

"Ho Ho Ho   Ho Ho Ho   Ho Ho Ho Ho   Ho Ho Ho"

Witch, Witch

Witch, witch, where do you fly?
Under the clouds and over the sky.

Witch, witch, what do you eat?
Little black apples from Hurricane Street.

Witch, witch, what do you drink?
Vinegar, blacking and good red ink.

Witch, witch, where do you sleep?
Up in the clouds where the pillows are cheap.

Activities

1. This poem may be done with two groups of children in a call and response arrangement.
2. Have the "witch" group make their voices old, cracked and scary.
3. Try an accompaniment background of drums scratched with fingernails and cymbals, lightly played, for a spooky effect.

The Little Witches

One little two little three little witches
Fly over haystacks, fly over ditches;
Slide down moonbeams without any hitches —
Heigh ho Hallowe'en's here!

Activity

You can sing this to the tune of *Ten Little Indians*.

G. GENERAL POEMS

Bumpety Bumpety Bump

A farmer went trotting upon his gray mare,
Bumpety, bumpety bump!
With his daughter behind him so rosy and fair,
Lumpety, lumpety lump!

A raven cried "Croak" and they all tumbled down,
Bumpety, bumpety bump!
The mare hit her knees and the farmer his crown,
Lumpety, lumpety lump!

The mischievous raven flew laughing away,
Bumpety, bumpety bump!
And vowed he would serve them the same the next day,
Lumpety, lumpety lump!

Activities

Rhythmic speech

1. Have a group of children recite the first and third lines of each verse while another group says the "Bumpety Bump" chorus.
2. A good introduction can be made from the words of the poem. For example, "Bumpety bump, bumpety bump, Bumpety bumpety bump!"
   This could be used as an ending also. Say it or play the rhythmic pattern on sticks or drum!
3. A group of children can make up an accompaniment by saying "bumpety" over and over, or by slapping their knees or playing instruments such as sticks or woodblocks to this rhythm.

4. Have the children act out the poem.

Snow

The snow fell softly all the night,
It made a blanket soft and white,
It covered houses, flowers and ground
But did not make a single sound.

Activities

1. This poem requires a very gentle treatment — perhaps just a simple downward figure played slowly with soft mallets on the glockenspiel or metallophone.
2. A group of children could make up a whispered accompaniment, such as "snow is soft, snow is soft".

The Big Bass Drum

The big bass drum,
Boom, boom, boom,
Beating, pounding,
Forever sounding
Beating out the rhythm
On the big bass drum.

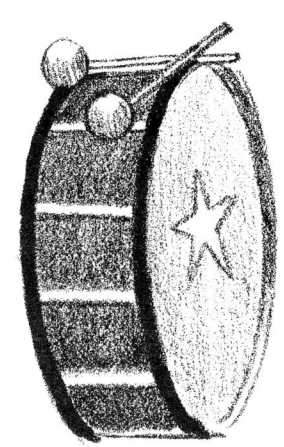

Activities

1. Say this vigorously and accompany it with a good beat on the drums.
2. You could use this poem for an "A" section of a rondo. Have the improvised parts played on different drums.

Creativity

The Train

The train goes running along the line
Jickety can, jickety can,
I wish it were mine, I wish it were mine,
Jickety can, jickety can,
Jickety jickety jickety can.

Activities

If you ask children "What sound does a train make?", the first thing they will invariably say is "choo choo choo choo." This is so, even though they have never seen or heard anything other than a diesel in their lives.
Other sounds they will suggest are:
the bell — "ding dong ding dong;"
the tracks — "click clack click clack" or "jickety can jickety can" from this poem;
the whistle — "whoo whoo whoo whoo".

1. One group of children could start the accompaniment by chanting, "choo choo" over and over.
2. Another group joins, saying, "ding dong, ding dong".
3. The third group says, very quietly, "jickety can, jickety can".
4. The rest of the children say the poem twice, allowing the spoken accompaniment to continue alone in the middle for an interlude.

5. At the end, the accompaniment becomes slower and slower. As the train comes to a stop everyone makes a "shhhhhhhh" sound for the escaping steam and one or two children can make the sound of the whistle.

Instruments

Pick percussion instruments which describe the sound *e.g:*
— a drumhead rubbed lightly for the "choo choo";
— a triangle for the bell;
— sticks or a woodblock for the "jickety can" or "click clack"

Movement

Spatial relationship

Have several children in a row move like a train, with the left hand on the shoulder of the person in front, the right hand making circles like the wheels. The train, of course, has to go more and more slowly and then stop.

Happiness

John had
Great Big
Waterproof
Boots on;
John had a
Great Big
Waterproof
Hat;
John had a
Great Big
Waterproof
Mackintosh —
And that
(said John)
Is
that

A.A. Milne

Activities

A spoken accompaniment could be devised:

Group 1. drip drop drip drop

Group 2. pitter patter pitter patter.

The rest of the children who are not in the groups could recite the poem.

My Sister Lettie

A wonderful thing happened to my sister Lettie.
Instead of hair she grew spaghetti.
And now when she wants a snack at night,
She combs it down and takes a bite.

The Umbrella Brigade

"Pitter patter" falls the rain
On the schoolroom window-pane.
Such a plashing. Such a dashing.
Will it ne'er be dry again?
Down the gutter rolls a flood,
And the crossing deep in mud;
And the puddles, oh, the puddles
Are a sight to stir the blood.

Chorus: But let it rain
        Tree-toads and frogs.
        Muskets and pitchforks,
        Kittens and dogs.
        Dash away, plash away.
        Who is afraid?
        Here we go,
        The Umbrella Brigade.

Pull the boots up to the knee.
Tie the hoods on merrily.
Such a hustling, such a jostling.
Out of breath with fun are we.
Clatter clatter down the street,
Greeting everyone we meet,
With our laughing and our chaffing,
Which the laughing drops repeat.

Chorus: But let it rain
        Tree-toads and frogs.
        Muskets and pitchforks,
        Kittens and dogs.
        Dash away, plash away.
        Who is afraid?
        Here we go,
        The Umbrella Brigade.

Laura E. Richards

Activities

This is a poem for older children and lends itself well to choral speaking.

One small group can read the verses while another can do the chorus.

Chorus: All say the first line: "But let it rain."
        One child says "tree-toads and frogs" in a great, nasty, slimy sort of voice.
        Another says "muskets and pitchforks" in a voice with a different quality.
        A third child says "kittens and dogs".
        Everyone joins together to finish the chorus with "who is afraid . . . ".

My Loose Tooth

I had a loose tooth, a wiggley, jiggley loose tooth
I had a loose tooth, hanging by a thread
So I pulled my loose tooth, this wiggley jiggley loose tooth
And put it 'neath the pillow and then I went to bed.
The fairies took my loose tooth, my wiggley jiggley loose tooth
So now I have a nickel and a hole in my head.

H. FUN POEMS TO HELP SPEECH

Pease Porridge Hot *(the letter "p")*

Pease porridge hot
Pease porridge cold
Pease porridge in the pot
Nine days old.

A Fly and a Flea *(the letter "f")*

A fly and a flea got caught in a flue
And they wondered what they should do.
Said the fly "Let us flee". Said the flea "Let us fly".
So they fled through a flaw in the flue.

The Rain *(the letter "r")*

Rain on the green grass
Rain on the tree
Rain on the house-top
But not on me!

To Market to Market *(the letter "j")*

To market to market to buy a fat pig
Home again home again jiggety jig
To market to market to buy a fat hog
Home again home again jiggety jog.

Rhythmic speech

Activities
1. Make an accompaniment figure of "jiggety jig, jiggety jog".
2. Have one group say it twice before the others start the poem, continue all the way through, and twice at the end, getting slower and slower.
3. You could play the rhythm of "jiggety jig, jiggety jog" on woodblocks and/or sticks.

4. Add a drum playing just the steady beat.

Fuzzy Wuzzy   *("f", "w" and "z")*

Fuzzy Wuzzy was a bear
Fuzzy Wuzzy had no hair
Fuzzy Wuzzy wasn't fuzzy
Was he?

Don't forget the popular old tongue twisters:
  She Sells Sea Shells ("s" and "sh")
  Peter Piper Picked a Peck of Pickled Peppers ("p")
  How Much Wood Could a Woodchuck Chuck?
    ("w", "ch" and "ck")
  Teddy Bear, Teddy Bear
    (see section of action poems) ("t")

PAINLESS LEARNING WITH SONGS, POETRY AND MOVEMENT

CONTENTS

It is my contention that many of the emotional and learning problems we are encountering in children today could be avoided if their earliest background was rich in songs, nursery rhymes, games and poetry. As I have stated before, this background lays the foundation in rhythm, speech, group participation, movement and coordination so necessary in later life, and gives practice in these skills at an early age when this learning should be acquired. These activities can also be used with great success to help handicapped children overcome their various problems.

All through the book I have tried to indicate the particular skill assisted by the individual exercise, song or poem. This chapter repeats these ideas somewhat, but here they are grouped under specific headings for easy reference.

Most of the songs and poems involve more than one child in the action. This aids group participation and often is the only way of reaching a withdrawn child.

Songs with a dance or movement pattern can help children to organize themselves to do a particular action. These songs have a governing force which is nonhuman and therefore easier for children to obey. The music says to "stop"; the music says to "take turns"; the music says "you're out". All children accept this, even those with emotional disturbances. In this way, children learn social skills and gain the practice needed in motor sensory development and auditory discrimination, but do not feel defeated because of a lack of skill on their part.

The songs and poems are grouped under headings. Those marked with an (*) can be found in **Songs** or **Poems** but these, of course, are just suggestions. Every teacher will have favourites of his or her own which will do the job as well.

A. SONGS USING CHILDREN'S NAMES

Children's names are of the utmost importance to them and songs and poems using their names are very popular. The individual child is singled out for attention and often this is the beginning of a feeling of self-worth.

Watch the look of delight and happiness which spreads over a child's face when "his" or "her" song is being sung.

Jim Along Josie
Mary Wore a Red Dress
Paw Paw Patch
Rig a Jig Jig
Sally Go Round the Sun

Change the name in the song to that of each child in turn.

B. BODY AWARENESS

The knowledge of the different parts of the body, what they can do and what they are called, is a very important part of every child's learning. Using these songs and poems can help. Some of them involve parts of the body directly by name, others indirectly, by using a certain part in performing the actions.

Songs

Deep and Wide
Do the Hokey Pokey
Ha, Ha Thisaway
Head and Shoulders
Head and Shoulders Baby
If You're Happy and You Know It
I'm a Little Teapot
Little Cabin in a Wood
Looby Loo
Making Valentines
Monkey See Monkey Do
Mulberry Bush
One Finger One Thumb Keep Moving
Paw Paw Patch
Punchinello
Push the Damper In
Put your Finger in the Air
She'll Be Coming Round the Mountain
Shoe Game
Tommy Thumb

Poems and Fingerplays

Grandma's Glasses
Eensy Weensy Spider (also a song)
There Was a Little Turtle
Tommy Thumb (also a song)
I'm a Little Teapot (also a song)
Hands on Shoulders
My Hands

---

*The songs and poems marked * can be found in **Songs**, page 55 or **Poems**, page 139.

164

C. COORDINATION AND SPATIAL RELATIONSHIPS

Children have to move. The "play" of early childhood is, in reality, the "school" where coordination skills (such as running, jumping, balancing, skipping) and concepts (such as over, under, beside, in, out, up, down) are learned.

The following game songs and poems are fun but they are, at the same time, a learning experience.

I.   Songs and poems with definite actions

Songs

A-Hunting We Will Go
Brother Come and Dance with Me
(The) Farmer in the Dell
*Go In and Out the Windows
*Going over the Sea
*Ha, Ha Thisaway
 Mulberry Bush
 I'm a Little Teapot
*Little Sally Water
*Li'l Liza Jane
 London Bridge
*Look at the Animals in the Zoo
 Oh Susanna
*(The) Elephant
*(The) Old Red Wagon (Circle to the Left)
*Punchinello
*Rig a Jig Jig
*Sally Go Round the Sun
*Shoo Fly
*Six Little Ducks
*Tideo (Jingle at the Windows)
*Witches in the Dark

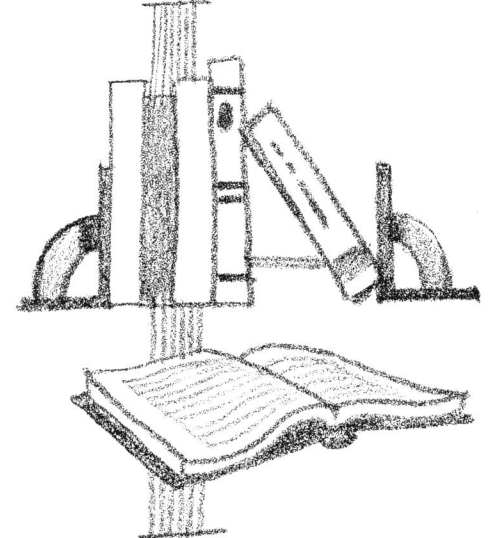

Poems

*Grand Old Duke of York
*Teddy Bear

II   Songs Describing Animals or Objects

Many songs and poems which do not have a set movement pattern describe animals (horses, dogs, rabbits) or objects (clocks, trains, airplanes) whose characteristics can be imitated

FIRST PATTERN

Start

First set of couples

Second set of couples

SECOND PATTERN

Start   Head couple leads off

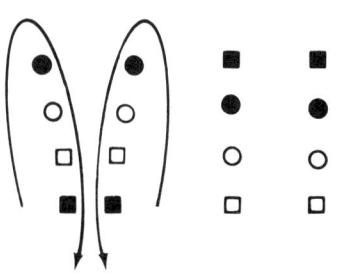

in movement. This fosters both coordination and body awareness as well as other kinds of associative and creative thinking.

Old Macdonald Had a Farm
*Bell Horses
*Pigs in the Farm
Hickory Dickory Dock
*The Train

III   Invent Your Own Movement Pattern

Many songs either do not have a set movement pattern or
the existing pattern might have to be adapted to the particular
needs of your children. There are very few basic types of movement but the possible combinations of them are limited only by
the abilities of the children with whom you are working.

The basic formations are the circle, the square and the line.
Some ideas follow:

Circle — Move around one way and then back again to the
start. (This is usually done holding hands.) Or:
— Move into the centre and back out. The children can
move together, individually or in partners.

Square — The patterns here can be essentially the same as in
the circle, as the square lends itself to all the basic circle formations.
— The square consists of four couples; the movements
involve a fairly complicated concept, and are not recommended for beginners in movement.
— Two couples move in towards each other and then
back to their places. The other two couples do the
same. Or:
— Two couples move in towards each other, one couple holding hands up high, the other passing under. The
two couples have now exchanged places. Repeat with
the second set of couples. Or:
— Two couples divide, one from each couple going
under the upraised arms of third and fourth couples,
then back to place. Repeat with the second set of couples.

Line — The lines move parallel to each other in the same
direction or in opposite directions, and then move back
to their starting positions. Or:
— Two lines move in towards each other then back out.
— One couple, holding hands, moves down the centre
of two lines then back. Or:
— The head couple goes around the outside of the
lines down to the bottom and
1. takes position at the end of the line, thereby making
a new head couple, or
2. holds hands up high to form an arch, while the rest
of the line, which has followed the first two children
goes under the arch and back to its original position.
This is "casting off" and also results in a new head
couple.

— One person from each of two opposite ends of two parallel lines comes to the middle diagonally then back out to his place at the end again. Repeat with children at the other ends of the lines. This movement is usually followed by a "casting off" movement (see above), so a new couple is available for the next repeat of the pattern.

Some basic types of movement are:
— walking
— skipping
— running (short steps always)
— slide stepping
— clapping own hands
— patting knees
— combining patting and clapping with partner by patting own knees and clapping partner's hands.
— joining hands with partner (one hand or both)
— linking arms with partner (good for circling around partner)
— "grand chain" type of movement (only for fairly advanced children)
— back to back (do si do).

Very often the type of song gives a clue for movement. For instance, a song about the sea such as *Haul Away Joe* or *Cape Cod Girls* might suggest movement describing the hauling in of the ropes for sail or anchor. A song about cowboys will give quite another clue as to the type of movement pattern possible.

Combine the above ideas for types of movement and movement patterns. Keep the patterns simple and remember that the children will also have ideas on what to do.

D. LEFT AND RIGHT

There are many opportunities for increasing awareness of left and right.

Songs
*Circle to the Right (The Old Red Wagon)
*Looby Loo (left hand in, right foot in, *etc.*)
Brother Come and Dance with Me
Hokey Pokey
*Pass this Shoe from Me to You (pass shoe from right to left)

Dance Patterns
When the movement is to the left or right, stress this by saying "to the left" or "to the right" as you do the action.

Notation
See **Notation**, page 191. These symbols move left to right and are excellent for helping to train the eye to move this way.

The "hands" and "feet" games are particularly good training.

Instruments

Devising accompaniments which move from left to right or playing accompaniments which alternate left hand and right hand helps to develop coordination in this area. (See **Instruments**, page 216, for more help here.)

Ball Bouncing

See **Coordination, Spatial Relationship and Body Rhythm**, part L, page 19.

E. REPETITIVE SONGS AND POEMS

Speech
Auditory sequencing

Repetitive songs and poems are excellent for speech training as well as auditory sequencing. I am not going to attempt to list all of these because they are so numerous, but here are a few which are especially good.

Songs

Bingo (Farmer Brown)
Did You Ever See a Lassie (Laddie)
Go In and Out the Window
*If You're Happy and You Know It
I know an Old Lady Who Swallowed a Fly
*Looby Loo
Monkey See Monkey Do
*Mulberry Bush
One Little Elephant Balancing

Poems

Donald Duck is a One-legged Duck
The Grand Old Duke of York
Pease Porridge Hot
*Teddy Bear Teddy Bear
*To Market to Market
This Little Pig Went to Market
This Is the House that Jack Built

F. COUNTING SONGS AND POEMS

Counting

There are literally hundreds of counting songs and poems, especially those used for skipping rope or ball bouncing. Some of the best known are:

Songs

(The) Ants Come Marching One by One
Elephants Marching One by One
One Bottle of Pop
One Elephant Went Out to Play

Ten Clay Pigeons (a hanging on the wall)
Ten in a Bed (Roll Over)
Ten Little Indians (both forward and backward)
This Old Man
The Twelve Days of Christmas

Poems

One, Two, Three, Alora
One, Two, Buckle My Shoe
One, Two, Three, Johnny Caught a Flea (See **Creativity**, page 182.)
*One, Two, Three, Four, Mary's at the Cottage Door
One Potato Two Potato

G. SPELLING BY RHYTHM

Rhythm helps in all learning and spelling is no exception. If children are having trouble with a particular word, make it into a rhythm pattern, say it, clap it and maybe play instruments to it. Repeat the pattern many times.

Spelling

a-l-l-i-g-a-t-o-r   f-i-n-i-s-h   j-u-s-t

V-e-n-e-z-u-e-l-a   W-i-n-n-i-p-e-g   p-o-t-a-t-o

C-h-i-c-a-g-o   c-a-r-r-o-t   f-a-t-h-e-r

These rhythms have been rather arbitrarily established, but they work.

H. SONGS OF THE WORLD AROUND US

The subject matter of songs (and poems) is absolutely unlimited. We have songs about colours, songs of counting, songs of the farm, of the zoo, of the circus, songs about astronauts, songs telling of the days of the week, songs telling of the months of the year, literally thousands of folk songs of other lands (which would be useful in geography lessons), songs about the atom, about food. If you can't think of a song about a particular topic, make one up. The children will probably like yours better anyway.

Any subject matter can be taught through song and poetry. It provides an excellent opportunity for integrated studies.

I. READING

This important phase of learning can be helped in many ways by an imaginative music program.

Listening, concentration and auditory sequencing all are skills which have to be learned before any real progress can be made in reading. See **Let's Listen**, page 25, and Auditory Sequencing, page 36, for games and ideas to help develop these skills.

Another precondition for learning to read is the acquisition of motor perceptual skills — laterality, directionality, spatial relationship, balancing, *etc*. In short, it requires the ability of the body to function effectively in the physical world.

Without this ability, many psychologists feel that little learning will take place, if only because the child, realizing his clumsiness and lack of ability, will develop emotional problems leading to failure in other types of learning. You can work with the ideas presented in the beginning of this book to help overcome some of these problems.

Rhythm is an integral part of reading. Playing the rhythm games, singing songs, reciting poems, all will help develop the necessary rhythmic skills.

Notation is the visual symbol of musical sound. Letters are the visual symbols of spoken sound. Working with the games outlined in **Notation**, page 191, helps to develop the idea of left to right progression, to heighten visual and auditory discrimination and to give training in visual and auditory similarities and differences.

Here are some extra ideas which help children learn to read:

Word Charts

Make charts of the key words in a song or poem. Hold these up at the appropriate place as the children sing the song or recite the poem. This leads to word recognition and the children learn the words like magic.

Concentration

1. Make two cards for each of the important words in a song or poem. Place them face down on table.
2. Each child turns up two cards and tries to say the words on the cards. If both cards have the same word he keeps the pair; if not, he puts them back face down and tries to remember where each word is so that he can possibly match cards on his next turn. The child with the most pairs at the end of the game is the winner.

Make charts of the whole song or poem, and use them for reading.

Use the words of a known song or poem to give the children practice in language skills — synonyms, homonyms, *etc*.

Word Jigsaw

Print the words of a short song on a card. If the song is very long, use only one phrase. Cut the card up into easily recognized shapes, each containing a word. As the children progress, the shapes can be made smaller and less easy to distinguish. The point of the game, of course, is to put the words together in the proper order.

These games capitalize on the fact that, with the aid of rhythm and music, children can learn twenty verses of a song or poem perfectly while at the same time have difficulty remembering their home address. So we use the words to a song for reading.

J. LANGUAGE DEVELOPMENT

Make Up Songs

This encourages language development as well as creativity. See **Creativity**, page 185.

Changing the Words in Songs

Make up endings to verses of songs — e.g., *Going Over the Sea:*
"When I was one, I ate a bun, going over the sea
When I was two, I buckled my shoe, going over the sea."
Find rhyming words for 3, 4, and 5, *etc.* and complete the story. Many songs, such as *The Ants Come Marching, Elephants Marching* or *Down by the Bay* can be developed with the same technique.

Other songs can have the words changed in the song itself. It is great fun for children to invent new words — the sillier the better. At the same time a lot of learning is taking place. See **Songs**, pages 78-86, for ideas and try the following:
Down by the Bay
Aiken Drum

K. SUB-VOCALIZATION

This is excellent preliminary training for silent reading.
Sing songs in which the words are dropped on the repeats and just the action is performed, or the rhythm of the dropped word is clapped.

Bingo (Farmer Brown's Dog)
*Deep and Wide
Oh You Push the Damper In

Sing a song silently until everyone gets to a specific word (decided upon in advance) then shout the word. Is everyone together?
Sing a song silently, singing only the first and the last words out loud. Did everyone end together?
Sing the first phrase of a song out loud, the second silently "inside the head", the third out loud, *etc.*, to the end.

L. ROUNDS TO HELP CONCENTRATION

Rounds (when one part starts first and the other repeats exactly the same thing starting slightly after the first) are a great help in developing concentration. Make sure the children know their parts thoroughly before attempting to perform them in a round. These can be done in many ways.

In Movement

A pattern consisting of several movements, done in sequence, is performed by the leader or one group. The rest start a little behind and do the same sequence.

| Group 1. | Walk 4 steps, | run 8 steps, | turn around twice, |
| | Group 2. | Walk 4 steps, | run 8 steps, |

| jump 4 times | walk 4 steps, | run 8 steps, |
| turn around twice, | jump 4 times, | walk 4 steps, |

| turn around twice, | jump 4 times, | |
| run 8 steps, | turn around twice, | jump 4 times. |

This is a very simple example. More complicated movement patterns can be devised.

Singing

See **Songs**, pages 77, 78.

Word Sequence

Speech rounds can be performed with word sequences, proverbs or short poems. Repeat as many times as you wish.
Here are just a few of the many possibilities.

| Buick, Buick, | Chevrolet, Chevrolet, | Volkswagen, Volkswagen, |
| | Buick,   Buick, | Chevrolet,   Chevrolet, |

| Ford, | Buick, Buick, | Chevrolet, Chevrolet, |
| Volkswagen, Volkswagen, | Ford, | Buick,   Buick, |

| Volkswagen, Volkswagen, | Ford, | |
| Chevrolet,   Chevrolet, | Volkswagen, Volkswagen, | Ford, |

Proverb

| Early to bed and | early to rise | makes a man healthy |
| | Early to bed and | early to rise |

| wealthy and wise. | | |
| makes a man healthy | wealthy and wise. | |

Poems

For a discussion of rounds using short poems, see **Poems**, page 144. Poems of other lengths can be used, but it is much easier to begin with four line poems.

Clapping and Body Sounds

This works best with one person as the leader or part 1. As the children become proficient they can be leaders.

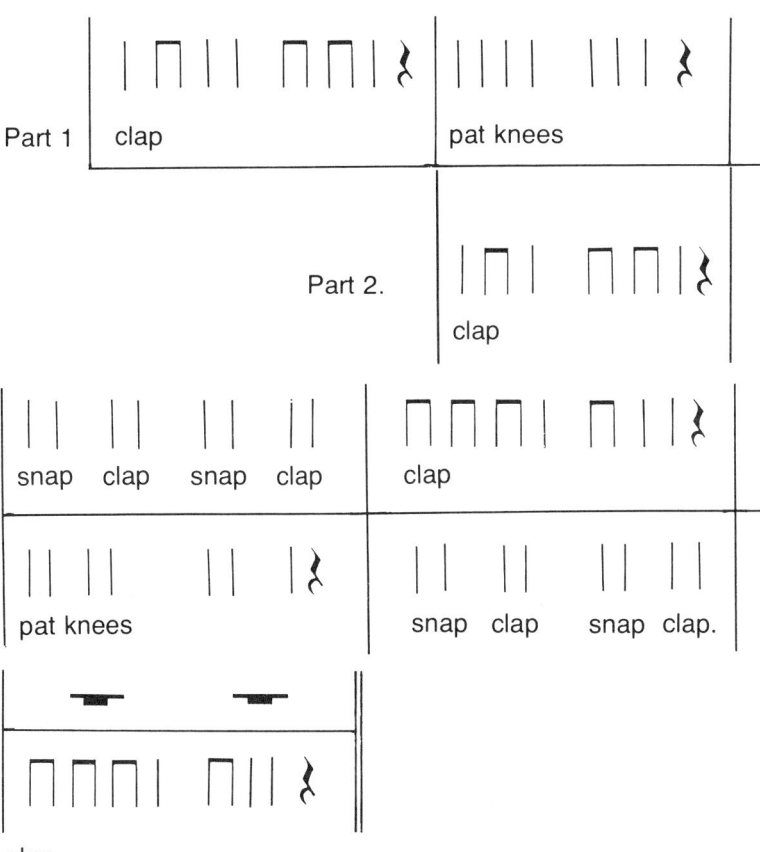

clap.

Many other patterns and combinations can be devised. At first it is wise to have a very easy pattern follow one that is more difficult. It gives the children time to catch up and helps to keep the whole exercise relaxed.

Patterns can be written on the board and clapped in a round. One part starts after the other.

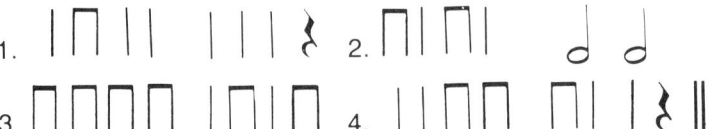

This exercise can be performed with two or four groups. With two groups, the first group would do two parts before the second group started. With four groups, each would start after the group before had done one part.

Percussion Instruments
Follow the same ideas as above only perform the rhythms on percussion instruments.

Melodic Instruments
A set piece of music is learned. One child or a group plays this on a melodic instrument such as a xylophone, glockenspiel or chime bars. Another child or group plays the same thing starting two or four measures after the first. Keep it very simple at first, starting with perhaps only one or two notes, gradually increasing the number until the full pentatonic scale is employed. See **Instruments**, page 217, for a full explanation of setting melodic instruments up in the pentatonic scale.

All rounds may be performed in two, three, four or more parts depending on the age and ability of the children taking part.

CREATIVITY

CONTENTS

The importance of having a child create his own music cannot be overemphasized. The music thus becomes part of the child because he "made it up". It is not just a copy of someone else's creation. It does not matter how small or how simple it is — just so long as it is his and his alone.

Children should first be given many opportunities to explore sounds. One can begin with sounds produced by various parts of the body, alone and in conjunction with other parts.

"How many sounds can you make with your mouth?" (clucking, sucking, smacking, blowing; the full range of "voiced" sounds: high, low, yelling, whispering, etc.).

"How many sounds can your hands make, just your two hands?" (clapping, snapping, flicking fingers, fist into palm, backs of hand clapped together, etc.). "With your feet?" (stamping, sliding, tapping with toes only, with heels, slapping them together, etc.). "With your hands and knees?" The possibilities are endless and produce a great amount of creative exploration and thinking, as well as developing listening skills.

Sounds can be brought from home, (see **Let's Listen** page 30, Found Sound) experimented with and moved to. "How does the sound make you want to move?" The more traditional instruments can be explored (see **Creativity,** page 187, Pure Improvisation) to see if they can be played in an unconventional manner to produce a different sound. This, too, develops a climate of freedom in which the child can explore creativity further.

Creativity in music does not, however, just happen. There must be some structure provided, if only that of saying, "No. Ten of you can *not* play drums and cymbals at the same time."

If our primary aim is to develop musical ability, then things must be organized so that a musical sound will result. If our primary aim is to develop other skills, such as listening, then the results cannot be so chaotic that no listening can take place. In either event, some structure must be provided.

The tools of music have to be learned. Some of the more important tools are: the ability to produce sound effectively on drums, xylophone, by singing, *etc.*; rhythmic ability; some knowledge of melody and a rudimentary knowledge of form.

There must be progressive steps leading to musical creativity and there must first be a foundation of rhythmic and melodic sureness which has been built up little by little, by having the child experience activities similar to those outlined in the previous sections. Especially important is a good foundation in singing.

When the children are ready, try some or all of the following ideas to help foster creativity.

A. QUESTION AND ANSWER

This activity is also called phrase completion or phrase building but is more easily understood by the children by the name Question and Answer. It follows along after the children are proficient in performing echoes. (See **Let's Listen**, pages 37-42.)

In Echoes, one person performs the first part of a phrase, the rest copy exactly what he has done. In Question and Answer, the second half is completely different. The first person "asks" a question and the second person completes it with his own pattern ("answer").

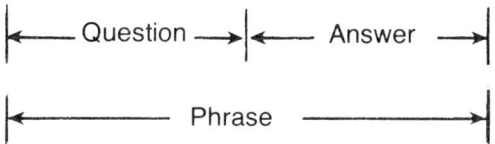

In contrast to echoes, there are many different answers that could be given and all of them would be correct.

One of the best ways to demonstrate Question and Answer is through a speech pattern. One person asks something and the other person answers.

"Where are you going?"	"To the show."
	or
	"I am going home on the subway."
	or
	"I am going out."

"Is it going to rain?"	"No, it is not."
	or
	"No, I think it will snow."

These word phrases can lead very quickly into clapping patterns. You clap the rhythm of the words.

"Where are you going?"   "To the show."

"I am going home on the subway."

"I am going out."

"Is it going to rain?"   "No, it is not."

"No, I think it will snow."

178

In Movement

One person performs a motion or a series of motions, the child creates a different one as a response. *e.g.* The first person shakes his hands over his head, then claps his hands and then turns around. The response might be to wave the hands down around the ankles, then jump up and down, and next make big circles with hands over the head. The possibilities are limited only by the space available for the movement.

Clapping and Different Body Sounds

Instead of copying the first person's patterns as in "Echo", the child makes up his own, clapping, stamping, patting knees, or snapping fingers.

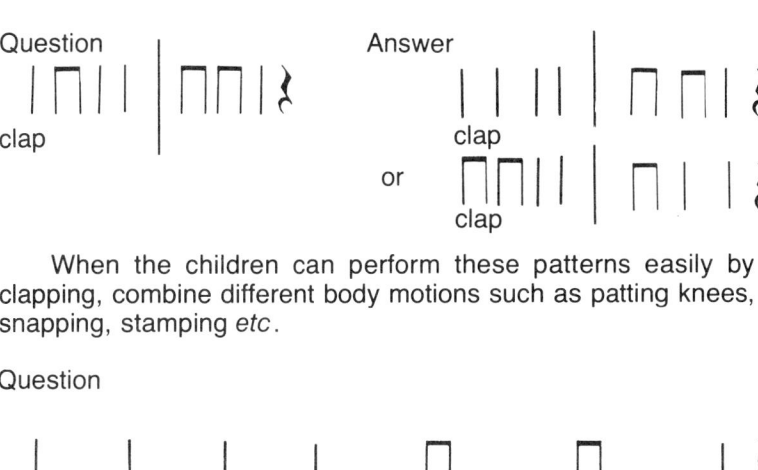

When the children can perform these patterns easily by clapping, combine different body motions such as patting knees, snapping, stamping *etc*.

Question

| | | | | | ∏ | ∏ | | ⁊

stamp   clap   stamp   clap   snap snap   snap snap   stamp

Answer

∏   ∏ | | ∏   ∏ | ⁊

clap clap   clap clap   stamp   stamp   clap clap   clap clap   stamp

or

| ∏ | ⁊ | | | ⁊

snap   clap clap clap   snap clap clap

Clap, stamp or snap these in different metres if you feel confident.

Question

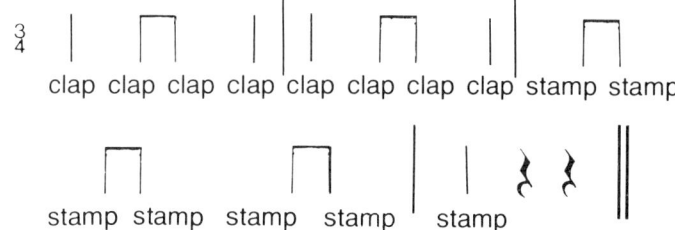

clap clap clap clap clap clap clap clap stamp stamp

stamp stamp stamp stamp stamp

Answer

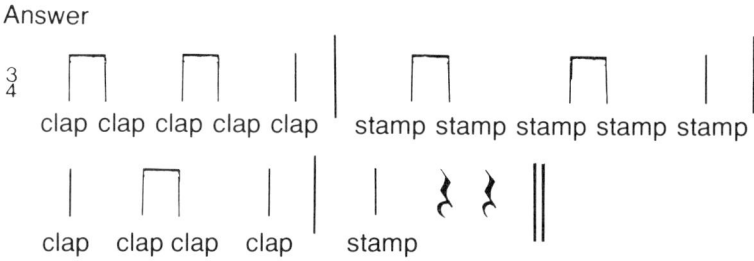

clap clap clap clap clap stamp stamp stamp stamp stamp

clap clap clap clap stamp

Percussion Instruments

Instead of clapping, stamping or snapping the Question and Answer, play these rhythms and others on percussion instruments such as drums, wood blocks, triangles, *etc.*

Singing

The section **Singing**, page 49, Call and Response, gives good examples of the Question and Answer type of technique. These examples can be sung to words or to neutral syllables such as "loo" or "lah".

Melodic Instruments

Begin simply by setting up the instruments such as xylophones, glockenspiels, chime bars, *etc.* with only one or two notes left on. The question is asked and answered on these notes. Gradually add notes until the five-note (pentatonic) scale is used. See **Instruments**, page 217, for an explanation of the pentatonic scale.

Some Examples of Melodic Questions and Answers

2 note

Xylophone   **Glockenspiel**

3 note

Xylophone   **Glockenspiel**

5 note
(pentatonic)

Xylophone   **Glockenspiel**

Let the children experiment with this technique. After a while, they will discover that ending the "question" on any note but the key note or doh, gives a feeling of incompleteness that really suggests a question.

Allow the children to end their "answer" on any note at first. When they gain more experience, they will find that ending on doh, gives a greater feeling of completion. Do not force this — after all, much 20th century music does not have a slavish attachment to doh.

(These above examples could be Questions and Answers for singing as well.)

"Question and Answer" leads to the creation of little melodies. Later on a child can make up both the Question and the Answer on one instrument while another child makes up a different Question and Answer on his own melodic instrument. Several of these can be joined to create a piece of music. If several of the Questions and Answers are played in sequence, accompanied very simply by other instruments, and an introduction and ending devised, the result is an attractive, small composition, of the child's own creation.

The instruments in the above exercises should all be set up in the same pentatonic scale so that whatever the child creates will fit in with the rest of the music.

Hand puppets can sometimes be used to give clapping or singing Questions. All children enjoy puppets and sometimes a withdrawn, autistic or emotionally disturbed child will respond to a puppet when he will not to a person.

B. RONDO

This is like a musical sandwich: first the bread, which is always the same; next a filling, which is different from the bread;

then another piece of bread, then another different filling, and so on, until it is large enough.

Children will understand the form very easily if it is presented to them in this way.

The form is A (bread), B (filling), A (bread), C (different filling), A (bread) and so on.

Build it up like a sandwich.

Group participation

bread	A
filling	D
bread	A
filling	C
bread	A
filling	B
bread	A

"A" can be a rhythmic pattern clapped, snapped or stamped by most of the children:

It can also be a movement pattern, a small song, a short poem or even a short instrument phrase but it should be the same each time it repeats.

"B", "C" and "D" are created in turn by different children clapping, stamping, singing or playing a pattern of their own devising. The whole piece can be accompanied, have an introduction and ending devised for it, and can be developed into a small composition in the same manner as was described in section A, Question and Answer (see above).

The following are some examples:

1. Use a short poem for the A section

Speech   A.   1, 2, 3,
Johnny caught a flea,
Flea died, Johnny cried,
Tee, hee, hee!

The class says the poem doing a "pat, clap, pat, clap" pattern as an accompaniment.

B.   One child plays a pattern he has made up on a drum.

A. Repeat the poem above (whole class).

C. A second child creates a pattern on a wood block.

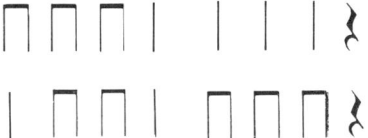

A. Repeat the poem above (whole class).

Add as many sections as you wish.

2. Use a short song for the A section

Sally Go Round the Sun

Key of C Major

Nursery Rhyme

Sal - ly go round the sun___ Sal - ly go round the moon___

Sal - ly go round the chim - ney tops Ev - ery af - ter - noon.___

A. The whole class sings this song.

B. One child makes up a short melody on a xylophone,
using only the three notes: G, E, A.

Xylophone

G E G A G E *(etc.)*

A. Repeat song above.

C. Second child plays a rhythm he has created on a drum.

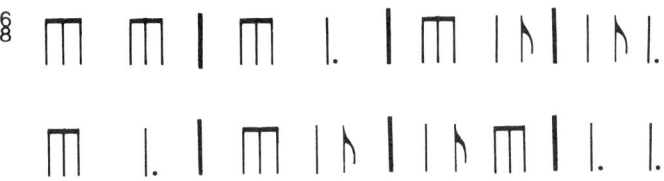

A. Repeat song above.

D. Third child (who, perhaps, has more proficiency in playing the instruments) makes up a small melody on five notes (C, D, E, G, A), using a glockenspiel:

Glockenspiel

The whole rondo could be accompanied by a very simple metallophone pattern just to keep the beat and add interest. For example:

Metallophone

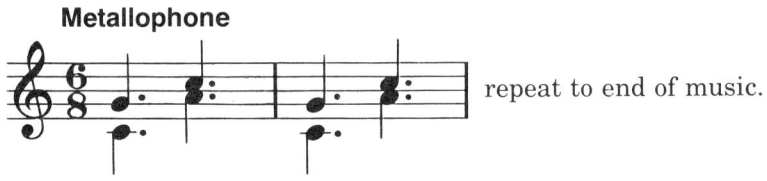 repeat to end of music.

If desired, have another child make up an introduction on a woodblock:

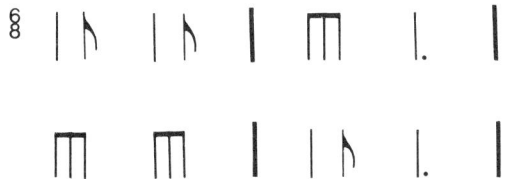

The whole exercise must be kept very simple so that the children have an opportunity to participate in a relaxed manner. It must also be simple enough so that the parts are able to be heard easily.

The rondo is so useful in working with a group of children because it involves the whole group in the A section while giving certain individuals a chance to create. There is a feeling of security engendered by always coming back to A, a home base.

Keep any accompaniment pattern very simple at first, so it does not intrude on the concentration of the improviser. Something as basic as a group of children patting their knees steadily on the beat, or someone playing the drum softly on the beat, often helps to hold the whole thing together.

C. MAKING UP SONGS

Children can make up their own songs about day-to-day activities such as swimming, walking to school or playing soccer at recess. It is generally better to restrict these to 3 notes or so at first (soh, me and lah or C, E and A in the C scale). Later, other notes can be added. (See **Singing**, under the heading Three-Note Songs, for further explanation.) Children will enjoy singing their own songs, sometimes more than the other songs they have learned. A song can be started one day, added to the next, changed again later in the week. It is a growing thing. Some very surprising songs will result.

One little girl sang her "news" to me one morning:

(long pause)

"Oh Yes."

While the following was a boy's contribution:

The following remarkable song was the joint effort of a group of junior and intermediate children from the Beverley Street School for Retarded Children in Toronto. The city of Toronto is building a fabulous new zoo and the children had been talking about animals particularly, in this case, about buffalo — where they came from, what they eat *etc*. When the classes came to music period, the discussion was directed into making up a song and one boy sang the first phrase quite spontaneously. From there the rest evolved, using the rhythmic and tonal pattern of that first phrase. Almost every phrase in the song is repeated — an excellent form for slow learners, who forget words so easily.

Buffalo

Myna Denov, music teacher
Classes of Mrs. Esson and Miss Hancoc

Buf- f'lo come a long way   Buf - f'lo come a long way

From an -oth - er coun - try   From an - oth - er coun - try

Buf - fa - lo was hun - gry   Buf - fa - lo was hun - gry

Thirs - ty and tired_   Thirs - ty and tired_   Buf - f'lo wants some

food_   Buf - f'lo wants some food_   Buf -f'lo saw some food and

now he's going to chase it   Now he has caught it

Now he has caught it   And he's going to eat it.

186

D. SOUND EFFECTS

Many songs and poems can have sound effects created for them using instruments. Here are some examples:

clocks ticking
> — wood block

flowers growing
> — an ascending scale played on xylophone, glockenspiel, "tuned" bottles filled with water, or piano.

giants sneaking up on someone
> — soft, slow drumbeats

rain
> — light fingers playing drum rapidly

spooky Hallowe'en sound of bells tolling
> — cymbals played very softly

skeletons
> — shaking maracas or tambourines

These are just a few ideas. The list is endless and the use of the instruments limited only by imagination and good taste.

A story such as *Chicken Little* can have different instruments to depict different animals. Chicken Little could be a fast repeated note on the xylophone, Duckey Daddle could be played on the sticks, and Turkey Lurkey could be depicted by a drum. Every time the animal is mentioned in the story, its instrument is played.

Gingerbread Boy is another story which can be treated in the same fashion. In addition to depicting each character by using a particular instrument, find a "running" sort of pattern of several notes in a row, repeated over and over, for "I can run from you, I can! I can!", and keep the cymbal or drum for the end, when the fox eats the gingerbread boy up.

E. PURE IMPROVISATION

Have children experiment with many different kinds of sounds. Ask them to find objects which produce interesting sounds at home and in the community. If it is possible, these can be brought to school for discussion and experimentation. See also **Let's Listen**, page 30, Found Sounds.

Allow children an opportunity to explore many kinds of instruments. They will experiment with different ways of playing them and produce many different sounds. After the children have had ample time for exploration and have also had some grounding in rhythmic and melodic work they are then ready to use the instruments for group improvisation.

I   Percussion

1. Several children pick percussion instruments to play. Try to have a variety of sound quality represented for interest's sake.

Group participation

187

2. Each child decides on a figure or rhythm that is short and easy enough for him to play over and over. (If trouble is encountered, use a word pattern to help hold everything steady.)
3. Decide who should begin first, in what order the others should come in, how many times they should play their patterns, who should drop out and in what order, and who should be left playing at the end. Try different combinations and ideas.

The following is just one example of the combinations that could be tried:

low drum begins ♩ ♩ 𝅗𝅥 ♩ ♩ 𝅗𝅥 ♩ ♩ 𝅗𝅥 ♩ ♩ 𝅗𝅥 and continues:

maracas enter after drum has played four patterns and continue:

wood block comes in, after maracas have played four patterns or with an improvised pattern which one child creates.

Have the improvisation work up to a climax and have all players stop at the same time, perhaps with a cymbal crash, or have the piece taper off by stopping the instruments one by one, until just the drum is playing.

One child could be the conductor of such an ensemble. He brings the instruments in and tells them when to stop. Children enjoy doing this and soon become very skilful.

Use just a few instruments at first, adding more as children become confident.

II   Melodic

Group participation

Do this in sequence.
1. Set several instruments, such as chime **bars,** xylophones, glockenspiels, and metallophones in **the** same five note or pentatonic scale. In C, this would **be** C, D, E, G, A. (See the section **Instruments**, page 217, for further explanation.)   If a child cannot cope with the five notes of the pentatonic scale, use as many as he can deal with efficiently — i.e., C D E or E G A or even G E.
2. Decide on the metre ($\frac{4}{4}$, $\frac{3}{4}$, $\frac{2}{4}$, *etc.*) and let several children improvise accompaniment figures in this metre on the melodic instruments or on drums, bells or other percussion. Play softly and be careful not to have too many playing at the same time. (See **Instruments**, pages 217-223, for ideas.)
3. One child playing a glockenspiel, recorder or xylophone improvises a melody above the accompaniment.

4. Later, several children could take turns improvising. Sometimes those playing the accompaniment can become soloists for a short time and then go back to playing the accompaniment while someone else takes over.

A beautiful sound can result. The children should be encouraged to improvise a dance to go with the music and can take turns conducting the group, indicating which person is to be the soloist, how loud or soft the group is to play, how fast or slow and so on.

F. CREATIVE DRAMA

Music can be the jumping off point for creative drama.

Instruments

Often the sound produced by different instruments will plant the seed of an idea for a song. A drum, for instance, rubbed with the hand, might suggest a wind blowing to the children. From this they could make up a story about a gale at sea, a boat in trouble, a shipwreck, *etc*. A cymbal played very softly with a mallet could be a church bell and could suggest a wedding, a funeral, a spooky Hallowe'en night, someone pulling the bell as a prank. The list is endless.

Self awareness
Group participation

Two contrasting instruments could suggest a dialogue between two people or even an argument if one is played loudly and the other softly or in a placating fashion. The argument could be over a dog, a car wreck, politics or almost anything.

Stories, Poems and Songs

Children, even in the earliest grades, can act out the story line of poems and songs. Be aware of the possibilities for this and give the children every encouragement. Children can act out the simplest nursery rhymes: *i.e. To Market to Market to Buy a Fat Pig, Baa Baa Black Sheep, The Grand Old Duke, Jack and Jill* or *The Queen of Hearts*.

Some other poems for dramatic action:
  *Bumpety Bumpety Bump
  *Hallowe'en
  Jonathan Bing
  *Snow
  Some One
  *A Fly and a Flea

Here are some good acting songs:
  Old Roger is Dead
    (children love to act songs about death)
  Miss Polly Had a Dolly
  The English Soldiers
  *Land of the Silver Birch
  *Donkey Riding
  Cobbler, Cobbler, Mend My Shoe

Mister Banjo
*C-C-C-C-Cold
Polly Put the Kettle On
There Was a Man (Pudding Bag)
*Witches on Their Broomsticks
*Crooked Man
The Fox Went Out on a Starlit Night

There are many excellent books dealing with creative drama in the schools (see **Books**, page 233 for titles) and there is no need to go into this in any more detail here. Suffice it to say: always be aware of the possibilities of music to add interest and to be a catalyst in the development and production of many wonderful activities. Creative drama can give all children a sense of self-confidence and in the case of special children can be the bridge to understanding and learning.

G. CREATING ACCOMPANIMENTS

Wherever possible, the children should create their own accompaniments, even to choosing the instruments which are the most suitable. See the section **Instruments**, page 219, for a further explanation of this and for examples to follow.

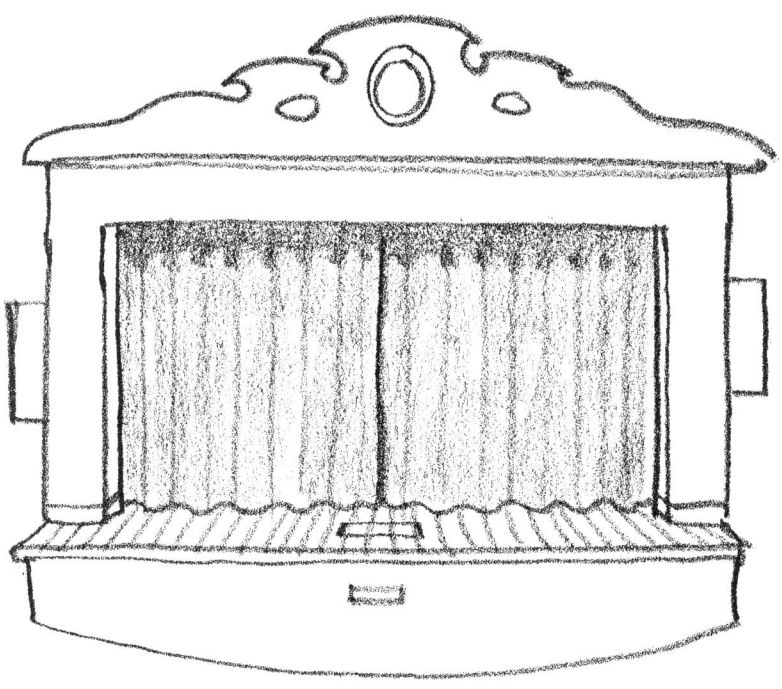

NOTATION

CONTENTS

Before a child begins the actual writing of notes, he must have been given plenty of opportunity to experience music. The sound and feel of music must be in the child's body first.

Music writing however, should not be ignored, as it is valuable in giving a visual representation to the sound. This is particularly true with rhythmic notation, when concepts of walking, running, stopping, *etc.* can be shown so graphically. Notation also opens musical doors which otherwise would always remain closed. These reasons aside, the children like to do notation, if it is presented in an interesting and enjoyable fashion.

Games using notation can be helpful in assisting the child in the developmental areas of visual and auditory discrimination, visual memory, laterality, midline skills and understanding the concepts of high and low.

A. RHYTHMIC NOTATION

I Learning Notation

Start with speech and pictures. Choose a picture subject which interests the children.

Use a quarter note or steady walking beat first.

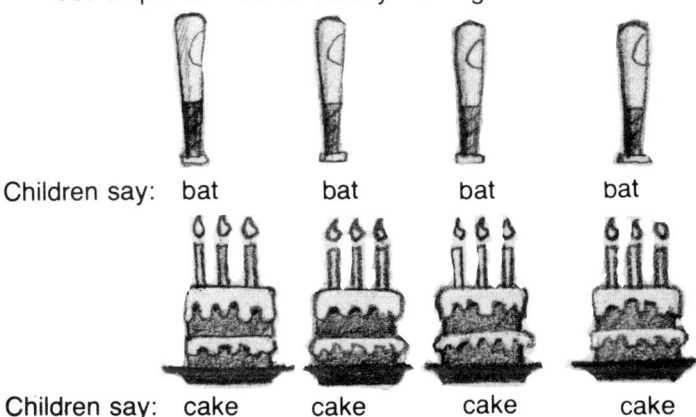

Children say: bat   bat   bat   bat

Children say: cake   cake   cake   cake

193

Children say: ball   ball   ball   ball

Children say: cat   cat   cat   cat

Children say these and clap them, walk them, and "play" them on their knees, shoulders, heads, *etc.* while they are saying the words.

When the children feel at home with these patterns, add the eighth note pattern.

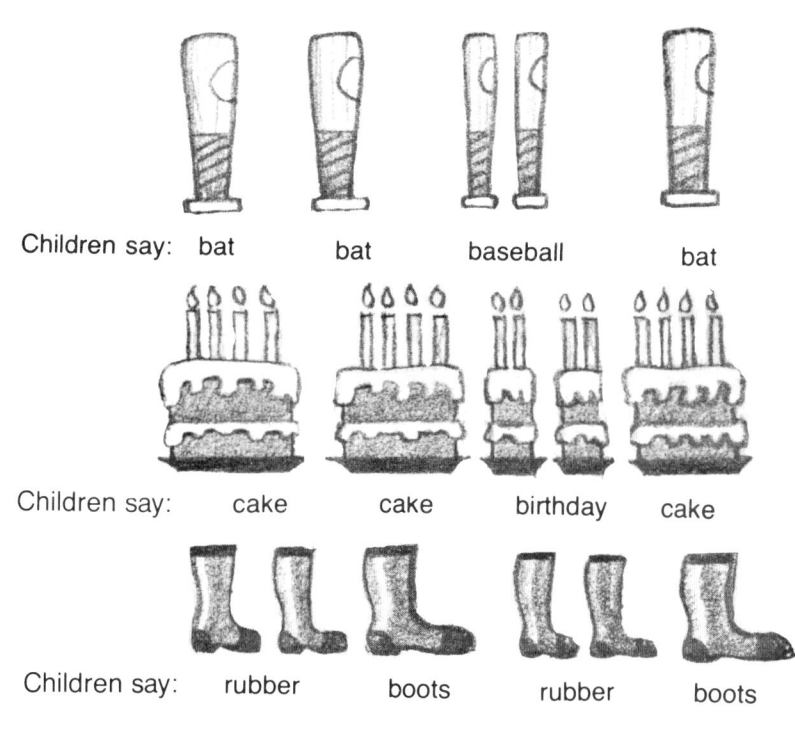

Children say: bat   bat   baseball   bat

Children say: cake   cake   birthday   cake

Children say: rubber   boots   rubber   boots

Then add rests.

Children say: dog   little   dog

194

These, of course, are only suggestions. Use your own ideas as well.

These patterns are also clapped, walked and tapped on all parts of the body at the same time as they are said.

Making the transition to notes, requires an intermediate step of relating short and long sounds to symbols. Use short lines for short sounds, and long lines for long sounds:

E.g.

___	___	___	____
boots	boots	boots	boots
___	___	_ _	____
boots	boots	rubber	boots
___	𝄽	_ _	____
dog		little	dog
___	_ _	_ _	____
walk	run run	run run	walk

The next step, that of relating the sound to conventional notation, is very easy for most children but should not be attempted until they have had a great amount of practice in the above.

Walking rhythms can be shown by quarter notes

Running rhythms can be shown by eighth notes

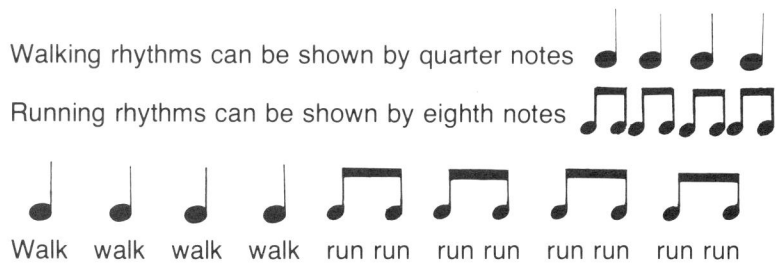

Walk walk walk walk run run run run run run run run

A stop can be shown by a rest.

Combine these, using first the quarter, then the eighth notes and then the rests. Use only the quarter note rest at first. It can be written either 𝄽 or 𝄽

walk walk run run walk run run run run walk walk

walk run run run run walk run run walk run run walk

walk   walk   walk (whist)   walk (whist) walk (whist)

An unvoiced "whist" for a rest, suggests the idea of no note but also fills in the space so that the time of the rest is not shortened. Saying "SAA" (suh) also fills the space. When clapping these patterns, have the children "Throw away" the rest with their hands while breathing.

For rhythmic notation, the "feet" of the quarter and eighth notes are not needed. They are only important for melodic notation. These, then, can be written:

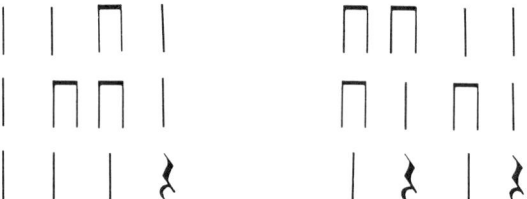

This type of notation is very easy and quick to write. Children love to make up their own rhythms for each other to clap.

Music educators realize the value of syllables in representing the rhythm of different note combinations and there are almost as many systems as there are books written about them. The originator of the idea was John Curwen and all later systems seem to be derivations from his original.

It really does not matter which is used as long as the system is kept consistent. I prefer to use Curwen's, as it always has the TAA on the first of each beat no matter what the divisions are.

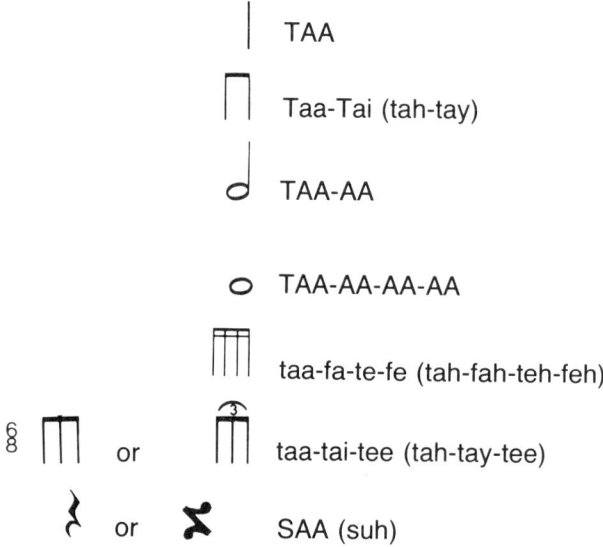

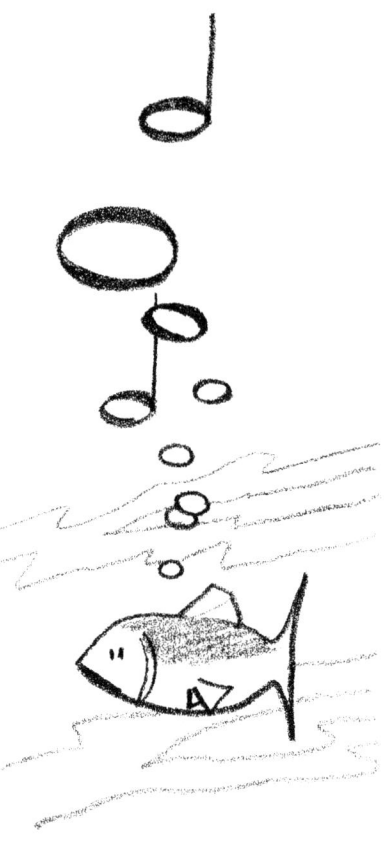

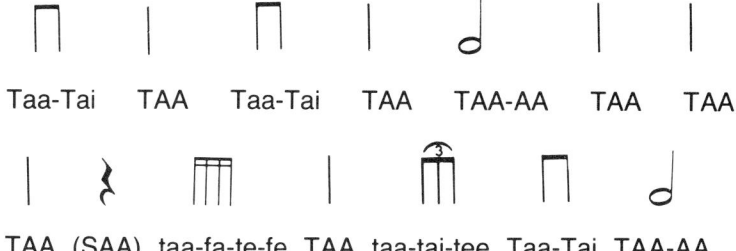

Taa-Tai   TAA   Taa-Tai   TAA   TAA-AA   TAA   TAA

TAA (SAA) taa-fa-te-fe   TAA   taa-tai-tee   Taa-Tai   TAA-AA

The Kodály Time Names are as follows:

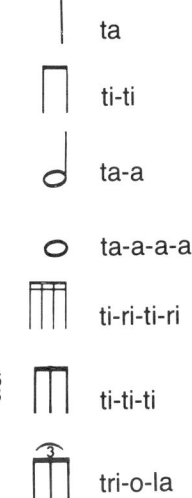

$\vert$	ta
$\sqcap$	ti-ti
♩	ta-a
○	ta-a-a-a
𝄘	ti-ri-ti-ri
⁶⁄₈ 𝄚	ti-ti-ti
³⌢𝄚	tri-o-la

When children are ready and have had a lot of experience with quarter and eighth notes and rests, add half notes (which get two beats) and whole notes (which get four beats). These note values are harder for children to express in movement because they require a more controlled and slower movement. The half note requires a "foot" as that is the only way to distinguish it from the quarter note.

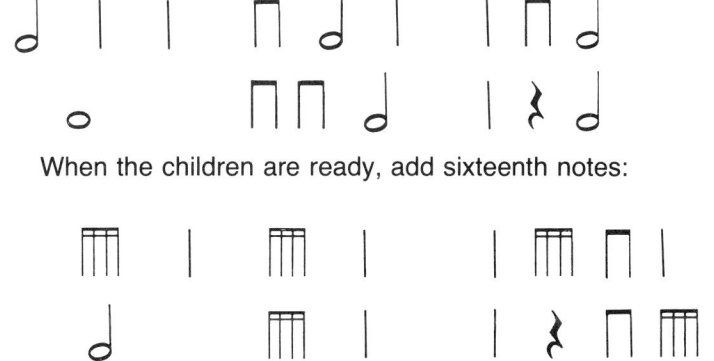

When the children are ready, add sixteenth notes:

197

Next, add triplets:

The triplet rhythm is very common in nursery rhymes, many of which are in $\frac{6}{8}$ time.

To Market to Market   (Jiggety Jig or Jiggety Jog)

Humpty Dumpty   (sat on a wall)

Much later, add dotted notes and syncopated beats:

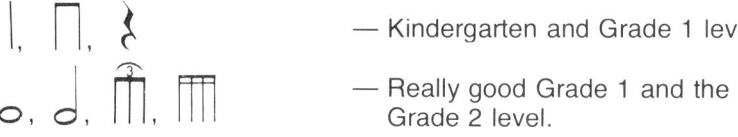

For more detailed explanation of this or the steps beyond this, please refer to a book specifically designed for teaching musical notation.*

It is difficult to say exactly at what level these individual note values should be introduced, because each group of children is completely different from any other and individual children within the group are also quite different from each other.

For purposes of this book, a general rule of thumb could be:

⏐, ⊓, ⸪   — Kindergarten and Grade 1 level

○, ⫟, ⫙, ⫚   — Really good Grade 1 and the Grade 2 level.

Syncopated and dotted notes — Grade 2 level and beyond.

These rules are not hard and fast. If you have a group of Grade 3 age children who are operating musically on a Grade 1 level or below, either because of lack of ability or lack of exposure to musical training, of course you do not plunge into dotted notes and syncopation without preparation. The same is true in reverse. Don't keep bright Kindergarten children who have very high IQ's at the quarter- and eighth-note level all year. Use your own discretion.

*Perrin, Kovacs, Daley and Allin *The New Approach to Music* Primary Division (1970); Junior Division (1972). Holt, Rinehart and Winston of Canada, Limited, Toronto.

II Notation Games

There are many games to play using rhythmic notation. Always be careful to use those rhythms at the level of the children's ability.

Guess Which One

1. Make a set of cards with different rhythms drawn on them:

   e.g.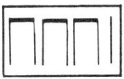

   Visual discrimination
   Auditory discrimination

2. Put several of these up in a row. The children clap each one, so that they are sure they know how it sounds.
3. Clap or play one. Ask "Which one is it?" The children guess.

Can You Write My Rhythm?

Someone claps a rhythm, others write it down.

Auditory discrimination

Note Concentration

1. Make cards for different rhythms. Place them face down on the floor or a table. Have two cards for each rhythm.

   Visual and auditory memory

2. Each child turns up two cards and tries to clap the rhythm on each. If they are the same, he keeps the pair. If not, he puts them face down again and tries to remember where each rhythm is, so that he can, perhaps, match cards on his next turn. The child with the most pairs at the end of the game is the winner. Keep some very simple, so everyone can have success in matching the cards.

Rhythm, Rhythm, Who's Got the Rhythm?

Make up several cards with different rhythms. Give one to each child (allow about eight children at a time to play — a large number becomes unwieldy). Each child keeps his rhythm secret. One person plays one of the rhythms; if a child thinks it is his, he turns his card over and can play his rhythm on the drum if he is correct. Repeat until everyone has had a turn.

Which One Is Different?

Make a stencil of several rows of rhythms. Have every rhythm in each row the same, except one. Children have to circle the one that is different. Using a stencil makes it easy to supply a large group with material.

Visual discrimination

Music Bingo

This is, of course a variation of the old bingo game but also involves listening. Children love to play it and at the same time they are practising skills.

Visual discrimination

1. Have the children clap all the rhythms — "under the M..." "under the I..." and so on. If they have learned the time names, these can be said at the same time:

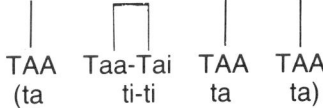

TAA Taa-Tai TAA TAA
(ta   ti-ti   ta   ta)

This ensures that the children know the sounds of the rhythms in the game beforehand.

2. Have small cards printed with each rhythm in a box and pull them out one at a time saying "under the S . . ." and then clap or play the rhythm on a drum or sticks.
3. If children have that rhythm on their card they put a marker on it. The first one to get a row completed is the winner.

This game takes a bit of preparation but is a good one. Make up card forms and run them off on the duplicating machine. Fill in three or four with the rhythms given in the sample or make up your own.

Change the rhythms around but be sure you have each rhythm printed on little cards in the box. After three or four card forms are ready it is a simple matter to run off enough for the class. They can be used over and over.

M	U	S	I	C

People Rhythms

Rhythms can be shown by using people. This gives the child a clear concept of the rhythms and also helps awareness of body in space.

Have a group of seven or eight children stand in a line. Another child "arranges" them into a rhythm.

Children standing are quarter notes.

Two children standing and linking arms are two eighth notes.

A child squatting down makes a rest.

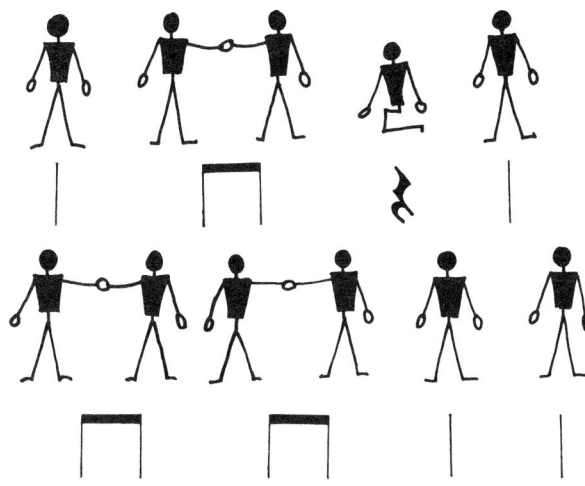

After one child has "arranged" the others, the rhythm is clapped by the rest of the children. The different rhythmic arrangements are endless.

After children have had experience clapping, saying and writing rhythms, the following games can be tried.

Hands

Make hands from coloured paper: use one colour for the left and another colour for the right. Children can trace their own hands for this.

Make large hands for the quarter notes and smaller ones for the eighth notes.

If the children have trouble remembering which is left and which is right it might help if the words "left" and "right" or even "L" and "R" were printed on the hands.

Laterality
Directionality
Coordination
Midline

Do the following in sequence:
1. Have the children work with large hands first. Arrange them in order on a table keeping left on the left side and right on the right side.

 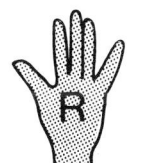 

The children put their own left or right hands on the corresponding paper ones and say *left, left: right, right* in even time.

2. The next pattern is a crossover one.

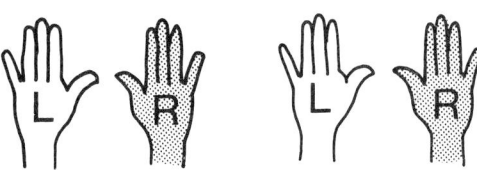

The children say *left, right: left, right* while putting their hands on top of the paper ones.

or

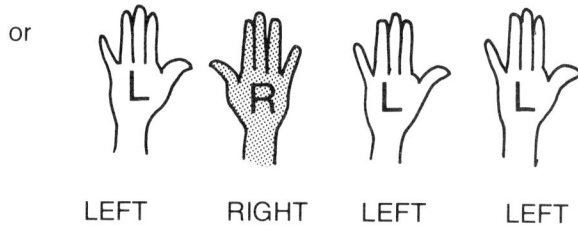

LEFT   RIGHT   LEFT   LEFT

3. Introduce the smaller hands for the eighth notes.

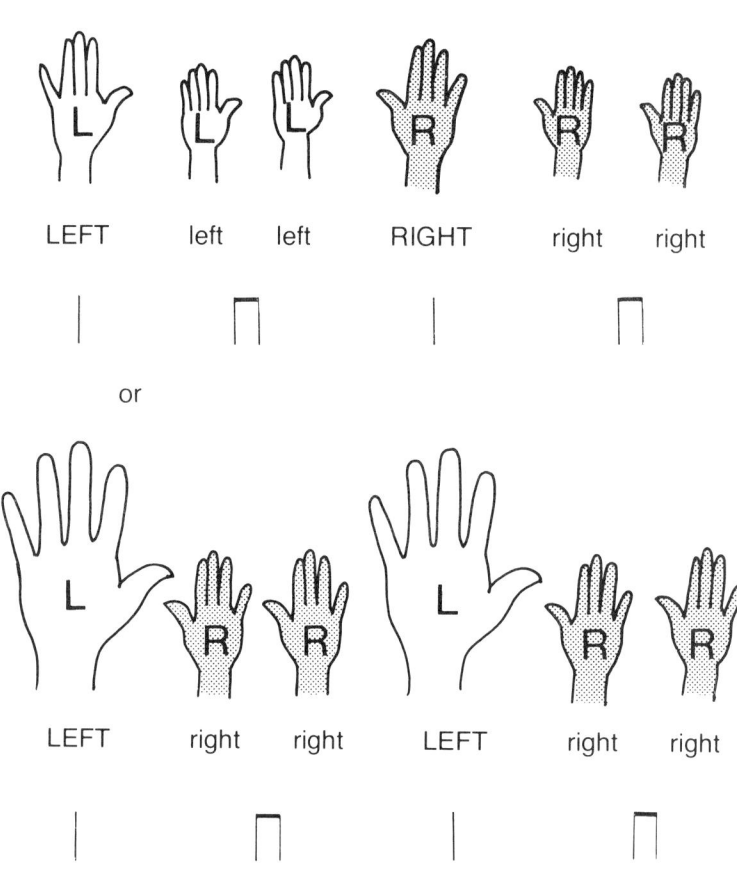

202

4. When the children are ready, something like the following can be tried:

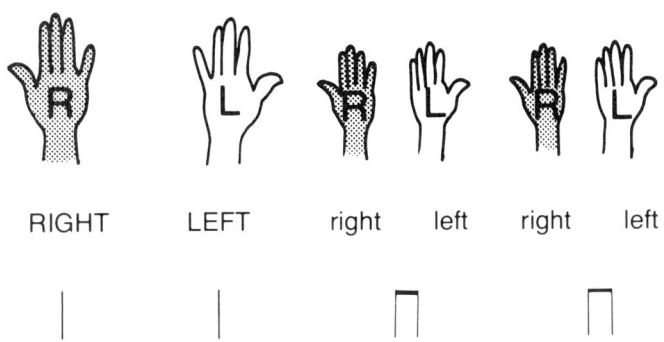

RIGHT   LEFT   right   left   right   left

This pattern is, of course, very difficult and should not be attempted without a great amount of preliminary work.

The beauty of this game ("Hands") is that it can be structured to make it as easy or as difficult as the children are able to manage. It is also a game that they can do without supervision, alone or in pairs. It is very popular and, at the same time, is a painless way to practise coordination skills.

Feet

Have the children cut out silhouettes of their feet from coloured paper — one colour for right and another for left.

If children have trouble remembering which colour is which, it might help to print the words "right" and "left" on the matching "feet" or even an "L" and an "R".

Coordination
Laterality
Balance
Directionality
Midline

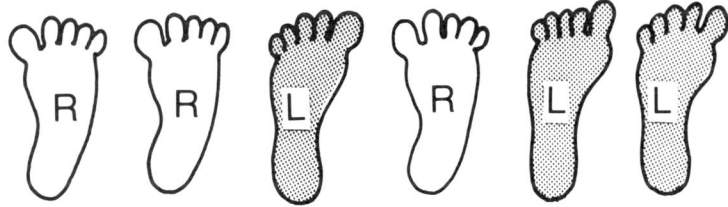

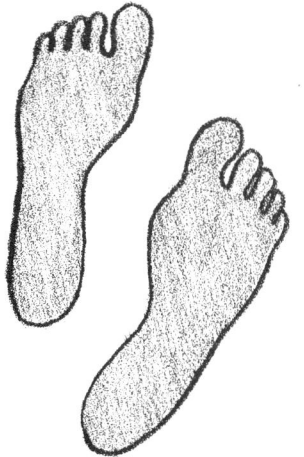

Follow the steps above for "Hands", using feet instead.

This game will have to be played on the floor in a fairly large space and it might be necessary to tape the "feet" down so that they will not slide.

It is more difficult with feet than with hands to coordinate a fast rhythm, changing over left and right but if the limitations of the individual children are kept in mind, it can be good practice and fun.

Speech Rhythms

Speech rhythms can be written in rhythmic notation. The child can then *see* as well as *hear* how the word should sound.

203

This is important for all children but especially for the deaf, the hard of hearing and those with speech disorders. Syllables are easy to master if the word rhythm is clapped and written.

Adding accents shows clearly where the stress should be placed:

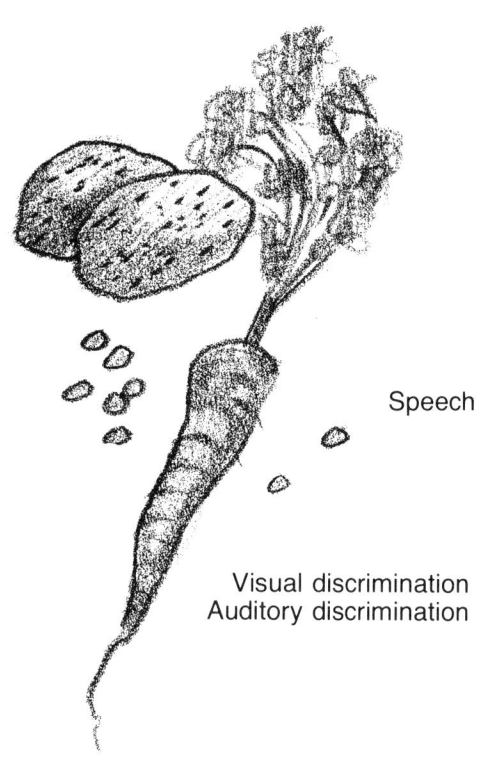

Speech

Visual discrimination
Auditory discrimination

potatoes   carrots   cauliflower   beans

Guess the Word

Print two, three or even more words on the board (the number depends on how advanced the children are). The children clap the rhythm as they say each word. Then you clap just the rhythm and the children guess which word was clapped.

Match the Rhythm

This next game is basically the same as the one above, but is harder. Write the rhythmic notation of each word on the chalkboard or on cards. The corresponding words are on other cards or in a separate space on the board. Children have to match these up.

After the children have mastered individual word rhythms, progress to phrases:

elephant   zebra   kangaroo   sloth

Australia   Asia   Africa   Europe

Then move on to sentences:

May I have a donut please?   It's not your turn!

B. MELODIC NOTATION

Many good books have been written on the teaching of melodic notation, especially those by Zoltán Kodály and teachers of his method. I do not intend to delve into this aspect of music teaching very deeply, as this book is mainly for fun games and music, and not for teaching theory.

Melodic notation, however, is very useful in the early grades for showing the concepts of high and low visually. After much work has been done in listening to and moving to high and low sounds (see **Let's Listen**, pages 33-36), the following steps could be followed:

Do these steps in sequence:
1. Draw a bird high up on the chalkboard or chart and an elephant down below. Have the children say which is high and which is low using high and low voices, pointing with their hands to high and low and, perhaps, placing cards with "high" and "low" written on them beside the picture.
2. Draw a note high up on the board and one down low. Follow the same steps as in number 1.
3. Draw two "telephone lines"

    and put birds or notes on the "wires". Play two notes to correspond with these two "birds", on piano, pitch pipe, xylophone or other instrument. (The notes could be G and E, or C and A, or D and B.) These notes are *soh* and *me* in the solfa scale. Have the children indicate which is high and which is low, both with their hands and by saying the words.
4. Draw these notes next in the spaces between the lines and follow steps 1, 2 and 3 again.
5. Finally, move on to a 5 line staff with your high and low notes.

The next steps, of course, involve learning the names of the lines and spaces, and entail a great amount of work familiarizing the children with the sounds which accompany these names.

The use of hand signs (one for every degree of the scale), which is an important part of the Kodály method, gives valuable clues as to the visual and kinesthetic representation of high and low.

I would again refer anyone interested in pursuing the note reading aspect further to a good text on the subject, such as *The New Approach to Music* (see page 198 above).

INSTRUMENTS

CONTENTS

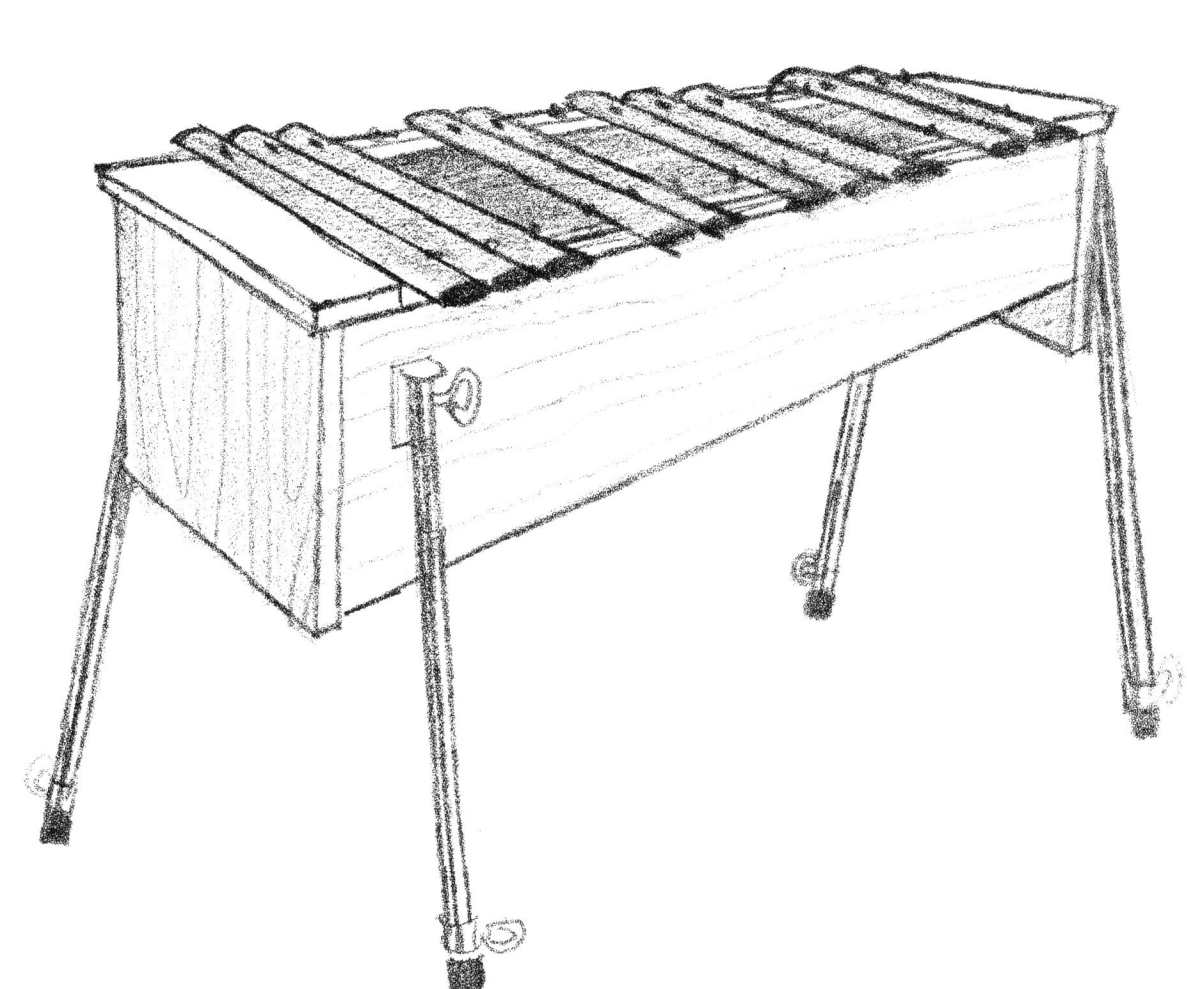

Instruments can be of great assistance in a music program. Those played by the teacher, such as a piano or guitar, can facilitate learning and give support and interest whether played alone, or as an accompaniment to a song. Those played by children, such as tuned or hand percussion, ukelele, recorder, zither *etc.*, aid coordination, musical independence, learning and also add enjoyment.

Children should be given the opportunity to discover the different properties and sounds of instruments. Discuss with them both the more formal group of instruments which may be bought by the school, and those brought by the children from home, such as flower pots (suspended from string), lengths of pipe to blow, bottles filled with different levels of water, metal spikes to bang, ropes pulled taut for plucking, *etc.*

If the exploration time is fairly relaxed and time is taken for discussion, much useful *speech* and *language* will result. Children come up with some beautiful words to describe sounds, such as scrunching, whizzing, sploshing and shimmering. These descriptive words can be written on charts and used for *reading*.

Decide how the sound is produced from instruments — bowed, plucked, hit or blown and develop categories for all the instruments. A discussion of orchestral instruments divided according to category can follow.

The home-made instruments as well those at the school can be used creatively for sound effects, or, in combination, in little compositions. (See **Creativity**, Improvisation, pages 187-189, for ideas.)

A. PIANO

This is perhaps the most versatile of all the instruments, as it can play both the melody line and the accompaniment. It is capable of many moods and is tremendously expressive.

It has some drawbacks, however, and should not be used exclusively. It is very large and impersonal and very sophisticated. Children cannot relate to it easily and small children, of course, find it impossible to play. When playing the piano, the teacher has to face away from the children and is, of necessity, sitting above them. This takes away from the intimacy of the music period.

However, concepts of high and low, fast and slow, loud and soft, can be shown easily on the piano without any great technical skill being required. Sound effects, such as thunder (big groups of notes played together in the bass) or rain (repeated, soft, high notes), are also easy.

B. GUITAR AND UKELELE

These are excellent instruments. They have a lovely quiet sound that children relate to easily. They are small enough to present no barrier to communication. The teacher can face the children and, indeed, have them around her.

The guitar is fairly difficult to play but a ukelele is easily mastered. The baritone ukelele has just four strings but has a lower tone than a regular ukelele and a quality similar to a guitar. It is a most useful instrument.

Children can learn to play at least the first chord of the ukelele and failing that, the instrument can be tuned so that the first string is the same note as the fourth. A child can then strum along and accompany very simple songs, requiring a one-chord accompaniment, such as songs with three notes or pentatonic songs.

Children who are very withdrawn, such as autistic children, or those with emotional problems can often be reached using a guitar or a baritone ukelele. If the instrument is held close to them or put in their laps and the strings strummed softly, they will often strum along themselves. You can finger the chords and let them pluck the strings or tune the instrument so that it makes one chord.

The teacher needs to know only two or three cords to accompany most songs children sing. These important chords are I, IV and V₇. There are many excellent books available on learning to play the ukelele but most of these set the instrument up in the key of D major (strings tuned to A D F♯ and B). I have found it much easier to work with children's songs if the ukelele is tuned to C major (strings tuned to G C E A). More songs are written in the key of C major than in D major and C major is the same basic key as the percussion instruments — xylophone, glockenspiel, *etc*. are tuned to. They can thus be used together.

Two-chord Songs

The following is a list of songs which can be accompanied by using only the two chords, I and V₇.

*Aiken Drum
A-Hunting We Will Go
Alouette
Augustine
Aunt Rhody
Billy Boy
Buffalo Gals
Clementine
Did You Ever See a Lassie?
Everyone Loves Saturday Night
Green Grass Grew All Around
*Go In and Out the Windows
*Ha, Ha Thisaway
He's Got the Whole World
*Hot Potato Pass It On
*If You're Happy and You Know It
*Looby Loo
Look at the Animals in the Zoo
Lukey's Boat
Michael Finnegan
*Mister Banjo
One Elephant Went Out to Play
*Paw Paw Patch
Polly Wolly Doodle
*Rig a Jig Jig
Skip to My Loo
Susy Little Susy
This Old Man

Three-chord Songs

These songs can be accompanied with the three chords, I, IV, and V₇.

Camptown Races
Catch a Falling Star
Cindy
Comin' Round the Mountain
Dinah
*Donkey Riding
Ezekiel Saw a Wheel
Grandfather's Clock
Goodnight Irene
I Saw Three Ships
I've Got Sixpence
John Brown's Body
Kum Bah Yah
Little Brown Jug

*Songs marked * can be found in **Songs**, page 55.

Moonlight Bay
Oh Susanna
Old MacDonald
One More River
On Top of Old Smokey
So Long, It's Been Good to Know You
Streets of Laredo
Tavern in the Town
There's a Hole in My Bucket
This Land Is Your Land
Yankee Doodle
Yellow Bird
You Are My Sunshine

These are just suggestions. I'm sure you will find more.

C. DRUMS, STICKS, BELLS, WOODBLOCKS AND OTHER HAND PERCUSSION

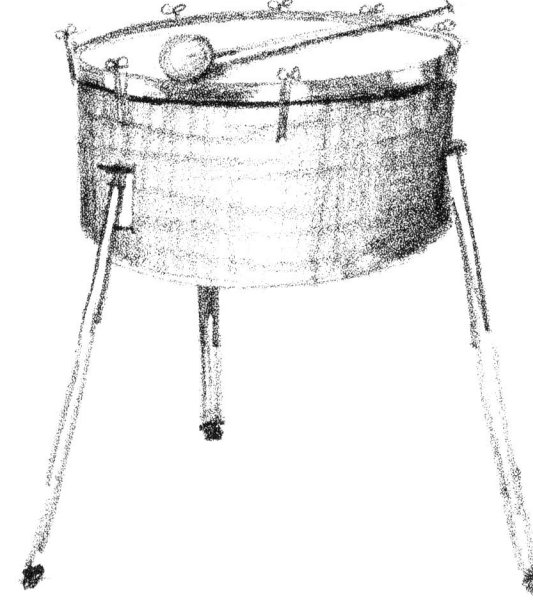

These are excellent, inexpensive and easy for children to play.

Care must be taken to avoid monotony in accompaniments. The old technique, which had one group always playing the beat for the first part and another set group playing the beat for the second part, for instance, is fine to begin with, but with a little imagination, more interesting accompaniments can be devised.

Avoid having too many instruments playing at the same time.

Have some instruments play only once or twice to heighten an effect.

Combine these instruments with others, such as tuned percussion (xylophones, glockenspiels, chime bars, *etc*.).

Use instruments to create a mood for sound effects in poetry and creative drama.

Collect bells, maracas, *etc*. from gift shops, secondhand shops, other people's basements and attics. Just be sure that those you select have a good sound. Drums and tambourines are obtainable from local instrument supply houses. The best kind have tuneable heads. It is thus possible to obtain a good sound and the heads are replaceable, which saves money in the long run.

Fun with Drums
Boys, in particular, like to work with drums. The following are games which have proven popular.

Echo
One person plays a rhythm on a drum, another repeats it. (See **Auditory Sequencing**, B., page 37, for a fuller explanation.)

Question and Answer

One person plays a rhythm on a drum; another replies with a different related rhythm. (See **Creativity**, A. Question and Answer, page 178, for a fuller explanation.)

Children can thus have a dialogue on drums — another way of communicating.

Moving Partners

Partners face each other. One holds a hand drum, the other a drumstick. On the count of 1, the first person moves the drum and then holds that position. On the count of 2, the second person plays a rhythm on the drum to complete the bar. On the next count of 1 the first person moves, and so on:

Coordination

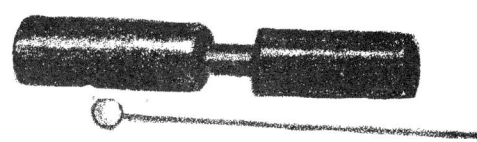

$\frac{2}{4}$ time

1. first person moves ⸗ partner plays ⊓
2. first person moves ⸗ partner plays |

$\frac{3}{4}$ time

1. first person moves ⸗ partner plays ⊓ |
2. first person moves ⸗ partner plays | ⊓

$\frac{4}{4}$ time

1. first person moves ⸗ partner plays ⊓ ⊓ |
2. first person moves ⸗ partner plays | ⊓ | |

Repeat as often as you wish.

Rondos

These can be performed entirely on drums.

A. B. A. C. A. D. A.

A. section.
This should be a set rhythm learned beforehand and played on drums by two or more children: ⊓ | ⊓ | ⊓ ⊓ | ⸗

or

The sections B., C., D. *etc*.
These are improvised on drums by the children. The whole exercise could be accompanied by a steady beat played on a big bass drum. (See **Creativity**, Rondo, page 181, for a fuller explanation.)

Alternating Drums

For this game, the group will need several hand drums. You need as many drums as children playing the game. Eight is a

213

good number. If there are many more the circle becomes too big.

One person stands in the middle of a circle holding a drum and a drumstick. Other children make a circle around him, holding drums between them and slightly in front of them, facing up. The person in the centre walks around playing a pattern on their drums and his, alternating between the two. Decide in advance on the total number of patterns to be played.

The trick is for the drummer to play only one beat on each child's drum, alternating every time with his own drum. The rhythm can be very simple in the beginning and gradually, as the children gain confidence, they will invent more complicated patterns.

The game can be made harder by having children in the circle move slowly in the opposite direction to the child in the centre as he is trying to play the rhythm. It takes a lot of concentration and coordination not to miss a beat.

It is possible (but very difficult) to reverse direction after one pattern, and do another in the opposite direction. Both the circle and the person in the middle must change direction. Let everyone have a turn in the centre.

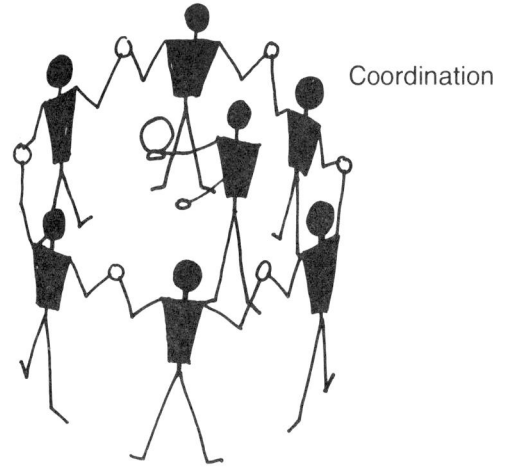
Coordination

Mixed Up Beats

This is a good brain teaser. Four students stand in a row with drums. Have them each tap one note of a steady three-beat pattern, accenting the first beat of the bar strongly each time it comes around. The accent will fall to a different person each time. There can be no hesitations or stops.

3 beats
```
ⓧ  x  x  ⓧ
x  x  ⓧ  x
x  ⓧ  x  x
ⓧ  x  x  ⓧ        and so on.
```

The same can be done with a line of five children and a pattern of four beats.

4 beats
```
ⓧ  x  x  x  ⓧ
x  x  x  ⓧ  x
x  x  ⓧ  x  x
x  ⓧ  x  x  x        and so on.
```

Any number can be played this way as long as there is one more or fewer persons than the number of beats in the pattern. If the number of beats in the pattern is the same as the number of children, one child will always have the strong beat and the game will no longer be a challenge.

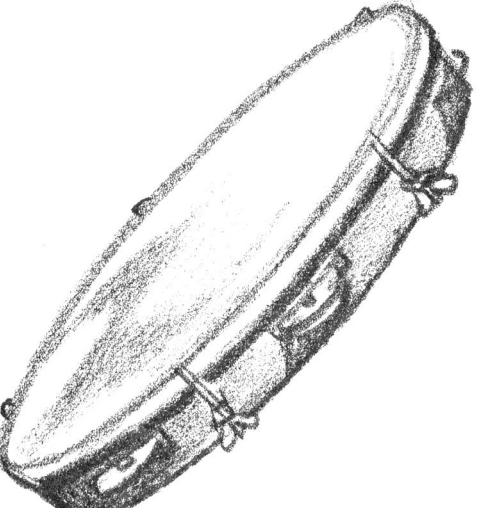

D. LYRES AND ZITHERS

These have a nice quality of sound, soft and yet satisfying. They are fairly easy to play but are somewhat difficult to tune and are also rather expensive.

E. AUTOHARP

This is an excellent instrument for teacher and children. It is easier to play than the lyre although it does not have as beautiful a tone. The chords are written on the "keys" and all one has to do is press the correct key for the correct sound to come forth. It can be strummed with pick or fingers or, in the case of the very young or handicapped, a tongue depressor wrapped in masking tape makes a good sound and is easier to hold.

The autoharp is fairly difficult to tune but it stays in tune for weeks.

F. RECORDERS

These instruments are very useful in the classroom. If the teacher can play fairly efficiently, a recorder will help in teaching and will also arouse interest. Children from ages eight to ten can learn to play easily. The advantages of the recorder are that it is cheap, there is no tuning problem and the children learn to read music while learning to play.

G. KAZOOS

It might be considered strange to include kazoos in a list of musical instruments but I have found them to be very effective in working with non-singers.

The principle on which the kazoo operates, of course, is that of the humming of a melody into the mouthpiece; this produces the sound. Some children (particularly handicapped children or slow learners) who will not sing, will hum enough to play the kazoo. They are intrigued by the off-beat sound. Later, this intermediate stage (using a kazoo), can be dispensed with because the non-singers have now become singers.

This is, of course, just a gimmick and should be used very sparingly.

H. TUNED PERCUSSION

These instruments include:
xylophones — bass, alto and soprano
glockenspiels — alto or soprano
metallophones — bass, alto and soprano

These are excellent for all children and are primarily used for straight improvisation, sound effects and for accompaniments to songs. The notes are removable, so that accompaniments ranging in difficulty from one note to complicated patterns with many notes can be devised.

These instruments (particularly the alto and soprano) are small enough to move around, sit on desks, or even be put on hospital beds or lapboards of wheel chairs.

They have a beautiful sound which is very appealing to all children. They were developed by Carl Orff for use with his system of teaching music to children. Although they are rather expensive, they are carefully made, last for years and require virtually no maintenance and no tuning. It is better to use only one or two instruments which produce a truly beautiful sound than to be satisfied with a greater number which are second rate but perhaps less expensive.

All children can learn to play on the beat on one or two notes. Even severely crippled children can play with the head-piece they use for typing.

When introducing the instruments, have children in all grades play, with both hands (if possible), a quarter note or walking pattern on the xylophone or glockenspiel. The two notes used will most often be *doh* and *soh* in the key you are working in:

in C	C and G
in F	F and C
in G	G and D

Leave all the notes on if the children are capable of hitting the correct ones, otherwise take off as many as is necessary.

With very small children, it might be necessary to take off all notes except those actually being played.

If the children you work with are perceptually impaired, they will, in most cases, be distracted by the other notes. Emotionally disturbed children will want to play the other notes just because they are there and physically handicapped youngsters will hit the wrong note by accident. It may be necessary in all these cases to arrange the notes so that the child playing will achieve success, even if this means there are only two notes left.

This two-note basic beat pattern can be accompanied later on with a quarter note pattern on another instrument (percussion or melodic) or in the older grades with a half and/or whole-note pattern on metallophone or glockenspiel.

For children with problems, the instruments may always have to be set up with just a few notes left on, so that anything they hit will sound appropriate. Another way to do this is to use the notes *doh, me* and *soh.*

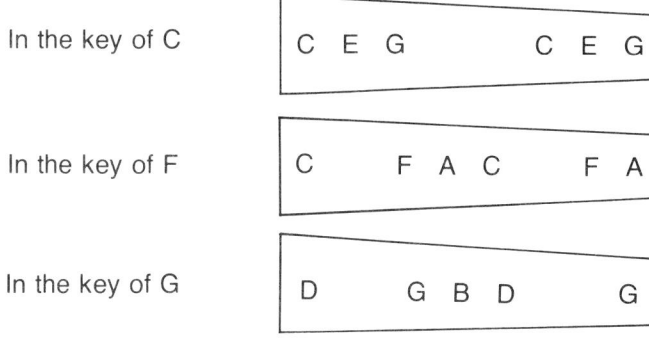

In the key of C	C E G C E G
In the key of F	C F A C F A
In the key of G	D G B D G

Pentatonic Scale

The next step for children who are able is to set the instruments up in the pentatonic or five-note scale. This is *doh, ray, me, soh, lah* in solfa, or notes 1, 2, 3, 5, 6 of the scale.

In the key of C

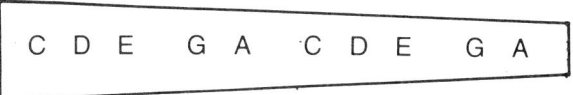

In the key of F

In the key of G

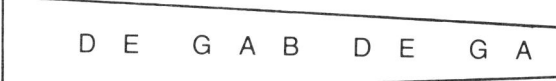

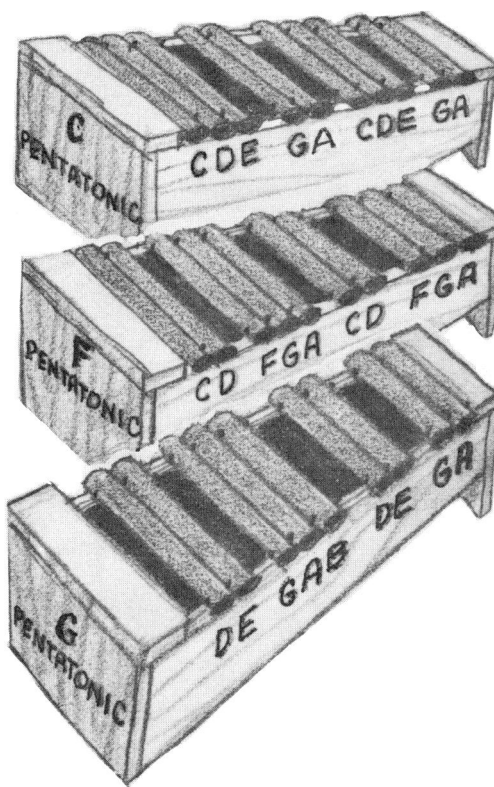

The instruments can thus be set up in the scales of C, F, and G. If the songs are written in one of these major keys, use the appropriate setting. If the song is written in another key, teach it in the original key and then sing it in the key nearest to the original of those above, using the setting suggested.

Most of the songs in **Songs**, have been written in C, F, or G, to make it easier to find an accompaniment. The suggested accompaniments which follow are written in the same three keys — C, F and G.

The instruments also come with F# and B♭. By interchanging these with F or B it is possible to use other keys.

In tie scale of D

| D | E | F# | | A | B | | D | E | F# | A |

In the scale of B♭

| F | G | | | B♭ | C | D | | F | G | |

But this is getting complex. For further explanation see Doreen Hall's *Teacher's Manual*. (See **Books**, page 231.)

It is easy to teach children to set the instruments up. Tell the class which note is *doh*. Have one child play up the scale, starting on *doh*, while the class sings the notes to the tonic solfa — *doh, ray, me, fah, soh, lah, te, doh*. The children quickly learn that the notes to be taken off are *fah* and *te* and when they come to them, they stop and take them off. Notes can also be taken off by having the children sing up the scale to numbers, taking off the fourth and seventh notes.

The pentatonic scale is used because it does not give a definite feeling of "key". When the children make up patterns, they can pick any combination of notes and play these together or in sequence. Several instruments can play together in a straight improvisation (see **Creativity**, page 188) or as an accompaniment to a song and providing that they are all set up in the same pentatonic scale the whole thing will sound possible.

The Metallophone

The metallophone has a very ringing quality and will drown out all the other instruments, as well as the singing. Introduce it last in accompaniments, and use it sparingly, when the children are able to sustain slow note values. Xylophones and glockenspiels are more useful as their sound is not as penetrating.

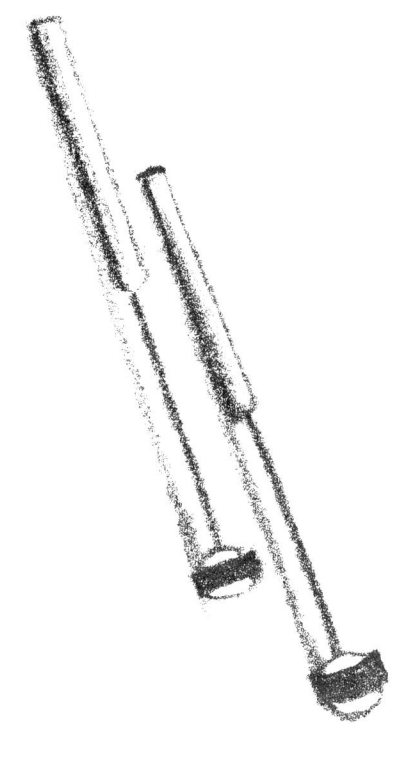

Mallet Technique

The mallets should be held loosely with the palms of the hands curved around the base of the mallet. This is especially true of the index finger. If it is allowed to rest "pointing" up the mallet the whole hand and arm will become stiff and this will result in a hard tone. The keys should be struck in the middle and the mallet should always bounce off quickly as soon as the note is played so the sound is not muffled.

Always prepare the accompaniments first by having the children pretend to play them on their knees or in the air, in time, and with relaxed arms. If the player is still stiff and tends to "poke" at the instrument give him some arm and shoulder relaxing exercises before allowing him to continue. Children who are tense or who have learning or coordination problems will require a great amount of practice in playing instruments before they can do so in a relaxed manner.

Try as much as possible to play with two hands to develop coordination on both sides of the body

Proceed very slowly — do not attempt to introduce too many instruments at once. It is always better to have one or two people playing something very simple and beautiful and in rhythm, than to have many playing who are uncertain. Chaos develops quickly unless control is exercised.

The rhythm may often be kept steady by introducing a drum or woodblock, *etc.* along with the melodic instruments.

Keep the accompaniments to the songs simple. In introductions, interludes (between verses) and endings, it is possible to introduce more instruments and more complicated rhythms. Always make these extra "bits" a definite length — two or four bars each usually works very well.

It is often possible to have a different treatment for different verses. A different combination of instruments, or a slightly different accompaniment will accomplish this effect.

Always make sure the children know the song well before attempting any instrumental accompaniment.

The following are some suggested accompaniments. They are only suggestions because the children should be encouraged to create as many as possible of their own. The accompaniment should be repeated throughout the song.

They are given in the three most useful keys for the instruments: C, F, and G.

When the sticks on the notes are pointing down, this means play with the left hand. Sticks pointing up means play with the right hand.

Suggested Accompaniments for $\frac{4}{4}$ Time

Xylophone or Glockenspiel

Xylophone or Glockenspiel

Xylophone or Glockenspiel

Metallophone Accompaniment

(Could be played on xylophone or glockenspiel as well.)

Key of C

Metallophone

(xylophone and glockenspiel)

Key of F

Metallophone

(xylophone and glockenspiel)

Key of G

Suggested Accompaniments for $\frac{3}{4}$ Time

Xylophone or Glockenspiel

Key of C

Xylophone or Glockenspiel

Key of F

Xylophone or Glockenspiel

Key of G

221

Metallophone Accompaniments
(Could be played on xylophone or glockenspiel as well.)

Key of C

Metallophone
(xylophone and glockenspiel)

Key of F

Metallophone
(or xylophone and glockenspiel)

Key of G

The tuned percussion instruments are available from:

New Era Instruments (by Premier)
Canada: Bishop Music Ltd., 1983 Leslie St. Don Mills, Ontario M3B 2M3

U.S.: Rhythm Band Inc., P.O. Box 126, Fort Worth, Texas 76101.
Selmer Music Co., P.O. Box 310, Elkhart, Indiana 46514.

England: Premier Drum Co., Blaby Road, Wigston, Leicester.

Studio 49 Instruments
Canada: Waterloo Music Co., Waterloo, Ontario.

U.S.A.: Magnamusic Baton Inc., 10370 Page Industrial Blvd., St. Louis, Missouri 63132

Sonar
Canada: Hohner Canada Inc., 1969 Leslie St., Don Mills, Ontario M3B 2M3

U.S.A.: M. Horner Inc., Andrews Rd., Hicksville, L.I., New York.

These instruments can also be obtained very easily in England, all over Europe and in many other countries such as Japan and Australia.

Chime Bars
These are also known as resonator bells or tone bars. They can be used in the same manner as the xylophones or glockenspiels. They are good because they can be divided among more children.

I. MAKE YOUR OWN INSTRUMENTS

Children love to make instruments. Care must be taken, if these are used in a musical setting, that a good sound is obtained. There are some good books on the subject listed in **Books**.

RECORDS

CONTENTS

A. SONGS — FOLK AND OTHER

Folk song recordings are so numerous today that it is very difficult to make a choice. The following records are very clear and very relaxed in style. Most of the songs they contain are authentic folk songs or good child centred songs composed in modern times. Many of the singers are men, and the women singers have quite low voices. Children relate to this pitch more than to higher voices. They will readily sing along with the record.

Tom Glazer	*Activity and Game Songs* C.M.S. 657.
Pete Seeger	*Abiyoyo* Folkways 31500.
Pete Seeger	*Birds and Beasts and Bugs and Little Fishes* Folkways 7011.
Ella Jenkins	*Call and Response* Folkways FC7308. (Rhythmic Group Singing)
Pete Seeger	*Children's Concert at Town Hall* Harmony H30399. Contains many old favourites such as: *Put Your Finger in the Air* *Ha, Ha Thisaway*
Ed McCurdy	*Children's Songs* Tradition TLP 1027.
Bob Hastings	*45 Songs Children Love to Sing* RCA Camden CAS 1038e.
Ella Jenkins	*Rhythm and Game Songs for Little Ones* Folkways FC7057.
Ella Jenkins	*Rhythms of Childhood* Scholastic SC 7653.
Edith Fowke	*Sally Go Round the Sun* McClelland and Stewart (publishers) T-56666-67. (Companion record to book of the same name.)
——	*Small Musician* series Bowmar *The Small Singer* Vol. I (021) *The Small Singer* Vol. II (022) *The Small Listener* (393) *The Small Dancer* (391) *The Small Player* (392) (An excellent set of records.)
Pete Seeger	*Song and Playtime* Folkways 7526.

B. RECORDS FOR TEACHING

These are good for all children — handicapped or normal. Many of the records in the Folk Song section are also good for teaching.

Hap Palmer	*Creative Movement and Rhythmic Exploration* (533) Educational Activities Inc., Freeport, L.I., U.S.A.
——	*Dance a Story* RCA Victor There are several of these records.

These are particularly good:
> *About Balloons* (RCA LE 104)
> *The Magic Mountain* (RCA LE 103)
> *The Little Duck* (RCA LE 101)

Hap Palmer — *Learning Basic Skills Through Music* Educational Activities Inc., Freeport, L.I., U.S.A.
Vol. 1 — 514   Vol. 2 — 522
Vol. 3 — 521   Vol. 4 — 526
These records have many good songs for teaching the alphabet, colours, shapes, numbers, *etc.*

Ella Jenkins — *Play Your Instruments and Make a Pretty Sound* Folkways 7665.
Excellent for the four-year-old level — allows free experimentation with instruments

Edna Doll, Mary Jarman Nelson — Records that teach selected songs, narration and music from *Rhythms Today* Silver Burdett Records 8118 P.

C. RECORDS FOR SPECIAL CHILDREN

—— *Basic Concepts Through Dance* Educational Activities Inc., Freeport, L.I., U.S.A.
> *Body Image* (EALP 601)
> *Position of Body in Space* (EALP 603)
Excellent for slow learners. Instructions are very clear and are given very slowly.

Winifred Stiles, David Gingland — *Learning as We Play* Folkways FC 7659.
This record contains many songs from their book *Play Activities For The Retarded Child*.

—— *Music for Exceptional Children* Summy Birchard (publishers)
Companion to book of same name
Two records: (839 S 9776 and 839 S 9778).

—— *Simplified Folk Dance Favourites* 602 Educational Activities Inc., Freeport, L.I., U.S.A.
Gives very simple, clear directions all can understand.

—— *Songs for Children with Special Needs* Bowmar
Album 1 (011)
Album 2 (012)
Album 3 (013)

D. GOOD RECORDS FOR LISTENING AND MOVING

This short list is given only to suggest some of the countless good recordings available. Any record shop will have lists of many more and the children themselves will love to bring some of their recordings from home for listening.

I have not attempted to give specific references to particular recordings, as there are many recordings of each piece available. In addition, each company keeps changing its lists, so it is difficult to keep up to date.

Bartók	— excerpts from *Mikrokosmos*
Benjamin	— *Jamaican Rumba*
Debussy	— *Children's Corner Suite* — *La Mer*
Dukás	— *The Sorcerer's Apprentice*
Gershwin	— *An American in Paris*
Grieg	— *Peer Gynt Suite*, especially *Anitra's Dance* and *In the Hall of the Mountain King*
Grofé	— *Grand Canyon Suite* — *Mississippi Suite*
Holst	— *The Planets*
Mendelssohn	— *A Midsummer Night's Dream* -- *Fingal's Cave Overture*
Prokofiev	— *Peter and the Wolf* — March from *The Love of Three Oranges*
Ravel	— *Bolero* — *Mother Goose Suite*
Saint-Saëns	— *The Carnival of the Animals*
Smetana	— *The Moldau*
Stravinsky	— *Petrouchka* — *The Rite of Spring*
Tchaïkowsky	— *The Nutcracker Suite*
Warlock	— *Capriol Suite*
Weinberger	— Polka from *Schwanda the Bagpiper*
——	— *Adventures in Music* (RCA Victor) This series has records chosen for listening for Grades I through VI. The selections and commentaries are excellent.

BOOKS

CONTENTS

A. USEFUL GENERAL BOOKS

Andrews, Gladys	*Creative Rhythmic Movement for Children* Prentice-Hall, New York, 1954.
Blishen, Edward	*Oxford Book of Poetry for Children* Oxford University Press, London, 1963.
Boorman, Joyce	*Creative Dance in the First Three Grades,* Longmans Canada Ltd., Don Mills, Ontario, 1967.
Boorman, Joyce	*Creative Dance in Grades Four to Six* Longmans Canada Ltd., Don Mills, Ontario, 1971.
Boorman, Joyce	*Dance and Language Experiences With Children* Longmans Canada Ltd., Don Mills, Ontario, 1973. These three books give valuable practical help to anyone planning movement experiences with children.
Briggs, Raymond	*The Mother Goose Treasury* Hamish Hamilton, London, 1966. A beautifully illustrated, very complete book of nursery rhymes.
Davis, Flora	*Inside Intuition: What We Know About Non-verbal Communication* McGraw-Hill Ryerson, Ltd., 1973.
de la Mare, Walter	*Poems for Children* Holt, Rinehart and Winston, Inc., New York, 1930.
Doll, Edna and Nelson, Mary Jarman	*Rhythms Today* Silver Burdett Company, a Division of General Learning Corp., Morristown, New Jersey, 1965.
Findlay, Elsa	*Rhythm and Movement — Applications of Dalcroze Eurhythmics* Summy Birchard Co., Evanston, Illinois 60204, 1971.
Fowke, Edith	*Sally Go Round the Sun* McClelland and Stewart, Toronto, 1969. This is the best source of poems, folklore and song material for children I have ever discovered, and it is beautifully illustrated. Small children like to use it as a picture book. A recording of some of the material is available under the same name (see **Records**, page 225).
Grayson, Marion F.	*Let's Do Finger Plays* Robt. B. Luce Inc., Washington, 1962.
Grey, Vera and Percival, Rachel	*Music, Movement and Mime for Children* Oxford University Press, London, 1962.
Goulding, Dorothy-Jane	*Play-acting in the Schools* Ryerson, Toronto, 1970. This is a very easy book to read, crammed with many excellent ideas.
Hall, Doreen	*Music for Children* (A Teacher's Manual) Schott and Sons, Mainz, Germany, 1960. A great help for anyone using ideas from Carl Orff's "Music for Children".
Ireson, Barbara	*Faber Book of Nursery Verse* Faber & Faber, London, 1958.
Keetman, Gunild	*Elementaria,* Schott and Co. Ltd., London, England, 1974 (English translation by Margaret Murray). A "must" for those interested in working with the Orff approach.

Lee, Dennis	*Alligator Pie,* Macmillan of Canada, Toronto, 1974.
Mandell, Muriel and Wood, Robert E.	*Make Your Own Musical Instruments* Sterling, New York, 1959.
Murray, Margaret	*Wee Willie Winkie,* Schott and Co. Ltd., London, England, 1965. Miss Murray has published many excellent Orff materials. This little book has very easy settings of well known songs.
Opie, Iona and Opie, Peter	*The Oxford Dictionary of Nursery Rhymes* Oxford University Press, London, 1951. A definitive collection of English nursery rhymes with delightful histories of the origins of the verses.
	The Oxford Nursery Rhyme Book Oxford University Press, London, 1965. An excellent collection of nursery rhymes, beautifully illustrated and grouped into categories such as lullabies, riddles, catch rhymes, *etc.*
Orff, Carl and Hall, Doreen	*Music for Children,* Pentatonic Book I. Schott and Sons, Mainz, Germany, 1951.
Perrin, Kovacs, Daley and Allin	*The New Approach to Music,* Primary Division, © 1969, 1970, Junior Division, © 1972. Holt, Rinehart and Winston of Canada, Limited, Toronto. Excellent books for teaching a comprehensive music program at the primary and junior levels.
Slade, Peter	*An Introduction to Child Drama* Lawrence Verry, Mystic, Connecticut, 1958.
Untermeyer, Louis	*Rainbow in the Sky* Harcourt Brace, New York, 1935.
Williams, Peter	*Making Musical Instruments* Mills and Boon, Foley St., London, 1970. These are craft cards put together in book form, treated with plastic to withstand paint, paste and grubby fingers. Well illustrated and containing many good ideas.
Withers, Carl	*A Rocket in My Pocket* Holt, Rinehart and Winston, Inc., New York, 1948. A good collection of verses for children.

B. USEFUL SONG BOOKS

Bissell, Keith	*Let's Sing and Play* Waterloo Music Co. Ltd., Waterloo, Ontario, 1973. Songs with voice and percussion accompaniment.
Boni, Margaret B.	*The Fireside Book of Folk Songs* Simon and Schuster, New York, 1947.
Brocklehurst, Brian	*Pentatonic Song Book* Schott and Co., Ltd., London, England, 1968. This little book has a lot of good material.
Cooperative Recreation Services	*Open Road Song Book* Delaware, Ohio. Distributed in Canada by Gordon V. Thompson, Toronto. A small pocketbook with many familiar songs for group singing.

Fowke, Edith	*Sally Go Round the Sun* McClelland and Stewart, Toronto, 1968. The best all-round source book for children's games, poems and songs, in my opinion. See **Records**, page 227, for a description of the accompanying record.
Fowke, Edith and Johnson, Richard	*Folk Songs of Canada* Waterloo Music Co., Waterloo, Ontario, 1954. An excellent collection of Canadian folk songs.
Glazer, Tom and Seiden, Art	*Tom Glazer's Treasury of Folk Songs for the Family* Grosset and Dunlap, New York, 1946.
Guthrie, Woody	*Woody Guthrie Folk Songs* Ludlow, New York, 1963.
Heller, Ruth	*Christmas, Its Carols, Customs and Legends* Schmitt, Hall & McCreary, Minneapolis, 1948.
Lloyd, Norman	*The New Golden Song Book* Golden Press, New York, 1955.
Nichols, Elizabeth	*Orff Instrument Source Book I, 1970 and II, 1971.* Silver Burdett (G.L.C.), Morristown, New Jersey. Orff accompaniments for an excellent choice of folk songs. Perhaps more useful with fairly advanced classes.
Panabaker, Lucile	*Lucile Panabaker's Song Book* Peter Martin Associates, Toronto, 1968. Excellent material for very young or slow learning children.
Seegar, Ruth Crawford	*American Folk Songs for Children* Doubleday, Garden City, New York, 1948.
Tobitt, Janet E. (arr.)	*Singing Rhymes for Recreation* Books 1, 2, 3, 4, A & C Black Ltd., London, 1936-1951.
Wessels, Katherine Tyler	*The Golden Song Book* Simon & Schuster, New York, 1945.
Winn, Marie (editor)	*The Fireside Book of Folksongs* Simon & Schuster, New York, 1947.
Wuytack, Jos. and Aaron, Tossi	*Joy* (play, sing, dance). A. Leduc, Paris, 1972. The Orff accompaniments are excellent and the dance patterns very clear.

C. USEFUL BOOKS FOR WORKING WITH HANDICAPPED CHILDREN

Alvin, Juliette	*Music and the Handicapped Child* Oxford University Press, London, 1965.
Canner, Norma	*And a Time to Dance* Beacon Press, Boston, Massachusetts, 1968.
Carlson, Bernice and Gingland, David	*Play Activities for the Retarded Child* Abingdon Press, New York, 1961.
Dobbs, J.P.B.	*The Slow Learner and Music* Oxford University Press, London, 1966.
Gingland, David and Stiles, Winifred	*Music Activities for Retarded Children* Abingdon Press, New York, 1965.
Nordoff, Paul and Robbins, Clive	*Music Therapy in Special Education* John Day Co., New York, 1971.

Robins, Ferris and Robins, Jennet   *Educational Rhythmics for Mentally and Physically Handicapped Children* Association Press, (National Council Y.M.C.A.), New York, 1968.
A very comprehensive book of games, ideas and suggestions.

Schattner, Regina   *Creative Dramatics for Handicapped Children* John Day Co., New York, 1966.

D. GENERAL MUSIC PROGRAMS

The books in these series give a wide choice of good material suitable for grades Kindergarten to eight and can usually be found in the schools.

Exploring Music   Holt, Rinehart and Winston, Inc., New York.

Making Music Your Own   Silver Burdett Co., A Division of General Learning Corporation, Morristown, New Jersey.

Songs for Today   Waterloo Music Company, Waterloo, Ontario.

Songtime   Holt, Rinehart and Winston of Canada, Limited, Toronto

SAMPLE LESSON PLANS

CONTENTS

This chapter is an attempt to organize some of the ideas found in this book into some sample lesson plans.

I have hesitated to include such a chapter in the book because I feel that lesson plans are dangerous for two reasons.

The first is that the teacher, or any person working with children, by following lesson plans tends to formalize the "music period" into 20 or 30 min slots each day, three times a week, or what have you. As I have said many times throughout the book, an active music program should be an integral part of the child's whole experience each day, every day, whether at school, at home, at camp or wherever. This is especially true when working with very small children.

A sort of mini-opera can take place all day with requests being *sung* to put boots on, to tidy up, have juice, etc. Songs can be sung for good morning, good bye and about the topics of current interest. Music can be used for resting, for dancing, for creative movement or for the physical education period. The happiest homes, classrooms and camps I have ever visited were planned this way.

My second objection to lesson plans is that each group of children is different and people working with children have to plan their own lessons to suit the needs of the particular children in the group. The emphasis might be on listening games with some; coordinative skills might take priority for others. Any outline or lesson plan must be carefully adapted.

With the forgoing reservations then, here are some plans, not to be followed slavishly, but to be used as examples or sign posts along the way.

General Observations

Children should have the joy of singing every day and preferably many times a day.

Each day should include some listening experiences using both records and active listening games involving the whole child. Each day should include some activities aimed at sensory motor development, some rhythmic work and some speech and poetry.

All of these do not have to be included in a 30 min session, but might be fitted in at different times during the day: e.g. a lesson in Geography might include a song or some other music of the country, speech and poetry could be included in the English lesson and the coordinative and motor sensory work could be included in the physical education period.

These lesson plans have attempted to show the progression in each of the main areas. Some children will not be able to progress as quickly as the lessons suggest, and should take longer on each step. Others might have to go at a much faster rate.

I have tried to organize the work under specific headings, but as with everything else in this approach to learning through music, the activities spill over into other categories. This, of course, is part of the great joy and excitement in teaching music.

239

The basic categories are as follows:

Warm Up
Let's Move
Let's Listen
Speech and Poetry
Songs
Extra Songs and Poetry Which Might Be Tried
Notation
Instruments

I have also arbitrarily picked some topics, around which to organize the activities. These, also, could be changed to suit the needs of the group.

There are two groups of lessons. Level I is for very young children who have had very little experience with music before. Level II is designed for slightly older children who may or may not be familiar with the earliest musical concepts.

The Setting

The setting for music for young children should be very informal and relaxed. If it is possible, they should sit in a group on a mat with the piano, record player and other materials close to hand, and there should also be room for free movement, games and dancing.

Materials available ideally should include:

Instruments, page 207

a) A selection of rhythm instruments such as hand drums, maracas, sticks and triangles. Later, xylophones, chime bars, metallophones, glockenspiels, etc. can be introduced.

b) A piano, guitar or ukelele if the leader can play these.

c) An autoharp (especially if the leader cannot play one of the above).

Records, page 225

d) A record player with a good selection of records for listening to, singing with (folk songs, etc.) and/or moving to (either freely or following directions for games and activities).

Notation, page 191

Let's listen, page 25

e) A chalkboard for the introduction of visual concepts of fast and slow, loud and soft, high and low, and notation.

f) Charts for the introduction of note reading in later lessons.

g) Art materials for expressing musical concepts and the subject material of songs, records and poems.

h) A small selection of "props" such as hats, canes, brooms, etc., to help in acting out the songs and poems.

LEVEL I

Lesson I

Names

Warm Up

Listen to some favourite records, either instrumental or folk songs. Move to these or sing along with them.

Sing some songs most of the children would know such as *Baa Baa Black Sheep, Twinkle Twinkle Little Star, etc.*

Have the children seated around you in an informal group on a mat and just sing as many songs as they know at first.

Have the children move in any way they wish to a song. Pick one child who is performing an action on the beat and have the others move his way if possible. Do not force this.

The children could act out the story of a song.

Let's Move

Play a steady walking pattern on a drum and have the children move any way they wish to the sound in their own space. Next, have them take their own space with them and move around the room in random fashion to the drum beat, stopping when the drum stops. You might suggest forward, back, to the side, etc., to add variety in their movement. Stress that each child has his or her own space and that he or she must not go into anyone else's space. This, hopefully eliminates bumping and pushing.

Coordination
Spatial relationship
Body rhythm

Let's Listen

Try the "Follow Me" game (page 12) changing as often as the children are able. Make sure they have enough space around them to enable them to move freely.

Coordination
Spatial relationship
Body rhythm

Explore the different sounds the body can make — first just hands, just feet, mouth, knees, then making different combinations — hands and knees, feet and knees and hands (page 12).

Speech

For page 132, clap the names of different children. Have all the children listen and tell you the number of claps in each name. Group the names according to the number of claps. Combine as many names as the children are able to cope with, and try some of the activities suggested on page 132. Do not introduce notation at this stage as most young children need the experience of clapping, saying and walking the rhythms first. After a set number of repetitions an ending might be devised such as — "That's my name.

Speech

Song

Songs

Introduce the song *Rig a Jig Jig* (page 102) substituting different children's names for "I".

Extra Songs and Poems

Mary Wore A Red Dress
Paw Paw Patch (page 87)
Dairy Charm (page 150) (Change "Peter" to each child's name in turn.)
Mary At The Door (page 143)

Instruments

Have one or two children play a drum, sticks or other simple percussion instrument on the beat of the song.

Lesson II   Animals

Warm Up

Play some recorded music as a listening experience. As the theme for this lesson is **Animals,** a suggestion might be one of the selections from Saint-Saëns *Carnival Of The Animals.* Talk about how the animals move and how the sound of the music makes us want to move. Let the children express their feelings about the music with their bodies.

Let's Move

Coordination
Spatial relationship
Body rhythm

Have the children move to fast and slow beats played on a drum (page 14).

Do some of the exercises for developing awareness of fast and slow (page 31).

Discuss the movement of different animals. Have the children describe the particular movement in language (thus helping language development), then imitating the movement (page 32). Lists could be made of "fast" animals and "slow" animals and these lists could be used for reading experiences.

Let's Listen

Coordination
Spatial relationship
Body rhythm

The "Mirror" activity (pages 17-18), is excellent training in concentration as well as coordination. Continue with "Follow Me". Combine the two or allow one to flow from and into the other. Contrast fast and slow activities describing the movement as "fast" and "slow" thus reinforcing the concepts introduced in **Let's Move.**

Speech

Instead of using children's names (page 132), the same technique can be used with animals. "When you go to the zoo what animals do you see?" You might develop something such as the following:

The zoo, the zoo, we're going to the zoo. The zoo, the zoo, we're going to the zoo. What kind of animals will we see? Rhinoceroses, tigers, elephants, bears, Camels, giraffes and monkeys eating pears. The zoo, the zoo, we're going to the zoo. The zoo, the zoo, we're going to the zoo.	(all say this with rhythmic vitality) (one child speaks) (different children speak each animal's name)	Speech

The poems *(The) Elephant* and *Six Little Ducks* (pages 21-22), are fun and have good movement patterns.

Coordination
Spatial relationship
Body Rhythm

Songs

Following along on the animal theme, the song *Rover* (page 65) could be taught here.

Songs

After the children have learned the song they can be encouraged to put the "beat" in their hands, feet, knees, on the floor, etc. (page 51) while singing.

Singing

If any children have trouble doing this, have one half of the group clap and say a word pattern such as "Rover Rover Rover Rover" over and over as the other half sings the song (page 52). Alternate groups.

When the children are proficient in the above, let one or two play drums or sticks on the beat as an accompaniment to the singing.

Extra Songs and Poetry

(The) Ants Come Marching
At The Farm (page 80)
Bell Horses (page 62)
Bingo
Horses Horses (page 90)
Eensy Weensy Spider (page 152)
Teddy Bear (page 148)

Instruments

Imitate the sounds animals make on instruments. Move to these.

Have children experiment with different percussion instruments playing them fast and slow.

Lesson III   Transportation

Warm Up

Play records which describe trains, cars, busses, etc. Gershwin's *An American In Paris* is a good choice as it describes the hustle and bustle of a great city with its cars and taxies.

Sing songs such as *The Bus* (The wheels on the bus go round, round, round . . .) or *Row Row Row Your Boat* which have a transportation theme. Review other songs the children know.

Let's Move

Have the children divide up into teams and "become" different modes of transportation: row boats, sail boats, trains, dog sleds, horses, bicycles, scooters, etc. These "constructions", of course, must be able to move and could have spoken or instrumental sound effects as accompaniments.

See **Speech** and **Song** for other movement ideas.

Let's Listen

Most children have no difficulty distinguishing between loud and soft sounds but just to make sure, some of the activities described on pages 31-32 might be tried. They are fun to do.

Have the children talk about and make the sounds produced by different modes of transportation. Think about their properties; soft, loud, fast, slow, high, low, raucous, grating, pleasing and so on. Lists could be made describing the sounds e.g. clunking, hissing, purring (as in a Rolls Royce), screeching. This kind of activity helps language development and reading.

Start "Echos" (page 37) with some movement echos first then using clapping, stamping, etc.

Let's listen

Speech

The poem *The Train* (pages 155-156) brings in many different activities: movement (especially fast and slow), instrumental, both saying the poem and in the word accompaniment); and is a favourite of all children.

Poems

Song

Try *Jig Jog Jig Jog* (page 67). This is a very popular song with young children and as it is sung many times during the year(s), progressively more difficult accompaniments can be tried.

Songs

Extra Songs and Poems

(The) Bus
Down by The Station
Going Over The Sea (page 84)
New River Train
(The) Old Red Wagon (page 68)

Notation

Have the children say "jig jog jig jog" over and over again, "writing" the sound in the air. They will most often make a downward movement which looks like this: | \ | | | |

Notation

Next have them write the "beat" on the board (the beat is, of course jig jog jig jog). The result might look like this:

Discuss left to right progression in reading. Music does the same so the next time the picture might look like this:

This is the start of music reading and is just a shorthand way of writing: ♩ ♩ ♩ ♩ ♩ ♩ ♩   (See pages 194-198.)

Instruments

Experiment with different instruments to find which produce the sounds of the modes of transportation discussed (page 87).

Instruments

Use the instrumental accompaniments suggested for *The Train* and *Jig Jog Jig Jog.*

Lesson IV   Instruments

Warm Up

Listen to records such as *The Young Persons Guide To The Orchestra* by Benjamin Britten or *Peter And The Wolf* by Prokofiev which point out the different instruments of the orchestra.

Discuss the sounds of the instruments and if possible take the children to hear an orchestra playing. The older children in Junior High or High School are often delighted to come and play for their younger brothers and sisters.

Let's Move and Let's Listen

Let's listen

Instruments

I have combined these for this section because it was impossible to do one without the other.

Go on a sound walk and collect sounds either on a tape recorder or in memory. Bring these back to the classroom and discuss them, contrast them, make a little composition of them, let them suggest ideas for movement, describe them in words (pages 30 and 209).

Suggest that the children bring sounds from home and work in a similiar way with these sounds (page 30).

Books

Make your own instruments in the class (see pages 233, Mandell and Wood, and page 234, Williams, for ideas). Use these for experimenting with sound.

Make sure that the sound of homemade instruments is good before using them musically. Art or physics might benefit from making a guitar from a cigar box and elastic bands but not music. Sticks, drums and shakers are all possible. Often bells etc., can be found in second-hand shops.

Have a music corner or table for all these instruments. Don't jumble them away in a box or the children will not treat them with respect.

Let's listen

Try Echos (page 38) on percussion instruments. The children enjoy using those they have made themselves.

Let's listen

While exploring the sounds of different instruments the concepts of high and low can be introduced very easily. Try some of the activities suggested on pages 33-36. High and low is a difficult concept for many children and must be worked at over a long period of time.

Singing

There are many opportunities during each day to "Call and Response" type of singing (putting on boots, lining up, etc.). These times should be exploited (page 49).

Songs

Change the words of songs to describe the playing of instruments. E.g. *Mulberry Bush* (page 79) could be:

Mary plays the big bass drum,
Big bass drum, big bass drum.
Mary plays the big bass drum,
Listen to her play.

Songs

Peter plays the xylophone,
The xylophone, the xylophone.
Peter plays the xylophone,
Listen to him play.

If You're Happy (page 99).

If you're happy and you know it play the sticks . . .
If you're happy and you know it shake the bells . . .

The advantage of this type of activity is that everyone gets a chance to play all the instruments.

Notation

It is wise to continue to teach conventional notation (page 193) but it is also fun to allow the children to use the art medium to explore to notation of sounds produced by the instruments.

Some of these which children have suggested are as follows:

One cymbal crash  or

Sticks hitting together

Drum beats ▼▼▼▼▼▼

Drums played with wire brushes

The designs can be combined and if you add colour a whole new world opens up.

Let the children examine scores of such modern composers as John Cage and Pendereki. We are, after all, in the last quarter of the 20th century but musically at least, we seem firmly rooted in the 19th or before.

Instruments

This whole unit has been concerned with instruments so there is not much more to be said here, except to present some suggestions as to how imaginative exploration might be encouraged without producing absolute chaos.

My first suggestion is to restrict the number of instruments available at any given time, but be sure to allow each child to explore every instrument at some time.

Often, the child can go to a quiet corner and find out how many different sounds he can make with his instrument, and then come back to the group to demonstrate these. Other children might have yet other ideas.

Suggest that they explore playing the sides, the bottom, the ends, with their hands, with their fingers, flicking with their fingers, playing with soft mallets, hard mallets, the ends of the mallets, etc.

"Can you change your sound?" "Make it louder, softer, higher, faster."

These are just a few ideas to use to spark imagination.

See page 187 for ideas of using instruments for sound effects for stories and poems.

Creativity

Lesson V   Hallowe'en

Warm Up

Play selections such as Dukás *The Sorcerer's Apprentice* or Grieg's *In The Hall Of The Mountain King* to set a spooky mood.

Let's Move

Have the children move like witches, ghosts, etc. Suitable sound effects can be produced by clattering sticks together or running fingernails across drum heads.

Do the actions suggested for *The Little Witches* (page 153) and the song *Witches In The Dark* (page 112).

Let's Listen

Continue with activities relating to high and low (pages 33-36). Witches flying high and low can be described on a piano, slide, whistle, one string on a guitar or xylophone.

Let's listen

The game "Hot and Cold" (page 36) is so popular with children, it might be played at the Hallowe'en party. It has the added advantage of being a quiet game.

Continue with Echos (page 37). These do not have to be done in the music period but could be a break between spelling and math or fill in time when everyone is lined up waiting for the bell to ring.

Speech

Discover words relating to Hallowe'en: spooky, scary, dark, skeleton, ghost, etc. Put these together in a rhythmic sequence and clap the pattern or play it on instruments.

Speech

E.g. spooky, skeleton, black cat, ghost.

Start very softly saying the pattern over four times or so getting louder and louder. Have "spooky" played on a drum, "skeleton" played on sticks, "black cat" played on maracas and "ghost", a glizzando from the lowest note to the highest played on a xylophone with a wooden mallet. At the end everyone could say, "ooooooooooooo Hallowe'en".

Poetry

The poem *Hallowe'en* (pages 152-153) is excellent as are many many other Hallowe'en poems.

Song

Songs

There Was An Old Witch (pages 115-116). Do the accompaniment suggested.

Extra Songs and Poems

Brownies and Witches (page 113)
The Witches Brew (page 113)
The Witch Rides (page 114)
Witch Witch (page 153)
The Little Witches (page 153)

Notation

Make charts of Hallowe'en words such as:

Notation

See if the children can guess which one you are clapping. Let them have turns clapping for the others to guess.

Instruments

Invent "sound effects" for the Hallowe'en songs and poems.

LEVEL II

Lesson I   Discovering Ourselves

Warm Up

Sing songs the children know. If these songs have action patterns, performing these will help develop directionality.

Let's Move

Let's listen

Do some of the activities suggested under *Presence and Absence of Sound* (page 28), especially "freezing" like an object or like the stick figures. These are excellent for listening as well as for developing body awareness and body image.

Let's Listen

Try "Musical Simon Says" (page 29). This game is lots of fun and can be made as complicated as you wish for older children.

Let's listen

Echos can be started if the children have had no previous experience. Use clapping, stamping, patting etc. (page 37). If they have already had a fair amount of exposure to echos, try some on melodic instruments (page 40). Keep this very simple at first.

Speech

Speech

Use names of parts of the body to give a rhythmic pattern to be clapped, stamped, etc. "Shoulders, head, ankle bone, chin" for example. End with something like, **That's me.**

Poems

Hinges (page 147) is an excellent poem for body awareness. Proceed it by a discussion of all the hinges of the body: fingers, elbows, jaw, knee, shoulders, etc.
Do actions to it by moving all your hinges at once, then bending forward for "in front" and back for "in back" then collapsing in a heap for "crack".

Song

Songs

One of the all time favourites is *Head and Shoulders Baby* (pages 69-70). If you make up verses just using body parts it becomes a complete body awareness song. All children from Kindergarten to Grade VI enjoy this song.

Extra Songs And Poems

Going Over The Sea (page 84)
Looby Loo (page 97)

Hands on Shoulders (page 151)
My Hands (page 151)

Notation

If the children you are working with have not had notation, introduce quarter note notation and rests, using the names of the parts of the body.

Notation

E.g. shoulders   shoulders   back   back

If they have had some experience already, then this will be a review and you can proceed to eighth notes, half notes, etc. (pages 194-196).

Instruments

Instruments are not stressed in this lesson except as already mentioned in **Let's Move** and **Let's Listen.**

Lesson II   Weather

Warm Up

Listen to *Fingal's Cave Overture* by Mendelssohn. Suggest that the children try to bring other records of music describing weather, from their collections at home or from the libraries.

Let's Move

See **Speech.**

Let's Listen

Continue developing echos (pages 37-42), singing, clapping, playing, etc.

Let's listen

Devising instrumental sound effects for the weather words sharpens the listening sense as the sound must be listened to and considered carefully before it is accepted.

Speech

Find weather words. Describe the sound, if possible, with instruments (see **Instruments** below). Then create movement describing the words and sounds. Sometimes one word repeated over and over such as splashing, splashing, splashing, splashing, will evoke a series of interesting movements as the children discover different "ways" of splashing. Other times movement for a series of words such as flashing, floating, dripping, freeze, can be worked out singly or by a group of children.

Speech

Ask each child to find a weather proverb. Our folklore has many of these. Some examples are:

— April showers bring May flowers.

— Red sky at night, sailor's delight,
Red sky in the morning, sailor's take warning.

— Rain before seven,
Clear by eleven.

Pick some of these and work out a pattern using stamping, patting, clapping and snapping accompaniments.

Painless learning

These proverbs can be said in unison and also in canon (or a round, pages 172-174). In the second example the second part could come in when the first part reached the word "sailor". It could also be done as a four-part round. This is very effective if the whole is accompanied by a clapping, stamping pattern.

Try *The Snowman* (page 147). Have children pretend to make the snowman, rolling the balls (a large one for the bottom, smaller for the middle and a very small one for the head). This activity could

Poems

be done to a drum beat – fast at first, because the ball is tiny, then slower and slower and slower as the ball gets bigger. The children have to get down on their knees eventually and "push".

If you live where there is no snow, try *Rain* (page 158).

Song

Songs

C C C C Cold (page 110) is a good song which children love even though they live in warm climates.

Extra Songs and Poems

Fog — Carl Sandburg
Happiness (page 156)
The Snow (page 154)
The Umbrella Brigade (page 156)

Notation

Describe the sound effects of the weather words in graphic pictures using large sheets of paper and colours if possible. See **Lesson IV Level I.**

Instruments

Devise sound effects for different weather words. Some suggestions:

— fog: very soft and slow playing on gong or metallophone

Instruments

— flash of lightning: a sudden, loud playing of cymbal or triangle, with the sound stopped quickly.

— thunder: loud drum sound.

— rain: fingers playing on a drum very softly.

Use the suggested instrumental accompaniment to *C C C C Cold* or make up your own.

Lesson III Let's Do Our Own Thing

Warm Up

Review many of the songs the children have sung previously.

Let's Move, Let's Listen and Creativity

These topics are combined because of their interdependence.

Phrase Completion, or in simple terms, **Question and Answer,** is the natural follow up to the rhythmic independence gained through work with echos.

Creativity

Introduce the concept as on page 178 with word patterns, then go on to performing some with movement and with clapping, patting, snapping, etc. (page 179).

A dialogue can ensue between two drums. One person "asking the Question" and the other "answering" it.

See pages 212-213 for further ideas of **Question and Answer,** using percussion instruments.

Instruments

Speech

Try the poem *Alligator Pie* (page 79) and have the children make up many other verses. It might also be sung to the tune of *Skip To My Loo.*

E.g.

Alligator pickles, alligator pickles,
If I don't get some I think it's going to tickle.
Give away my quarters, give away my nickles,
But don't give away my alligator pickles.

Songs

Song

Down By The Bay (page 83) can be sung for a whole afternoon without exhausting the possibilities of verses. It is also a great song to teach rhyming words.

Songs

Have the children make up their own songs. See page 185 for one explanation as to how to proceed. The song must have some relevence to the child's world or to the subject matter under discussion, or it will not be interesting enough to capture the attention of the group.

Creativity

Extra Songs and Poems

Aiken Drum (page 85)
Old House (page 81)
Rig A Jig Jig (page 102)

Notation

Notate the rhythms of some of the words from *Alligator Pie*. If eighth notes have not been introduced they can be at this stage (see pages 194-198).

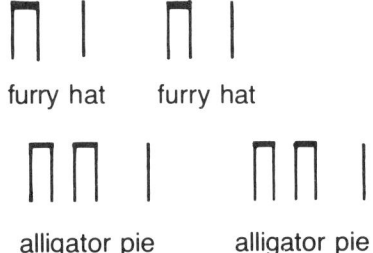

furry hat   furry hat

alligator pie   alligator pie

Instruments

See pages 187-188 and follow the suggestions there for helping the children make up their own instrumental piece.

Make your own instruments. See the section **Books** on pages 233 and 234 for books to give ideas on this subject. Refer also to page 209. Children really enjoy this kind of activity.

Creative Drama

The section on pages 189-190, gives a very few ideas of how creative drama can be enhanced or even initiated by music.

Lesson IV   Our Land

Warm Up

Listen to music such as *The Grand Canyon Suite* by Grofé and records of folk songs of many countries.

Let's Move

Do the actions or dance patterns associated with the songs above.

Try some simple, traditional square dances.

Instruments   Do some of the games suggested under *Fun With Drums* (page 212). These are good for coordination and movement as well as developing drum technique.

Creativity

Develop **Question and Answer** further using melodic instruments, xylophones, glockenspiels, etc. Start with two or three notes at first, gradually adding until the full pentatonic range is used (page 181). Small compositions can be devised and the concept of form taught very early through this technique. Several children make up their own phrases (Question plus Answer) and these are played in a definite order: A B A, A B B A, A B C A, or A B A B. Accompaniments can be created to accompany the whole.

Creativity

Start Rondo form as it is explained on pages 181-185. Use the suggested poem *(Johnny Caught a Flea)* for the A section and either have the children make up clapping patterns for the episode or play these on percussion instruments.

Song

Land of The Silver Birch (pages 108-109) is a beautiful Canadian folk song describing the peace and quiet of the north woods. The accompaniment could be changed but try to have the children keep the simple feeling that the song requires.

Songs

Extra Songs and Poems

Sing folk songs of different countries.

Jimmy Crack Corn
Kookaburra
Liza Jane (page 71)
Mr. Banjo (page 111)
Oh Susannah
Shoo Fly (page 92)

Notation

Continue with notation games similiar to those on pages 199-200. When children are ready, introduce sixteenth notes and triplets. The easiest way to do this is with word patterns.

Notation

Instruments

Use the instruments suggested in the song accompaniments.

Investigate the traditional instruments of our land but also those from other countries. There are excellent resource books and records available for reference. Try to find some group which is playing these instruments and take the children to hear them.

Lesson V   The Sea

Warm Up

Water has always had a fascination for poets and song writers and there are countless songs, instrumental pieces and stories about the sea.

Review some well-known sea chanties. Listen to them on records and sing as many as possible.

Listen to records such as *La Mer* by Debussy and *The Moldau* by Smetena.

Let's Move and Creativity

Make up a movement pattern for the song *Cape Cod Chanty.*

Do a movement Rondo (page 181) using a set pattern for the "A" section. E.g. Starting with a circle formation, skip eight steps to the right and eight back to the left. Each child in turn makes up his or her own short movement pattern for the episodes, B, C, D, etc.

Creativity   Another Rondo can be devised using an "A" section derived from the rhythm of a word pattern of "sea" words such as:

swirling	crashing	phosphorescent	calm

Have the episodes played on percussion instruments.

Speech

Find unusual words which describe the sea and things to do with it. Move to these either singly or in a group effort. One group could be each of the properties of the sea.

E.g.

Speech   sea weed: drifting, wafting, floating.
fish: quick, darting, poised.
the water: crashing, foaming, shimmering, swirling.
rocks: hard, unwielding, stuck

Song

Songs   *Cape Cod Chanty* (page 75). Have the children make their own verses using all parts of the fish.

Extra Songs and Poems

Donkey Riding (page 106)
I'se The B'y (that builds the boat)
Jack Was Every Inch A Sailor
Lukey's Boat

Notation

Continue with notation games perhaps using sea words to give the exact rhythm. "People Rhythms" are fun to do (pages 202-204).

Instruments

Use instruments for accompaniment. Always have the children experiment to devise their own accompaniments if possible. Use those in the book as models (pages 219-223).

Describe some of the sea sounds and words with instruments.

Notation

INDEX

261

265

T

U

V

W

X

Z